A Promising Problem

A Promising Problem

The New Chicana/o History

EDITED BY CARLOS KEVIN BLANTON

University of Texas Press ⬥ *Austin*

Requests for permission to reproduce material from this work should be sent to:
   Permissions
   University of Texas Press
   P.O. Box 7819
   Austin, TX 78713-7819
   http://utpress.utexas.edu/index.php/rp-form

♾ The paper used in this book meets the minimum requirements of
ANSI/NISO Z39.48-1992 (R1997) (Permanence of Paper).

Library of Congress Cataloging-in-Publication Data

A promising problem : the new Chicana/o history / edited by Carlos Kevin
Blanton. — First edition.
      pages   cm
   Includes bibliographical references and index.
      ISBN 978-1-4773-0896-7 (cloth : alk. paper) — ISBN 978-1-4773-0903-2 (pbk. :
alk. paper) — ISBN 978-1-4773-1011-3 (library e-book) — ISBN 978-1-4773-1012-0
(nonlibrary e-book)
      1. Mexican Americans—Ethnic identity.   2. Mexican Americans—
Historiography.   3. Mexican Americans—Social conditions.   4. Mexican
Americans—Study and teaching—History.   I. Blanton, Carlos Kevin,
1970– editor.
      E184.M5P76   2016
      973'.046872—dc23   2015034520

doi:10.7560/308967

Contents

Preface

Chicana/o history is at an exciting juncture. My own experience over the last decade is that the new developments in the field dominate friendly conversations among colleagues at conferences, libraries, archives, and other places where historians congregate. My Texas A&M University colleagues and students have long suffered my incessant need to discuss these trends. I have found it curious that these academic and intellectual advances in the field are occurring simultaneously with a negative external political context. My colleagues and I feel that this situation reflects both the problem and promise of Chicana/o history.

One such discussion in the fall of 2012 stemmed from an event for Hispanic Heritage Month at my university. Though happy with the wide student interest, my history department colleagues Lisa Ramos, Felipe Hinojosa, and I wondered why such events focused on celebrity speakers instead of the exciting academic developments in the field of Chicana/o history. We decided to do something about it. We organized what would eventually become the one-day symposium *Breaking Free, Breaking Down: The New Chicana/o History in the Twenty-First Century*, held almost a year later on September 27, 2013, at Texas A&M. And we decided to "flip the script" in how these kinds of professional gatherings work. Rather than invite one or two eminent senior speakers to contextualize the new directions in the field and then subsequently ask a host of up-and-coming scholars to confine themselves to the narrower subfields in which they operate to support those directions, we instead tasked mostly emerging talents and relative newcomers to the field to discuss the big interpretive changes from their vantage point. For many of these scholars, it was their first opportunity to write a broader, more explorative analysis about Chicana/o history. The enthusiasm and momentum for the project was palpable.

The symposium was wonderful, and in the process of preparing for it, the group decided to turn these tentative explorative pieces into longer, freestanding essays for an edited collection. Several of the original symposium contributors have remained on this book project, one joined the project after the symposium, and other colleagues have moved on to other projects. Every one of them at each stage of this long discussion, from the planning of the symposium in the fall of 2012 to the submission of the final manuscript to the University of Texas Press in the spring of 2015, has been an inspiration. As the symposium co-organizer and the principal editor of this volume, it has been my responsibility to communicate the project's scope and deadlines, as well as to direct the line-by-line editing of these chapters. I am thus perhaps in the best position to appreciate the convivial sharing of scholarship and engaging debate with these wonderful colleagues. This entire process has reminded me that it is real people of flesh and blood who make ideas and shape the fields they inhabit.

A few caveats are in order. What follows here in *A Promising Problem* are deeply personalized intellectual attempts to come to terms with the exciting new developments in Chicana/o history. This is not a collection of traditional bibliographic essays for narrower subfields or of expressly historiographical pieces. We acknowledge the vital utility of both. But *A Promising Problem*'s chapters mean to explore rather than comprehensively catalogue. They demonstrate the development of the field instead of limiting themselves to merely describing that development. The contributors to this collection are highly active in different topical aspects of Chicana/o history. This diverse selection is intentional. However, these chapters cannot cover all topics. For those questions and subfields that have gotten left out of the chapters that follow, we can only express regret that time, space, and the increasing richness of the field make the task of fully covering everything of importance impossible. From different subfields and interdisciplinary perspectives, the chapters in *A Promising Problem* continue the ongoing project of enlarging Chicana/o history. The scholars' task is to use their own work as a springboard to address the larger changes in the field and the promise these new directions have for future scholars. These chapters address and further some aspect (or several) of the most recent developments in the fertile academic field of Chicana/o history.

This growing complexity of the field is daunting. A myriad of seemingly cacophonous ruptures and continuities characterize the new Chicana/o history of the twenty-first century. Coming to terms with Chicana/o history's rapid development is a going concern in the field. Two recent and impressive attempts are the *Pacific Historical Review*'s special issue in November 2013 devoted to Chicana/o history with essays by Albert Camarillo, Ernesto Chávez, Natalia Molina, Miroslava Chávez-García, Raúl Ramos, and Alexandra Minna Stern, and Mario T. García's 2014 edited collection with Routledge, *The Chicano Movement: Perspectives from the Twenty-First Century.*

It is not the purpose here to spell out in finality the substance of these changes in the field that we designate, with some caution, as the *new* Chicana/o history of the early twenty-first century. All of the contributors consciously remark upon one or several aspects of these larger shifts, and my own chapter will discuss the shifts more broadly. What is the new Chicana/o history of the twenty-first century? In brief (this is the subject of the next chapter), the field's big changes can be confined to four thematic concepts: (1) the proliferation of new and stimulating conceptualizations of identity; (2) the decentering of a traditional sense of place in the field; (3) a deeper, inward-looking, critical reflection by historians about the meaning of the field, something of a field-wide historiographic turn; and (4) the field's continued connection to its defining characteristic of the past, tying Chicana/o scholarship to social realities and the quest for justice.

My chapter, "Looking In while Stepping Out: Growth, Reassessment, and the Promising Problem of the New Chicana/o History," explores how the current problems of Chicana/o history stand in stark contrast to the vital promise of the field. I find that as Chicana/o scholars step out in bold, creative new interpretive directions, they are empowered by constantly reexamining the field's axioms while connecting their academic work to a wider struggle for justice. I examine the origins of Chicana/o history in the late 1960s and 1970s, the development of a *traditional* interpretive paradigm in the field, and that paradigm's gradual unraveling in the face of what I call the *new* Chicana/o history of recent years. Michael A. Olivas's "The Accidental Historian; or, How I Found My Groove in Legal History" is an insightful autobiographical approach that plumbs deeper personal meaning in Chicana/o history. A longtime legal scholar and activist attorney who is a relative newcomer to publishing Chicana/o history, Olivas writes because of the deep connection this shared past has to his experiences as an activist-intellectual. He demonstrates as well as anyone that Chicana/o history is for everyone (not just historians) and that the investigation of the past can be the engine driving today's activist passions. His inspiring, instructive chapter challenges Chicana/o historians to be wary of divorcing the world of scholarship from the pursuit of social justice.

Lilia Fernández's chapter, "Moving beyond Aztlán: Disrupting Nationalism and Geographic Essentialism in Chicana/o History," is stimulated by the need to expand beyond a traditional and confining sense of place within the Chicana/o imagination. Her focus is on the US Midwest, particularly Chicago. Fernández further expands the historical imagination by exploring the connections between Chicana/o and Puerto Rican populations and their historiographical traditions, pushing the field further away from cultural nationalism and toward a Chicana/o historical reality that is both more accurate and more ambitious. "Chicana/o History as Southern History: Race, Place, and the US South" by Perla M. Guerrero continues this decentering of traditional notions of geographic space by looking at one of the fastest-growing Chicana/o populations in the nation. Guerrero addresses core assumptions of cultural nationalism by asking important relational questions about other Latina/o immigrant groups and their connection to Chicana/o populations. She finds that adapting Chicana/o history to include recent Latina/o immigrant groups, which may or may not have any connection to Mexico, is one of the field's central tasks if it is to maintain its sense of authenticity and relevance.

Felipe Hinojosa's chapter, "Sacred Spaces: Race, Resistance, and the Politics of Chicana/o and Latina/o Religious History," embraces the relational turn, the growing multiplicity of identities and perspectives in the field, and the reorientation of its physical and geographic space. Hinojosa examines church occupations in 1969 and 1970 in Los Angeles, New York City, and Houston among multiple Latina/o groups and over several different religious denominations, demonstrating how the scholarly concern with religion enlivens and complicates traditional narratives in Chicana/o history and upends old assumptions about the sources of cultural identity and community activism. Sonia Hernández's "Chicanas in the US-Mexican Borderlands: Transborder Conversations of Feminism and Anarchism, 1905–1938" also pushes the traditional boundaries of Chicana/o history. Hernández breaks away from conceiving the US Southwest within a North/South framework in her analysis of Mexican and Latin American intellectual and ideological connections to Chicana/o identity. The vehicle for these transborder discourses is the ideological language and organizational work of anarcho-syndicalism before, during, and after the Mexican Revolution. This focus expands the Chicana's presence beyond the home, the workplace, and the US side of the Rio Grande.

Finally, Luis Alvarez's chapter, "Eastside Imaginaries: Toward a Relational and Transnational Chicana/o Cultural History," examines how the ultimate meaning of Chicana/o identity and community depends in part on relationships outside the internal community. By focusing on the prominent role of non-Chicanas/os in shaping Chicana/o culture in East Los Angeles, Alvarez demonstrates new ways of conceptualizing the Chicana/o community, who is in it, and how it is constructed and reconstructed over time and through a relational lens. Not only is this work a compelling example of the new ways in which multiple identity formation enriches the field, but it also contributes to the heightened sense of internal criticism about the ultimate meaning of Chicana/o history, what it is, and who it studies.

We conclude with a select bibliography of recent (since 1995) publications in the field of Chicana/o history. The books and articles in this bibliography appear in the following chapters, often multiple times. The bibliography is intended not just for ease of reference but also as a way of demonstrating the field's vitality. And this vitality is not simply a matter of what has happened in the past couple decades. This is a crucial point. The success of the field today rests upon a foundation of outstanding work in Chicana/o history. We are quite cognizant of the massive intellectual debt we owe to those pioneering Chicana/o historians who labored for decades with little support and, in many cases, in the face of outright hostility. Without this earlier work, today's historians could not possibly do what we do. Earlier I hinted at the awkwardness of using the phrase "the new Chicana/o history of the twenty-first century." It might seem triumphalist. It is not meant to be so. We hope that our honest enthusiasm—perhaps it is simply pride for what we do, for our field, and for each other—is not off-putting to anyone. What we are doing in this collection honors what earlier scholars began. Paraphrasing very loosely from the twelfth-century English and French humanists John of Salisbury and Bernard of Chartres: "We sit on the shoulders of giants. We see more and things that are more distant than they, not because our sight is superior or because we are taller, but because they raise us up and by their great stature add to ours." We hope that someday future scholars will be able to say some version of the same thing for all of us. We aspire to that too. Chicana/o history is for everyone and is as important as ever, as these chapters strive to communicate. It is our sincere hope that readers of this volume will agree and will find something of use or interest in the chapters that follow.

Acknowledgments

As the editor of *A Promising Problem: The New Chicana/o History*, it falls on me to ensure that the many friends and colleagues who have helped us in this journey receive some well-deserved gratitude. I apologize for anyone I have neglected.

This book grew out of a 2013 symposium that had many helping hands enabling its success. Many thanks to the Glasscock Center for Humanities Research at Texas A&M University—and to Joe Golsan, Sarah Mismer, Donna Malak, and Elsa Hernández—for generous financial sponsorship and for housing our meeting. From the fall of 2012 to the fall of 2013 the Glasscock Center took care of many of the little but important things that allowed us to realize our aspirations for this project. The History Department at Texas A&M University under department head David Vaught made a serious commitment to this symposium and came through with generous support during a time of fiscal constraint. History Department business coordinator Barbara Dawson made the travel, lodging, and honorarium arrangements, handling all requests with grace and enthusiasm. Other sponsors who deserve a big thanks are Texas A&M University's Office of Multicultural Services and the Office of the Vice President and Associate Provost for Diversity, especially Becky Petitte and Kristine Stanley. Several colleagues at Texas A&M University and elsewhere—Armando Alonzo, Walter Buenger, Brian Rouleau, Kate Untermann, Angela Hudson, Cynthia Bouton, Rebecca Schloss, Tommy Curry, Nancy Plankey Videla, Joseph Jewell, José Villalobos, and Anne Martínez—and many graduate students, including my fall 2013 Race, Ethnicity, and Migration graduate seminar, deserve tremendous thanks for the stimulating exchanges and penetrating questions.

I thank the two external reviewers whose patient and encouraging analyses have made this book a much better effort. The University of Texas Press has been wonderful throughout this process. Before she retired, Theresa May took a chance on this idea for yet another edited collection arising out of yet another conference. The encouraging Kerry Webb has taken the reins this past year and has enthusiastically continued that support. Their confidence and belief in this project has been vital and unwavering. Also, we owe many thanks to John Brenner for his copyediting expertise.

There are countless colleagues, friends, and relatives who have suffered with us as we wrote these essays, and we thank them for their willingness to read our work and talk to us about it. And if I may be permitted to express a more personal gratitude, thank you, Kristine, for your patience throughout this project and for your sage advice.

My contributors, from the symposium planning in 2012 to the final submission of this manuscript in 2015, have been wonderful. Thank you Luis Alvarez, Gerry Cadava, Lilia Fernández, Perla M. Guerrero, Sonia Hernández, Felipe Hinojosa, Michael Olivas, Lisa Ramos, Marc Simon Rodriguez, and Ana Elizabeth Rosas. And I must single out two of these colleagues, Lisa Ramos and Felipe Hinojosa, for listening to me in the early fall of 2012 when I had this odd idea for a conference and maybe even a book. They codirected the symposium with me. They cheerfully and valuably contributed to its direction, and to the final shape of this book today.

I would like to dedicate this collection to our teachers. I hope what we are doing in this work honors the many wonderful people who have challenged and inspired us in and out of the classroom.

CHAPTER ONE

Looking In while Stepping Out: Growth, Reassessment, and the Promising Problem of the New Chicana/o History

CARLOS KEVIN BLANTON

The field of Chicana/o history[1] is nearing the half-century mark. It began as a field of bright promise dealing with serious problems. It remains so today. At this very moment Chicana/o historians are stepping out into bold new kinds of studies, interpretations, and subfields; yet a part of this stepping out is enabled by how these historians also look inward to debate the meaning of the field and to maintain one of the defining characteristics of Chicana/o history's past—the persistent connection of academic research to real social concerns and the pursuit of justice. So problems and promise are inseparable in Chicana/o history.

Some scholars may find this dualism odd, as it seems like an exciting time to work in Chicana/o history. The new Chicana/o history of the twenty-first century has become a successful and growing historical field and continues to be engaged with the central intellectual currents of the historical profession. Chicana/o historians from across rank and region are winning awards from professional history associations as well as major grants. Top journals, including the *Journal of American History*, the *Pacific Historical Review*, the *Western Historical Quarterly*, and the *Journal of Southern History*, now publish (some with frequency) Chicana/o history essays. Chicana/o scholars are regularly asked to serve on major committees in the profession. They have assumed the presidencies of the largest history associations as well as editorial positions in major history journals. Chicana/o historians hold positions at many (but not enough) of the top research universities in the nation. Chicana/o history's growing influence enlivens the inquiries of other fields such as the Southwest borderlands, US western history, and the history of Mexico. And it continues to be interdisciplinary, as evidenced by its growing connection to American studies, religious studies, legal studies, and the social sciences. The field is vibrant enough to draw historians from other fields (one scholar enthusiastically refers to this as being a "fellow traveler") and to enter debates beyond the discipline of history.[2]

Yet crisis surrounds the field. Consider this: there are no laws or organized mass movements in this country against the study or teaching of the US Gilded Age and Progressive Era, of medieval Europe, ancient Greece, or colonial Latin America. But there is such resistance to Chicana/o Studies and, by extension, Chicana/o history. While academic endeavors such as other ethnic studies, area studies, and GLBT programs and groups are often controversial and face significant hostility, the academic subject of Chicana/o history and Chicana/o Studies—despite the nation's rapidly changing demographics (or perhaps because of them)—continues to experience exceptionally high and sustained levels of fear and anger. The nation's liberality of academic pursuits is curiously suspended with Chicana/o history, it would seem. The deportation of immigrant students, themselves vital consumers and producers of Chicana/o-Latina/o history, continues at alarming rates despite the mild election-year holding action of the 2012 DREAM Act. These deportations today represent a living, breathing connection to the state-sanctioned oppressions of the past so vividly documented in those very Chicana/o history books that so many Americans find disconcerting. This connection between past and present, between problem and promise, is long-standing and inherent to the field of Chicana/o history.

So what do I mean by the *new* in Chicana/o history? I define this as the field's current state of intellectual rigor and direction dating to the mid-1990s. For me, the *new* has a relational definition. It is not an organized faction or generational cohort with membership based on birth, place, or age. Instead, the *new* is measured by the movement of its interpretations away from what I define as those *traditional* interpretations in Chicana/o history that derive from the field's birth in the late 1960s and 1970s. My conceptualization of these terms has to do solely with the academic field's state of being that is shaped by the participation of scholars of all ages, backgrounds, and training. The field of Chicana/o history has experienced remarkable intellectual development in recent decades. This chapter attempts to explain that development and explore its meaning. It is my firm conviction that this is a sign of the field's strength, maturity, and vitality, not an indicator of discord or declension.[3]

This chapter briefly examines the roots of Chicana/o history, analyzes its interpretive definition, and reflects on an order to these myriad new directions. It is not enough to preemptively conclude that because the times have changed, so too must the history. An explanation of the meaning of these changes is absolutely necessary. I propose that these directions coalesce around four general themes that, not coincidentally, the scholars in this collection address: 1) the proliferation of new and stimulating conceptualizations of identity; 2) the decentering of a traditional sense of place; 3) a deeper, inward-looking, critical level of reflection on the field and its meaning, something of a field-wide historiographic turn; and 4) the field's continual, vibrant connection to its defining characteristic of the past, tying academic research to Chicana/o realities and the pursuit of social justice. The first two themes on identity and place represent how Chicana/o history in the last two decades has stepped out in new and creative ways that push the boundaries of the field and vitally connect it with other academic fields and interpretive concerns. The final two themes represent how recent Chicana/o history has been aided by deep reflection on the development of the field and the social meaning of the knowledge it produces. Taken together, these themes are sides of the same coin. Each contributor to this collection addresses more than one of these themes; they look in while they step out.[4]

The Social Context of Chicana/o History Today

Knowledge about Chicana/o topics today has become subject to serious governmental scrutiny. In 2010 and 2011, for example, public officials in the state of Arizona and in the Tucson Unified School District took legislative and administrative steps to outlaw ethnic studies programs directed toward Chicana/o students.[5] In a stunning example of ahistoricism, reactionary activists in Arizona sought to eradicate the incorporation of Chicana/o content into school curricula by alleging it was racist. They made these claims nearly forty years after Chicana/o activists first clamored for the creation of such programs to combat the very Jim Crow racism so amply documented by the nation's federal court system. These same courts also advocated the idea of Chicana/o Studies as one of several remedies for long-standing societal racism. That the mostly Mexican and Mexican American students taking such courses were 45 to 150 percent more likely to graduate from high school than those who did not made no difference to the ethnic studies opponents.

For them, this was never about educating children or debating the effectiveness of the curriculum. It was, and remains, about targeting Chicanas/os and Mexican immigrants.[6]

This hostile attitude is real and frightening. And it exists not just in Arizona, but across the United States. This antipathy does not distinguish between US-born Mexican American citizens and Latina/o immigrants. And this prejudice is girded with guns. For example, armed white militia groups have been patrolling the US-Mexico border with the avowed purpose of hunting down undocumented immigrants. Conversely, those very immigrants must also satisfy the demands of rapacious economic interests in the United States that seek bound labor at far less cost than any minimum wage. The extensive militarization of the border by the US government through Operation Gatekeeper, which has funneled border crossers away from settled areas and toward the most isolated, dangerous entry points, makes these crossings a more harrowing prospect even if one can avoid the armed domestic terror groups. The US government conservatively estimates a death toll of as many as 5,500 undocumented immigrants from border crossings since 1998; every one of these persons possessed a universe of human experience and potential.[7] All this has occurred as the federal government has intensified to alarming levels its efforts to deport immigrant workers and their families. These deportations include children who are honor students, many of whom have been US residents for most of their lives.[8]

This uptick in angry rhetoric, so much of it directed at defenseless children, is on the rise. A number of national and state officials routinely and publicly threaten to unleash militarized force against the thousands of refugee children in detention centers across the nation. The former Texas governor Rick Perry authorized a thousand National Guard troops to protect this side of the Rio Grande, ostensibly from such children. The rhetoric from the political right on the immigration issue and the nation's long-term demographic trends is replete with biological crudities and apocalyptic fears of white cultural extinction, while an allegedly left-wing president and political party do remarkably little to address the situation. This problematic rise in hostility toward Latina/o immigrants and Chicanas/os in the United States transcends class status and ideology. It forms the social context for the new Chicana/o history of this century.[9]

It is easy to focus on extremists. A few rotten apples one could dismiss. But this hostility toward Chicana/o peoples goes far beyond just the obviously disreputable. The nation's *thinkers*, its intellectuals, its policy makers, reflect this widespread, systematic hostility.[10] In fact, they have created the academic discourses that structure and house such prejudice. Intellectuals in the United States have consistently regarded Chicana/o peoples in a negative and stereotypical light. And while one can readily argue that the nation has always had serious problems with race, its discourse on Mexican-origin peoples is unique in its unthinking, reflexive nature as well as its remarkable persistence and durability over time. One can spot these ideas today with little difficulty. However Chicana/o people assert their identity or identities—as white, as a separate race, as an ethnicity, as citizens, as immigrants, as men or women, as gay or straight, as workers, as students—they are perceived in US intellectual discourses in remarkably uniform terms of negativity and deficiency.

For example, the national scholar Samuel Huntington of Harvard University (a conservative) and the best-selling author and public intellectual Arthur Schlesinger Jr. (a liberal) in recent decades have written anti-Mexican, anti-Chicana/o screeds filled with dyspeptic fantasies and hysterical fears about the group's unwillingness or inability to assimilate to white, Anglo-Saxon, Protestant US culture. Despite numerous scholarly refutations, this intellectual perspective, which one scholar refers to as a "veiled, 'politically correct' racism," has mainstream intellectual support.[11]

A more recent case in point is the uproar in 2013 over Jason Richwine, a Heritage Foundation staffer, and his arguments over the supposed intellectual inferiority of Mexican immigrants and Mexican Americans. He used his academic work to advance his restrictionist activism. It is not his ideas that are surprising—their content is old hat—but that they derive from an approved 2009 Harvard dissertation. One senior scholar in the field of educational psychometrics describes this dissertation as having earned "the dubious distinction of being the most vicious and sustained pseudoscientific attack to date on Mexican-origin people in the U.S." The IQ discourse and its zombie-like reanimation every few decades (Jensen of the 1970s, Murray/Herrnstein of the 1990s, Richwine of the 2010s), regardless of the outraged academic debunking that follows in its wake, is just one more illustration of a strikingly deep structural antipathy toward Chicana/o peoples and other racialized groups. Yet these anti-Chicana/o discourses are not new. They are, in fact, a staple of intellectual life in the United States.[12]

The Sisyphean History of the Chicana/o in US Intellectual Life

It appears that no matter what Chicana/o peoples do, narratives about their alleged deficiency, corruption, and criminality appear and re-appear regardless of actual evidence. While deplorable, this intellectual hostility is not surprising. Intellectuals in the United States have always struggled with conceptualizing this group accurately and thus often re-sort to a priori assumptions that get proven in various intellectual dis-courses, for a while at least, as scientifically validated ideas. Then, pre-dictably, these notions get debunked. But in the meantime, whole other academic discourses appear in other disciplines and fields resuscitating the same old racist structures in a tragic (or comic) Sisyphean pattern.[13]

For example, in the first decades of this nation's existence, policy-makers and intellectuals subscribed wholly to old "Black Legend" stereotypes inherited from English colonial masters who in turn were informed by feelings of imperial rivalry, religious intolerance, and na-tional, dynastic insecurity. This ideological trope held Spanish peoples as cruel, corrupt, fanatical, weak, lazy, and bigoted; it held their *casta* subjects as far worse. Such attitudes readily bubbled to the surface of policy and intellectual discourse in the late eighteenth and early nine-teenth centuries. In many respects the Black Legend is a master trope of all the ultimately prejudicial discourses to come.[14]

The debate following the US-Mexican War over whether to annex all of Mexico or limit gains to the New Mexico and California territories is particularly instructive. This political controversy spurred politicians to modify older Black Legend discourses for a more specific discourse that regarded Mexico as an illegitimate nation whose not-quite-white peoples were inferior to Anglos. These same beliefs were used to ar-gue both for and against annexing all of Mexico. In other words, the belief in Mexican deficiency was shared by all parties. The arguments over annexation were not simply heated, momentary eruptions. For years they continued on as southern, pro-slavery expansionists filibus-tered throughout Latin America. The negative portrayal of Latinas/os flowed past international boundaries to apply equally to multiple peo-ples regardless of nationality or citizenship. The debate over whether to make New Mexico a state or keep it a territory, for example, spurred ar-guments throughout the nineteenth and early twentieth centuries for and against the racial fitness of New Mexico's ancient *Hispano* popula-tion for US citizenship.[15]

Chicanas/os in the century that followed remained a problem for

US thinkers. Racialist discourses of the early twentieth century permeated the professionalizing branches of US academia. Thinkers such as Madison Grant developed typologies of different *races*, mere conflations with what we might refer to today as *nationality*. Full of overgeneralizations about moral character, physical appearance, and blood mixture without any enduring scientific evidence, Grant's theories were a part of his larger effort to restrict immigration to the United States. He was not alone. Particularly prevalent in this discourse were biologists, criminologists, and economists who responded to the topic of immigration by forging classifications for all peoples. Even intellectuals who opposed such racialism and restrictionism formulated arguments that ultimately recognized the racial supremacy of some and the inferiority of others. The racist discourses over the immigration issue a century ago resembled today's debate. Indeed, Madison Grant's iconic piece of Progressive-era racism, *The Passing of the Great Race*, is not far afield from Huntington's "The Hispanic Challenge." This scientific discourse specifically impacted debate over Mexican immigration in the 1920s as opponents and supporters of restricting Mexican immigration based their arguments on fundamentally racialized ideas of Mexican deficiency.[16]

Another academic discourse in the twentieth century that affected Chicana/o peoples involved the effort to more fully segregate them as a deficient race. This discourse involved psychologists, sociologists, and education scholars. In the realm of education, the IQ test became a mechanism to justify the already preexisting racial segregation of Chicana/o children in the public schools. This intellectual rationalization was necessary since Mexican peoples were regarded officially in courts of law as *white*, confined as it was to this most formal and theoretical of legal contexts. This led to the Chicana/o experience of systematic de facto rather than de jure racial segregation. IQ tests were also used by eugenicists to justify the incarceration and sterilization of Chicana/o peoples, including children. While the science of educational testing had shifted away from IQ by the 1930s and 1940s, the kinds of content tests that replaced it still justified separate schooling for Chicanas/os due to alleged educational deficiencies such as an inherent *language handicap* or the need for *cultural enrichment*.[17]

A related complex of academic discourses emerged in the 1930s and extended well into the 1960s. These discourses involved sociologists, anthropologists, and psychologists who theorized about notions of cultural assimilation in the course of explaining persistent Chicana/o poverty. These ideas once again shifted the direct emphasis away from race and onto culture, but in a way that still reinforced what recent scholars refer to as *deficit thinking*. These new nonracial categories ended up neatly reflecting the old racial ones—different tune, same beat. The interpretation of Chicanas/os as deficient endured even when intellectuals supported sympathetic policies. Getting away from strict ideas of race did not banish the old hierarchies and sense of deficiency among mainstream academicians.[18]

Traditional Chicana/o History

The arrival of Chicana/o history in the late 1960s and 1970s ruptured these age-old Sisyphean patterns. In this moment, Chicana/o peoples spoke back, asserting their own ideas of who they were in response to these structural impositions of deficiency. In these heady days young men and women attended school and participated in community activism and protests. They thought long and hard about how traditional scholarship represented them in ways that were not only inaccurate but also racist and oppressive. It was a self-conscious, articulate form of personal and group liberation. Yet this fascinating moment did not materialize out of thin air. It too had an academic legacy, though the legacy was tenuous and fragmentary.

There were a handful of scholars who wrote Chicana/o history throughout the early and mid-twentieth century. They were precursors to the historical imagination of the Chicano Movement, though, in familiar fashion, they used their work as a way to engage deeply rooted racist notions in the national mind-set. Since the 1980s the study of such intellectual pioneers—George I. Sánchez, Ernesto Galarza, Carlos Castañeda, Adina de Zavala, Arthur Campa, Jovita Gonzalez, Américo Paredes, Carey McWilliams—has been prominent in the development of Chicana/o history as a field.[19] These talented, precocious thinkers documented the Chicana/o past while keeping a lively interest in the present as civil rights and labor activists, teachers, and cultural producers. On the whole their work was marginalized and conducted in relative isolation, with the certainty of little or no professional reward. Yet they wrote out of a love of history, a deep-seated need to set the record straight, and a deeper need to defend their *raza*.[20]

But these heroic efforts notwithstanding, there was no recognized body of scholars devoted to studying Chicana/o peoples in the early to mid-twentieth century. Chicana/o history as a self-consciously developed academic field began in the late 1960s and early 1970s when the Chicano Movement burst onto the national consciousness. The two—Chicana/o history and the Chicano Movement—are intimately bound. Chicana/o historians, indeed all Chicana/o scholars, were committed to a precise sense of community and activism. This was a history crafted by young intellectuals, most of whom considered themselves activists in *el Movimiento*. The intent of these activist scholars for Chicana/o history, indeed for all Chicano Studies, was to use this academic knowledge as a platform for cooperative action by the larger Chicano community, or action research.[21]

Thus, the initial explorers of Chicano history meant for their work to be highly politicized. Or perhaps it might be more diplomatically stated that they meant to create what a recent scholar refers to as a "usable past" with their historical work. One manifestation of the interconnection between academia and activism was *El Plan de Santa Barbara*, formulated in 1969 by a conference of Chicano students at the University of California at Santa Barbara. This document has iconic status in studies of the Chicano Movement and Chicana/o education. *El Plan de Santa Barbara* called for the creation of Chicano Studies programs and courses, as well as connecting the production of academic knowledge at higher education institutions to local communities.[22]

But the connection between *el Movimiento* and Chicana/o history goes beyond inspiration and timing. The Chicano history that was produced in the 1970s also mirrored the Chicano Movement in the content of its ideas. This is what I call *traditional* Chicana/o history. Interpretively, it meant assumptions of a far more universal experience and a more flattened sense of community than scholars today would assert. These ideas understandably came from the activist ethos of the era. This traditional framework emphasized the proletarian, revolutionary spirit in Chicana/o history and the theme of resistance against the overwhelming totality of structural racism and class exploitation. These works often couched community in terms of male leadership and in a shimmering, reimagined Aztlán homeland in the US Southwest. Chicana/o history was about reclaiming one's true self, as indicated by a historian who wrote in 1977 that through Chicana/o history *la raza* could reverse "such a degree of deranged assimilation" that had created "a monstrous distortion of our true past."[23]

I acknowledge painting with a broad brush here. It is true that some early Chicana/o historians affirmed the possibility of multiple claims of identity, thought of Chicana/o experiences outside the southwest, and discussed other aspects of intra-group diversity. And not everyone was comfortable with *Chicanismo*. Américo Paredes, whose magnificent *With His Pistol in His Hand* is, according to one recent scholar, "the ur-text in Chicano Studies," later dismissed what he felt was the exaggerated performativity of cultural nationalism and especially machismo. The pioneering labors of Chicana feminists vociferously opposed machismo and any sense of Chicanismo that promoted patriarchy. But these caveats are just technicalities. Any broader reading of the traditional scholarship clearly reveals that these scholars homogenized the Chicana/o experience for a more universal and useful (in terms of activism) interpretation. That some recent critics have occasionally presumed such critiques with little reflection and a pejorative tone is unfortunate; such sloppiness does not make this critique untrue, however.[24]

The recent historical attention to subjects such as cultural nationalism and internal colonialism gets at the meaning of Chicanismo. While rhetorically useful in quickly organizing large, diverse groups, the rhetoric of cultural nationalism homogenized the internal diversity of Chicana/o communities for a more advantageous imagining, according to the historian Ramón Gutiérrez. Also, early Chicano historians looked to Third World, anticolonialist thinking, especially the theory of internal colonialism inherited from Latin American scholars. Young Chicana/o intellectuals gravitated to internal colonialism to make sense of their own oppression and draw global connections to their experiences. While helpful in providing a structure to explain the interplay of race and class, this theoretical approach tied historical experiences along a narrow Marxist path of economic and social development that left little room for agency and internal or regional diversity.[25] One recent essay discusses how the study of Chicanas/os in the nineteenth century became a confluence of the intellectual models of internal colonialism and cultural nationalism: "Many of the first wave of self-identified Chicano/a historians located their research in the nineteenth century as part of a project to describe the roots of oppression and racialization."[26] Chicanismo had more immediate negative consequences. Many early Chicano historians downplayed or ignored women, much less notions of gender, replicating in their vision of the past the personal limitations of the present. Scholars in the 1980s and 1990s forcibly challenged such gender-privileged notions and opened up new avenues for discussing sexuality in the field.[27]

The traditional framework focused on New Left mainstays of interpretation such as community formation and the then-new urban studies approach, particularly in the southwestern states of the nineteenth and early twentieth centuries.[28] It analyzed state-sanctioned oppression and resistance to such oppression.[29] More often than not, it privileged Marxist models of class formation and labor history.[30] This body of work also emphasized the continuity of community and culture through time.[31] The portrayal of this traditional scholarship along these lines has become a stable, relatively orthodox perspective in the Chicana/o historiographical tradition since the late 1980s and 1990s.[32]

Although these Chicana/o era works had a higher national profile than those lonely groundbreaking works of the early to mid-twentieth century, they were never quite as influential as they should have been. The pioneering Chicano historian Al Camarillo recalls that while his cohort of early Chicano historians were profoundly influenced by the rise of that era's New Left intellectual currents, their work was "not in turn very influential on these newer historiographies." Despite the emergence of a more defined and rigorous field of Chicana/o history, it remained academically marginalized. This disregard even manifested itself around dismissive concerns of Chicana/o scholarly legitimacy. Camarillo briefly notes with satisfaction that he no longer has to answer accusatory questions at professional history conferences about his objectivity as a Chicana/o to work on Chicana/o history. This side comment hints at a wider universe, perhaps lost to time, of the daily microaggressions endured by early Chicana/o historians in their desire to contribute knowledge that mattered to their communities.[33]

This first wave of Chicana/o historians encountered many obstacles. They often experienced difficulties in publishing articles, locating supportive university presses, navigating the promotion and tenure process, and simply obtaining reading material for the new Chicana/o history courses they were creating. Breaking into other related fields was a challenge. For example, it took until the 1990s for the Texas State Historical Association, committed for so very long to a fundamentally anti-Mexican interpretive outlook, to recognize and officially encourage the work of Chicana/o historians. And still the trope of the disloyal, lying, thieving Mexican (or Chicana/o, as the trope makes no distinction) lingers in the publishing world of Texas history, often with only slight modification from the language of decades ago when open racism was far more tolerated in print.[34] To make matters more difficult, by the 1980s the national social and political terrain began to shift in ways more hostile to Chicana/o and Latina/o issues such as affirmative action, bilingual education, immigration, voting rights, unionization, and the responsiveness of the public schools, a trend that continues today.[35]

The Postmodern Intellectual Shift

This traditional perspective, which had been the field's unifying interpretive paradigm, began to unravel in the mid to late 1980s due in part to shifting intellectual currents within the US academy. Chicana/o scholars who had earlier created the traditional perspective began to fall away from it in their new works. Also, younger scholars expressed impatience with the interpretive confines of an earlier moment that did not always reflect their own. This was an internal debate. A scholarly backlash to the traditional perspective emerged, reaching an interpretive orthodoxy that decried the alleged combativeness and defensiveness of traditional perspectives, or what one historian at the time referred to as a "Them-versus-Us" mentality. These critics held that traditional notions distorted historical perception by overemphasizing internal consensus, group homogeneity, and shared experiences, and by implying a teleological history of the community culminating in glorious victory at the arrival of the Chicano Movement—what the scholar Randy Ontiveros refers to as "Whig" history.[36]

Out of this brewing internal tension, something of a brief transitional period emerged between the mid-1980s and the mid-1990s. If there was one thing that unified the work of this transitional period, it was the concept of *agency*. Most, but not all, Chicana/o historians during this shift contended with Chicana/o agency in new and diverse forms in their work. They also began to address neglected issues such as gender, which they rightfully concluded was woefully underappreciated in the traditional corpus.[37] Transitional scholarship came to more fully appreciate as well the complexities of race and class formation.[38]

There is much more to this transitional period in Chicana/o history. Historians during this brief era developed more focused topical investigations of the creation of the US-Mexico border as a physically defined and policed space.[39] The realm of Chicana/o culture became a focus among these scholars.[40] In-depth studies of immigration also appeared.[41] And the subject of education came under particular focus and attention.[42] The scholarship of this period took on topics outside the traditional Southwest region.[43] In addition, transitional scholarship deepened the theme of political and leadership generations as well as major activist groups.[44] The Chicana/o history produced during and after *el Movimiento* in the 1970s had traveled a significant distance by the 1980s and early 1990s. Scholars today fail to sufficiently appreciate these changes. This transitional period forms a crucial and intellectually formidable link connecting the traditional and the new in Chicana/o history.

But this shift away from traditional ideas requires additional explanation. It was the result of larger intellectual forces, particularly postmodern thought. The 1996 Michigan State University conference resulting in the collection *Voices of a New Chicana/o History*, for example, was a major attempt to grapple with the field's creation and development, as well as the impact of postmodernism. It illustrates how divisive postmodern intellectual thought was to many traditionalists two decades ago, accurately representing the muddle that was the transitional phase. In *Voices of a New Chicana/o History* the linguistic turn and the feminist agenda are points of serious contention. There is a palpable tension between traditional and new perspectives in this collection. Quite telling is the wistful lament by the collection's more pessimistic scholars of the absence of a single, overarching interpretive paradigm that would resuscitate the universal in the field over its increasing embrace of the particular and the nuanced.[45]

What was so divisive about postmodernism? For one, it led to a questioning or an unraveling of the traditional in a number of ways. At a basic level, it closed the door to a firm conviction of any sense of a single truth that can be commonly understood or divined. As the intellectual historian Daniel Wickberg writes of postmodernism's influence in several fields, one visible transformation is the shift from social history's search for the agency of the inarticulate to cultural history's unmasking of assumed categories and identities as well as its emphasis on power and the powerful.[46] More specifically to Chicana/o history, Ernesto Chávez identifies the postmodern turn in Chicana/o history as having to do with the demolition of the "universal male subject" by groundbreaking Chicana historians in the 1980s and 1990s. Postmodern thought was compelling to Chicana/o scholars for many reasons. Chicanas/os, once outsiders in their own academic representation, now contributed directly to that representation. Michel Foucault acknowledged this concept of the subject studying and, in effect, re-creating itself as a linchpin of the crisis of objectivity in the social sciences that, in turn,

structured the postmodern condition. This is an old experience for Chi-
canas/os. George J. Sánchez argues that their constant negotiation of
international boundaries, cultures, and stark differences between poverty and affluence meant that Chicana/o peoples, especially Mexican
immigrants, "have been among the first to experience what some have
called the 'postmodern condition.'"[47]

Even without subscribing to this novel argument, one must still conclude that many Chicana/o scholars have, self-consciously or not, embraced the intellectual tenets of postmodernity and that this has moved
them interpretively away from the traditional to the new. This shift entails an interest in multiple kinds of oppression and resistance, a commitment to embracing the complicated diversity of human experience,
an enhanced sensibility about the capacity for human agency, a disinter-
est for sweeping conclusions and universal assumptions, a preference for
more situational and strategic claims to individual and group identity, a
greater comfort with multicausality, and a preoccupation with language
and its often contended meaning. As Emma Pérez concludes, knowledge
is power, and breaking through older, colonial modes of thought that
are enmeshed in binaries of race, gender, sex, and class is itself a form
of liberation that enables the historian to "begin to build another story,
uncovering the untold to consciously remake the narrative."[48]

There is something inherently postmodern about Chicana/o history.
Partly, this condition can be explained by the contested social terrain
that Chicana/o historians occupy in academia. They bear a burdensome
intellectual legacy of having to defend their academic findings and the
respectability of their research subject, defend their ability and authority to perform their work, and connect that work to social realities. This
has created a sort of persistent intellectual presentism that defines the
field. I regard this persistent presentism positively. Scholarly passion for
one's community (no matter how imagined it might be or how authen-
tic one might be regarded by others) and the application of ideas to promote social justice are good and wholesome when bound by the accepted
scholarly constraints in regard to evidence and argument. But this sensibility was not in currency in academic circles forty and fifty years ago.
In the process of erecting the parameters of a new field of inquiry where
there had been nothing, early Chicana/o historians had to ask new questions, consider new evidence, and invent a new story. They did so while
addressing centuries of intellectual discourses on the alleged inferiority of Chicana/o peoples that directly impacted perception of their own
abilities. Theirs was a herculean task, and they had little help.

New Chicana/o History

Since the late 1990s and 2000s Chicana/o historians have continued the intellectual evolution first evinced by the transitional scholarship and further informed by emerging postmodern intellectual outlooks. The *new* Chicana/o history enlivens older topics and questions with fresh insight while exploring new topics and asking different questions. Several broad themes characterize these new directions: (1) the proliferation of different conceptions of identity; (2) the decentering of traditional notions of place; (3) a heightened reflection over the field of Chicana/o history, or a historiographical turn; and (4) the firm connection of historical investigations to present situations. The first two themes reflect how the new Chicana/o history is stepping out in new directions; the final two reflect how a rigorous, critical looking-in enables this act of stepping out.

Proliferation of Identity

The new Chicana/o history steps out to embrace multiple, overlapping, and contested forms of individual and group identity in place of the once-assumed universal, male, proletarian radical committed to resisting power and oppression in heroic ways from within a static culture. These new ways of seeing the past complicate older assumptions about internal homogeneity and the sameness of experience. This multiplicity of identity enriches the field. For example, traditional assumptions about Chicana/o religion are under serious scrutiny. No longer is the relationship of Chicanas/os to Catholicism embedded in a sweeping series of assumptions and structural models. And Chicana/o Protestantism has become far more appreciated and recognized by historians on its own terms and with greater interdisciplinary energy.[49] Felipe Hinojosa's chapter later in this volume adds significantly to this major development in the field.

Whiteness scholarship, an extension of critical race studies, has spurred trenchant criticism of the Chicana/o civil rights movement and its community leadership along lines of racial identity.[50] Yet the Manichean starkness of some whiteness critiques motivates other Chicana/o historians to undertake comparative, relational studies of Chicana/o civil rights and community activism as well as the processes that shape the formation of race in more complex ways.[51] In the next chapter of this volume, Michael Olivas discusses his growth as a historian and activist resulting from the rich Chicana/o civil rights tradition, so often under-appreciated and misunderstood by scholars. And innovative new studies of Chicana/o leaders, organizations, and strategies regularly appear.[52]

Yet the most noticeable and important development in this explosion of identity is the embrace of gender and women's history. The field of Chicana/o history has become more encouraging and supportive to the study of women and gender than it once was. Recent scholars have advanced sophisticated frameworks of gender, sexuality, and family in their research. The work of feminist and queer studies scholars illuminates the negotiation of power, history, and culture among men and women and within families.[53] Sonia Hernández's chapter in this book illustrates this shift by placing women and gender first in such a way that sheds new light on those subjects and on all those other related subjects that were once thought to be understood.

Decentering of Place

The second organizing theme is the demise of a traditional sense of place in the field. Chicana/o history still produces excellent and cutting-edge work on community formation in the Southwest United States as well as tried-and-true topics on culture and resistance to racial oppression.[54] Much of the work on the US-Mexican borderlands, however, has broadened in scope to more fully embrace transnationalism and the global reach of Chicana/o history.[55] This new borderlands scholarship also addresses the relationship between Chicanas/os and Native Americans, Anglos, and other migrants to the region.[56] The chapters by Luis Alvarez, Perla M. Guerrero, Lilia Fernández, and Sonia Hernández address in a broader manner this geographic expansion of constructed and negotiated boundaries and borders.

The demolition of a traditional sense of place extends to Chicana/o communities in other regions of the nation. Increasingly, the Chicana/o story is a national one, not regional. Perhaps ironically, this is demonstrated by regional incorporations of new (yet familiar) iterations of the Chicana/o historical experience in the US South and Midwest. Building upon an earlier but somewhat neglected foundation among Chicana/o scholars, work on the Midwest of late has taken flight.[57] An even newer manifestation of this eroding of traditional regional boundaries is the scholarship on Chicana/o and Latina/o peoples in the US South, often flippantly referred to as the *Nuevo* New South.[58] The subsequent chapters by Perla Guerrero and Lilia Fernández address this exciting and growing development.

Reflection on the Meaning of the Field

The third theme involves what I call a historiographic turn, the proliferation of serious reflections on the development and meaning of Chicana/o history. The new Chicana/o history goes far beyond politically useful but distorting interpretive assumptions of the traditional paradigm. Fittingly, among the richest and most promising subfields of Chicana/o history today are those that reexamine *el Movimiento*. Debating the Chicano Movement gets at the center of what Chicana/o history is today: who is included in it, where it is going, and why it exists. These works are interpretively nuanced and sophisticated.[59] Scholars now highlight the movement's compromises, tensions, and antecedents. This produces, according to the scholar Randy Ontiveros, far more complex narratives that avoid a kind of "movement elegy in which we are marching ever onward to glory." This means appreciating the movement for what it was at least as much as for what it claimed. As Felipe Hinojosa concludes in one recent study, "In the end, the Chicano movement was more reformist than revolutionary," contrary to its commonly understood posture.[60]

Asking questions about the meaning of the field initiates discussions of authority and representation that, though difficult, are ultimately beneficial and necessary. For example, Perla Guerrero in her chapter questions the meaning of Chicana/o history outside the US Southwest and for Latina/o students of increasingly non-Mexican heritage. These are issues with which the field must come to terms. Some scholars have viewed this evolution in the field in purely generational terms (often expressed pejoratively) or as a form of declension from an earlier purity.[61] This vital reflection on the changing nature of Chicana/o history demonstrates a heightened interest in traditional historiography as well as for other critical ruminations on the field's strengths and weaknesses. While this is perhaps the least developed of these themes and the most abstract to characterize, it too has momentum.[62]

Another manifestation of this new level of critical examination within the field is the effort to imagine Chicana/o historical experiences beyond a narrow ethnographic focus. The aim of this approach is to examine a more relational history that takes seriously how Chicanas/os are interconnected with other groups and how such relationships influence the historical experience. This changes the focus, scope, and basic assumptions behind the field. Specific manifestations of this general turn toward the relational are the recent emphasis on Latina/o history and inter-Latina/o relations.[63] It calls to mind Luis Alvarez's chapter later in this volume and its elucidation of the importance of the relational to Chicana/o history. That it does so in East Los Angeles, for many the supposed core of Chicana/o cultural authenticity, is a testament to the kind of radical possibilities the relational turn provides.

Connecting Past and Present

Yet the new Chicana/o history of the twenty-first century remains intimately connected to traditional Chicana/o history in its active linkage of past and present, often expressed through scholarly activism. For many in the field this entails participating in or helping to create Chicana/o or Latina/o studies programs, itself an important kind of scholarly activism. Here I take issue with George Mariscal's distrust of the notion that academic research is too personal a thing to qualify as activism or that this is somehow representative of a "generational anxiety" among younger scholars nervous about connecting activism to academic research. And no one is arguing that activism must stop there, or that this is the only kind of activism that matters.[64]

Beyond the issue of how activist-oriented a scholar may regard their own scholarship, without question many Chicana/o historians are involved in a wider advocacy for social justice. Today, for example, societal problems over civil rights, immigration, education, and poverty continue to animate the new Chicana/o history and the scholars who make it. The academic interests in transnationalism, in taking gender and sexual identity seriously, and in the relationship between Chicanas/os and other racialized groups are, not coincidentally, also matters directly at the forefront of civil rights today.[65] To push this point a little further, the contributors to this collection conduct serious and widely recognized academic work that nevertheless maintains the connection of past to present—that starting point of redressing contemporary problems. From the social invisibility of old and new populations, to the recognition of religious diversity and advocacy, to the possibility of radical and transformative ideas that cross borders, to the meaning of culture as it intersects with consumption, notions of authenticity, and globalism, to the plight of DREAMers, the contributors in this collection produce socially relevant scholarship. That basic connection between past and present—that faith in the empowering possibility of historical knowledge for self-awareness and collective action—is the most important theme in this field and unites Chicana/o historians of any period, connecting them with the timeless spirit of Chicana/o history, whatever the most recent changes in interpretation or method.

Chicana/o history is a crucial aspect of US and world history. It always was, even if at one time only its practitioners realized such claims. The new Chicana/o history of the twenty-first century continues to make that point. In fresh and intellectually stimulating ways, recent Chicana/o history recognizes the increasing proliferation of identity, furthers the decentering of place, engages in a deeper critical reflection about the meaning of the field, and maintains a connection to the present and to social justice. In doing so, Chicana/o history has built upon a productive and passionate foundation of prior works to extend the field. In the last few decades Chicana/o history has stepped out in bold new directions while continuing to look inward at the meaning of the field, where it has come from, and where it is going. This makes the Chicana/o history of the present as socially relevant as ever. Whatever the problems of Chicana/o history today, its promise is far more significant. That promise is something each of us involved in writing this volume strive to realize.

Notes

1. I use *Chicana/o* in an inclusive manner to denote Mexican Americans of the US Southwest, its traditional usage, and also to include Mexican immigrants. When national identity becomes important, I will use *Mexican* or *Mexican American*. I will occasionally use *Latina/o*. I employ the more gender-inclusive *a/o* ending, though I break with this practice when discussing the Chicano Movement of the late 1960s and 1970s out of respect for the conventions of that era. Activists at that time would have denied that *Chicano* was insufficiently inclusive, though such arguments have fallen flat in recent years. Finally, I realize that *Chicana/o* and *Latina/o*, while often overlapping terms, can be very different scholarly fields and bodies of knowledge. For more on connecting Chicana/o and Latina/o history, see David G. Gutiérrez, "Demography and the Shifting Boundaries of 'Community': Reflections on 'US Latinos' and the Evolution of Latino Studies," in *The Columbia History of Latinos in the United States since 1960*, ed. David G. Gutiérrez (New York: Columbia University Press, 2004), 1–42.
2. Alexandra Minna Stern, "On the Road with Chicana/o History: From

Aztlán to the Alamo and Back," *Pacific Historical Review* 82, no. 4 (November 2013): 581–587, quotation on p. 587.

3. While the designation "new Chicana/o history of the twenty-first century" may seem triumphalist, it is not so intended. I do not suggest the *new* is inherently better or more intellectually virtuous than the *traditional*, or vice versa—just different. And there remain commonalities between the *traditional* and the *new*. I do think it important, however, to discuss these differences with a critical, analytical perspective that is intended to leave aside any sense of moral judgment or personal negativism.

4. A caveat is in order. The chapter's final sections discuss subfields and directions within Chicana/o history and indicate significant works within them. In no way do they intend to be exhaustive. This chapter is more a thought piece than a comprehensive historiography. Also, in the later sections I list representative works as sparingly as possible. With some canonical studies—George J. Sánchez's *Becoming Mexican American*, for example—this is difficult. I acknowledge that most works could fit within more than just one historiographical niche and realize this decision misses out on additional complexity. It is, however, an editorial decision based on space constraints.

5. For more on these controversies in Arizona, see Darius V. Echeverría, *Aztlán Arizona: Mexican American Educational Empowerment, 1968–1978* (Tucson: University of Arizona Press, 2014); James A. Banks, "Ethnic Studies, Citizenship Education, and the Public Good," *Intercultural Education* 23, no. 6 (December 2012): 467–473.

6. Marc Lacey, "Rift in Arizona as Latino Class Is Found Illegal," *New York Times*, January 7, 2011, accessed November 22, 2013, http://nytimes.com/2011/01/08/us/08ethnic.html?pagewanted=print; Sophie Quinton, "Good Teachers Embrace Their Students' Cultural Backgrounds," *The Atlantic*, November 2013, accessed November 22, 2013, http://www.theatlantic.com/education/print/2013/11/good-teachers-embrace-their-students-cultural-backgrounds/281337/.

7. Greg Grandin, "History's Sinkhole," *The Nation*, October 22, 2013, accessed November 22, 2013, http://www.thenation.com/print/article/176782/historys-sinkhole.

8. "US Immigration Officials Deport Dreamer Activist. Rocio Hernandez Perez Surrendered to US Authorities at the Texas-Mexico Border Last Month to Protest Immigration Policies," *The Guardian*, October 29, 2013, accessed November 22, 2013, http://theguardian.com/world/2013/oct/29/us-immigration-deport-dreamer-activist/print.

9. Molly Hennessy-Fiske, "Texas Gov. Rick Perry Orders 1,000 National Guard Troops to Border," *Los Angeles Times*, July 21, 2014, accessed July 30, 2014, http://www.latimes.com/nation/la-na-texas-perry-national-guard-border-20140721-story.html; Ramón A. Gutiérrez, "Hispanic Identities in the Southwestern United States," in *Race and Classification: The Case of Mexican America*, ed. Ilona Katzew and Susan Deans-Smith (Stanford, CA: Stanford University Press, 2009), 188–190; Greg Richter, "Rep. Steve King: Numbers Show More Drug 'Mules' than Valedictorians," *Newsmax*, July 24, 2013, accessed November 26, 2013, http://www.newsmax.com/Newsfront/steve-king-drug-mules/2013/07/24/id/516905.

10. By *thinkers* I mean the specific class of people that, at any given point in time, are primarily "charged with the business of thinking" about meaningful debates and issues affecting society or policy. They debate ideas in an influential manner. For more on this, see Daniel Wickberg, "Intellectual History vs. the Social History of Intellectuals," *Rethinking History* 5, no. 3 (2001): 383–395, quotation on p. 385. For the intellectual as a social class in the United States, see Christopher Lasch, *The New Radicalism in America, 1889–1963: The Intellectual as a Social Type* (New York: Knopf, 1965).

11. Samuel P. Huntington, "The Hispanic Challenge," *Foreign Policy* 141 (March/April 2004): 30–45; Arthur M. Schlesinger Jr., *The Disuniting of America: Reflections on a Multicultural Society* (New York: W. W. Norton, 1991). For academic refutations of such arguments, particularly Huntington's, see Jorge Capetillo-Ponce, "From 'A Clash of Civilizations' to 'Internal Colonialism': Reactions to the Theoretical Bases of Samuel Huntington's 'The Hispanic Challenge,'" *Ethnicities* 7, no. 1 (2007): 116–134, quotation on p. 129; Rogelio Saenz, Janie Filoteo, and Aurelia Lorena Murga, "Are Mexicans in the United States a Threat to the American Way of Life? A Response to Huntington," *Du Bois Review* 4, no. 2 (2007): 375–393.

12. Commentary by Richard R. Valencia, "Jason Richwine's Dissertation, IQ and Immigration Policy: Neohereditarianism, Pseudoscience, and Deficit Thinking," *Teachers College Record*, May 29, 2013, 1–9, quotation on p. 4, http://www.tcrecord.org/printContent.asp?ContentID=17134; W. W. Houston, "The Richwine Affair," *The Economist*, May 14, 2013, accessed November 22, 2013, http://www.economist.com/blogs/democracyinamerica/2013/05/immigration-and-iq-0/print. For earlier IQ controversies, see Arthur R. Jensen, "How Much Can We Boost IQ and Scholastic Achievement?" *Harvard Educational Review* 39, no. 1 (Winter 1969): 1–123; Richard J. Herrnstein and Charles Murray, *The Bell Curve: Intelligence and Class Structure in American Life* (New York: Free Press, 1994).

13. For classic works on the subject, see Octavio I. Romano-V, "The Anthropology and Sociology of the Mexican-Americans: The Distortion of History," *El Grito* 2, no. 2 (Winter 1968): 13–26; Nick C. Vaca, "The Mexican-American in the Social Sciences, Pt. I: 1912–1935," and "Pt. II: 1936–1970," *El Grito* 3, nos. 1 and 2 (Spring and Fall 1970): 3–24 and 17–51. For a recent discussion of the construction of race through policy discourses, see Natalia Molina, *How Race Is Made in America: Immigration, Citizenship, and the Historical Power of Racial Scripts* (Berkeley: University of California Press, 2013).

14. Charles Gibson, *The Black Legend: Anti-Spanish Attitudes in the Old World and the New* (New York: Knopf, 1971); Richard L. Kagan, "Prescott's Paradigm: American Historical Scholarship and the Decline of Spain," *American Historical Review* 101, no. 2 (April 1996): 423–446; Kagan, "From Noah to Moses: The Genesis of Historical Scholarship on Spain in the United States," in *Spain in America: The Origins of Hispanism in the United States* (Urbana: University of Illinois Press, 2002), 21–48.

15. Robert E. May, *Manifest Destiny's Underworld: Filibustering in Antebellum America* (Chapel Hill: University of North Carolina Press, 2002); May, *John A. Quitman: Old South Crusader* (Baton Rouge: Louisiana State University Press,

1985); Reginald Horsman, *Race and Manifest Destiny: The Origins of American Racial Anglo-Saxonism* (Cambridge, MA: Harvard University Press, 1981); John C. Pinheiro, "'Religion without Restriction': Anti-Catholicism, All Mexico, and the Treaty of Guadalupe Hidalgo," *Journal of the Early Republic* 23, no. 1 (Spring 2003): 69–96; Arnoldo De León, *They Called Them Greasers: Anglo Attitudes toward Mexicans in Texas, 1821–1900* (Austin: University of Texas Press, 1983); Laura E. Gómez, *Manifest Destinies: The Making of the Mexican American Race* (New York: New York University Press, 2007).

16. Madison Grant, *The Passing of the Great Race; or, The Racial Bias of European History* (New York: Charles Scribner's Sons, 1916); Robert F. Zeidel, *Immigrants, Progressives, and Exclusion Politics: The Dillingham Commission, 1900–1927* (DeKalb: Northern Illinois University Press, 2004); Vernon J. Williams Jr., *Rethinking Race: Franz Boas and His Contemporaries* (Lexington: University of Kentucky Press, 1996); Daryl Michael Scott, *Contempt and Pity: Social Policy and the Image of the Damaged Black Psyche, 1880–1996* (Chapel Hill: University of North Carolina Press, 1997); Lynn M. Getz, "Biological Determinism in the Making of Immigration Policy in the 1920s," *International Science Review* 70, nos. 1–2 (1995): 26–33.

17. Miroslava Chávez-García, "Intelligence Testing at Whittier School, 1890–1920," *Pacific Historical Review* 76, no. 2 (May 2007): 193–228; Carlos Kevin Blanton, "From Intellectual Deficiency to Cultural Deficiency: Mexican Americans, Testing, and Public School Policy in the American Southwest, 1920–1940," *Pacific Historical Review* 72, no. 1 (February 2003): 39–62; Blanton, *The Strange Career of Bilingual Education in Texas, 1836–1981* (College Station: Texas A&M University Press, 2004); Richard R. Valencia, *Chicano Students and the Courts: The Mexican American Legal Struggle for Educational Equality* (New York: New York University Press, 2008).

18. Alice O'Connor, *Poverty Knowledge: Social Science, Social Policy, and the Poor in Twentieth-Century US History* (Princeton, NJ: Princeton University Press, 2001); Richard R. Valencia, *Dismantling Contemporary Deficit Thinking: Educational Thought and Practice* (New York: Routledge, 2010); Carlos Kevin Blanton, "A Legacy of Neglect: George I. Sánchez, Mexican American Education, and the Ideal of Integration, 1940–1970," *Teachers College Record* 114, no. 6 (June 2012): 1–34.

19. David G. Gutiérrez, "Significant to Whom? Mexican Americans and the History of the American West," *Western Historical Quarterly* 24, no. 4 (November 1993): 519–539; Mario T. García, *Mexican Americans: Leadership, Ideology, and Identity, 1930–1960* (New Haven, CT: Yale University Press, 1989); Félix D. Almaráz Jr., *Knight without Armor: Carlos Eduardo Castañeda, 1896–1958* (College Station: Texas A&M University Press, 1999); Leticia M. Garza-Falcón, *Gente Decente: A Borderlands Response to the Rhetoric of Dominance* (Austin: University of Texas Press, 1998); John Morán González, *Border Renaissance: The Texas Centennial and the Emergence of Mexican American Literature* (Austin: University of Texas Press, 2009); Ramón Saldívar, *The Borderlands of Culture: Américo Paredes and the Transnational Imaginary* (Durham, NC: Duke University Press, 2006); José E. Limón, *Américo Paredes: Culture and Critique* (Austin: University of Texas Press, 2012); Carlos Kevin Blanton, *George I. Sánchez: The*

Long Fight for Mexican American Integration (New Haven, CT: Yale University Press, 2014).

20. A few examples of this early scholarship include Carey McWilliams, *North from Mexico: The Spanish-Speaking People of the United States* (Philadelphia: J. B. Lippincott Co., 1949; repr., New York: Greenwood Press, 1968); George I. Sánchez, *Forgotten People: A Study of New Mexicans* (Albuquerque: University of New Mexico Press, 1940; repr., 1996); Jovita González, "Social Life in Cameron, Starr, and Zapata Counties" (master's thesis, University of Texas, 1930); Américo Paredes, *"With His Pistol in His Hand": A Border Ballad and Its Hero* (Austin: University of Texas Press, 1958); Carlos E. Castañeda, *Our Catholic Heritage in Texas, 1519–1936*, vols. 1–7 (Austin: Von Boeckmann-Jones Co., 1936–1958); Arthur L. Campa, *Spanish Folk-Poetry in New Mexico* (Albuquerque: University of New Mexico Press, 1946); Adina de Zavala, *History and Legends of the Alamo and Other Missions in and around San Antonio* (San Antonio: n.p., 1917); Ernesto Galarza, *Merchants of Labor: The Mexican Bracero Story. An Account of the Managed Migration of Mexican Farm Workers in California, 1942–1960* (San Jose, CA: Rosicrucian Press, 1964).

21. Mario Barrera and Geralda Vialpando, eds., *Action Research in Defense of the Barrio: Interviews with Ernesto Galarza, Guillermo Flores, and Rosalia Muñoz* (Los Angeles: Aztlán Publications, 1974).

22. Ramón A. Gutiérrez, "Internal Colonialism: An American Theory of Race," *Du Bois Review* 1, no. 2 (2004): 281–295; Michael Soldatenko, *Chicano Studies: The Genesis of a Discipline* (Tucson: University of Arizona Press, 2009), chap. 1; Lee Bebout, *Mythohistorical Interventions: The Chicano Movement and Its Legacies* (Minneapolis: University of Minnesota Press, 2011), quotation on p. 4; Rodolfo F. Acuña, *The Making of Chicana/o Studies: In the Trenches of Academe* (New Brunswick, NJ: Rutgers University Press, 2011), 59–63. Acuña has an excellent firsthand discussion of *El Plan de Santa Barbara*.

23. Jesus Chavarria, "On Chicano History: In Memorium, George I. Sánchez, 1906–1972," in *Humanidad: Essays in Honor of George I. Sánchez*, ed. Américo Paredes (Los Angeles: Chicano Studies Center Publications, UCLA, 1977), quotation on p. 44.

24. Américo Paredes, "Jorge Isidoro Sánchez y Sánchez, 1906–72," in *Humanidad*, 124–125; Américo Paredes, *A Texas-Mexican Cancionero: Folksongs of the Lower Border* (Urbana: University of Illinois Press, 1976), quotation on p. 171; González, *Border Renaissance*, quotation on p. 221, n. 3. For more on early Chicana critiques of sexism in the Chicano Movement see Maylei Blackwell, *¡Chicana Power! Contested Histories of Feminism in the Chicano Movement* (Austin: University of Texas Press, 2011).

25. Ernesto Chávez, *"¡Mi Raza Primero!" Nationalism, Identity, and Insurgency in the Chicano Movement in Los Angeles, 1966–1978* (Berkeley: University of California Press, 2002), 4–6; Gutiérrez, "Internal Colonialism," 281–295; Randy J. Ontiveros, *In the Spirit of a New People: The Cultural Politics of the Chicano Movement* (New York: New York University Press, 2014), 30.

26. Raúl A. Ramos, "Chicano/a Challenges to Nineteenth-Century History," *Pacific Historical Review* 82, no. 4 (November 2013): 566–580, quotation on p. 569.

27. Gloria Anzaldúa, *Borderlands/La Frontera: The New Mestiza* (San Francisco: Aunt Lute Books, 1987); Antonia I. Castañeda, "Women of Color and the Rewriting of Western History: The Discourse, Politics, and Decolonization of History," *Pacific Historical Review* 61, no. 4 (November 1992): 501–533; Ramón A. Gutiérrez, *When Jesus Came, the Corn Mothers Went Away: Marriage, Sexuality, and Power in New Mexico, 1500–1846* (Stanford, CA: Stanford University Press, 1991). For more on feminist challenges to Chicano patriarchy and the incorporation of Chicanas into feminist scholarship, see Blackwell, *¡Chicana Power!*; Amy Kaminsky, "Gender, Race, Raza," *Feminist Studies* 20, no. 1 (Spring 1994): 7–31.

28. Albert Camarillo, *Chicanos in a Changing Society: From Mexican Pueblos to American Barrios in Santa Barbara and Southern California, 1848–1930* (Cambridge, MA: Harvard University Press, 1979); Ricardo Romo, *East Los Angeles: History of a Barrio* (Austin: University of Texas Press, 1983); Mario T. García, *Desert Immigrants: The Mexicans of El Paso, 1880–1920* (New Haven, CT: Yale University Press, 1981); Richard Griswold del Castillo, *The Los Angeles Barrio, 1850–1890: A Social History* (Berkeley: University of California Press, 1979); Arnoldo De León, *The Tejano Community, 1836–1900* (Albuquerque: University of New Mexico Press, 1982).

29. Rodolfo Acuña, *Occupied America: The Chicano's Struggle toward Liberation* (San Francisco: Canfield Press, 1972); Robert J. Rosenbaum, *Mexicano Resistance in the Southwest: "The Sacred Right of Self-Preservation"* (Austin: University of Texas Press, 1981); Abraham Hoffman, *Unwanted Mexican Americans in the Great Depression: Repatriation Pressures, 1929–1939* (Tucson: University of Arizona Press, 1974); Juan R. García, *Operation Wetback: The Mass Deportation of Mexican Undocumented Workers in 1954* (New York: Praeger, 1980). Though it is much older, one could readily include in this vein Américo Paredes's *With His Pistol in His Hand*.

30. Mario Barrera, *Race and Class in the Southwest: A Theory of Racial Inequality* (Notre Dame, IN: University of Notre Dame Press, 1979); Emilio Zamora, "Chicano Socialist Labor Activity in Texas, 1900–1920," *Aztlán* 6 (Summer 1975): 221–236; Marc Reisler, *By the Sweat of Their Brow: Mexican Immigrant Labor in the United States, 1900–1940* (Westport, CT: Greenwood Press, 1976); Juan Gómez-Quiñones, "The First Steps: Chicano Labor Conflict and Organizing, 1900–1920," *Aztlán* 3 (Spring 1972): 13–49; Gilbert G. Gonzalez, *Progressive Education: A Marxist Interpretation* (Minneapolis: Marxist Educational Press, 1982).

31. Juan Gómez-Quiñones, "On Culture," *Revista Chicano-Riqueña* 5 (Spring 1977): 29–47; Acuña, *Occupied America*; John R. Chávez, *The Lost Land: The Chicano Image of the Southwest* (Albuquerque: University of New Mexico Press, 1984); Paredes, *Texas-Mexican Cancionero*.

32. Alex Saragoza, "Recent Chicano Historiography: An Interpretive Essay," *Aztlán* 19, no. 1 (1988–1990): 1–77; Gutiérrez, "Significant to Whom?" 519–539.

33. Albert M. Camarillo, "Looking Back on Chicano History: A Generational Perspective," *Pacific Historical Review* 82, no. 4 (November 2013): 496–504, quotation on p. 503.

34. Mario T. García, Foreword in Sánchez, *Forgotten People*, xi; Emilio Zamora, Cynthia Orozco, and Rodolfo Rocha, *Mexican Americans in Texas History: Selected Essays* (Austin: Texas State Historical Association Press, 2000); Walter L. Buenger, "Three Truths in Texas," in *Beyond Texas Through Time: Breaking Away from Past Interpretations*, ed. Walter L. Buenger and Arnoldo De León (College Station: Texas A&M University Press, 2011), 1–49.

35. For an overview of this increasingly negative political environment, see Kevin R. Johnson, "The Continuing Latino Quest for Full Membership and Equal Citizenship: Legal Progress, Social Setbacks, and Political Promise," in Gutiérrez, *The Columbia History of Latinos*, 391–420.

36. Saragoza, "Recent Chicano Historiography," 8–11, quotation on p. 8; Ontiveros, *In the Spirit of a New People*, quotation on p. 31.

37. Vicki L. Ruíz, *Cannery Women, Cannery Lives: Mexican Women, Unionization, and the California Food Processing Industry, 1930–1950* (Albuquerque: University of New Mexico Press, 1987); Sarah Deutsch, *No Separate Refuge: Culture, Class, and Gender on an Anglo-Hispanic Frontier in the American Southwest* (New York: Oxford University Press, 1987); Julia Kirk Blackwelder, *Women of the Depression: Caste and Culture in San Antonio, 1929–1939* (College Station: Texas A&M University Press, 1984); Gutiérrez, *When Jesus Came the Corn Mothers Went Away*.

38. David Montejano, *Anglos and Mexicans in the Making of Texas, 1836–1986* (Austin: University of Texas Press, 1987); Tomás Almaguer, *Racial Fault Lines: The Historical Origins of White Supremacy in California* (Berkeley: University of California Press, 1994); Lisbeth Haas, *Conquests and Historical Identities in California, 1769–1936* (Berkeley: University of California Press, 1996); Emilio Zamora, *The World of the Mexican Worker in Texas* (College Station: Texas A&M University Press, 1993); Arnoldo De León and Kenneth L. Stewart, *Not Room Enough: Mexicans, Anglos, and Socio-Economic Change in Texas, 1850–1900* (Albuquerque: University of New Mexico Press, 1993); Devra Weber, *Dark Sweat, White Gold: California Farm Workers, Cotton, and the New Deal* (Berkeley: University of California Press, 1994); Juan Gómez-Quiñones, *Mexican American Labor, 1790–1990* (Albuquerque: University of New Mexico Press, 1994); Gilbert G. Gonzalez, *Labor and Community: Mexican Citrus Worker Villages in a Southern California County, 1900–1950* (Urbana: University of Illinois Press, 1994).

39. Richard Griswold del Castillo, *The Treaty of Guadalupe Hidalgo: A Legacy of Conflict* (Norman: University of Oklahoma Press, 1990); James A. Sandos, *Rebellion in the Borderlands: Anarchism and the Plan of San Diego, 1904–1923* (Norman: University of Oklahoma Press, 1992).

40. George J. Sánchez, *Becoming Mexican American: Ethnicity, Culture, and Identity in Chicano Los Angeles, 1900–1945* (New York: Oxford University Press, 1993); Manuel Peña, *The Texas Mexican Conjunto: History of a Working-Class Music* (Austin: University of Texas Press, 1985); Mauricio Mazón, *The Zoot-Suit Riots: The Psychology of Symbolic Annihilation* (Austin: University of Texas Press, 1988); Richard Griswold del Castillo, *La Familia: Chicano Families in the Urban Southwest, 1848 to the Present* (Notre Dame, IN: University of Notre Dame Press, 1984).

41. Camille Guerin-Gonzales, *Mexican Workers and American Dreams: Immigration, Repatriation, and California Farm Labor, 1900–1939* (New Brunswick, NJ: Rutgers University Press, 1994); David G. Gutiérrez, *Walls and Mirrors: Mexican Americans, Mexican Immigrants, and the Politics of Ethnicity* (Berkeley: University of California Press, 1995).

42. Guadalupe San Miguel Jr., *"Let All of Them Take Heed": Mexican Americans and the Campaign for Educational Equality in Texas, 1910–1981* (Austin: University of Texas Press, 1987); Gilbert G. Gonzalez, *Chicano Education in the Era of Segregation* (Philadelphia: Balch Institute Press, 1990); Lynne Marie Getz, *Schools of Their Own: The Education of Hispanos in New Mexico, 1850–1940* (Albuquerque: University of New Mexico Press, 1997).

43. Dennis Nodín Valdéz, *Al Norte: Agricultural Workers in the Great Lakes Region, 1917–1970* (Austin: University of Texas Press, 1991); Zaragosa Vargas, *Proletarians of the North: A History of Mexican Industrial Workers in Detroit and the Midwest, 1917–1933* (Berkeley: University of California Press, 1993); Erasmo Gamboa, *Mexican Labor and World War II: Braceros in the Pacific Northwest, 1942–1947* (Austin: University of Texas Press, 1990).

44. García, *Mexican Americans*; Sánchez, *Becoming Mexican American*; Julie Leininger Pycior, *LBJ and Mexican Americans: The Paradox of Power* (Austin: University of Texas Press, 1997); Richard A. García, *Rise of the Mexican American Middle Class: San Antonio, 1929–1941* (College Station: Texas A&M University Press, 1991); Benjamín Márquez, *LULAC: The Evolution of a Mexican American Political Organization* (Austin: University of Texas Press, 1993); Carl Allsup, *The American G.I. Forum: Origins and Evolution* (Austin: University of Texas Press, 1982); Carlos Muñoz, *Youth, Identity, Power: The Chicano Movement* (New York: Verso Press, 1989); Armando Navarro, *Mexican American Youth Organization: Avant-Garde of the Chicano Movement in Texas* (Austin: University of Texas Press, 1995); Ignacio M. García, *United We Win: The Rise and Fall of La Raza Unida Party* (Tucson: University of Arizona Press, 1989); I. García, *Chicanismo: The Forging of a Militant Ethos among Mexican Americans* (Tucson: University of Arizona Press, 1997).

45. José Cuello, "Introduction: Chicano/a History as a Social Movement," in *Voices of a New Chicana/o History*, ed. Refugio I. Rochín and Dennis N. Valdés (East Lansing: Michigan State University Press, 2000), 1–22. The tension between the traditional and the new is striking. These camps could not even agree on what constituted Chicana/o history's success.

46. Daniel Wickberg, "Heterosexual White Male: Some Recent Inversions in American Cultural History," *Journal of American History* 92, no. 1 (June 2005): 136–157.

47. Michel Foucault, *The Order of Things: An Archaeology of the Human Sciences*, ed. R. D. Laing (New York: Pantheon Books, 1970); Ernesto Chávez, "Chicano/a History: Its Origins, Purpose, and Future," *Pacific Historical Review* 82, no. 4 (November 2013), quotation on p. 512; Sánchez, *Becoming Mexican American*, quotation on p. 9.

48. Emma Pérez, *The Decolonial Imaginary: Writing Chicanas into History* (Bloomington: Indiana University Press, 1999), quotation on p. 127. For postmodern intellectual trends and their effect upon the writing of history, see Eliz-

abeth A. Clark, *History, Theory, Text: Historians and the Linguistic Turn* (Cambridge, MA: Harvard University Press, 2004).

49. Roberto R. Treviño, *The Church in the Barrio: Mexican American Ethno-Catholicism in Houston* (Chapel Hill: University of North Carolina Press, 2006); Timothy Matovina, *Guadalupe and Her Faithful: Latino Catholics in San Antonio, from Colonial Origins to the Present* (Baltimore: Johns Hopkins University Press, 2005); Arlene Sánchez-Walsh, *Latino Pentecostal Identity: Evangelical Faith, Self, and Society* (New York: Columbia University Press, 2003); Felipe Hinojosa, *Latino Mennonites: Civil Rights, Faith, and Evangelical Culture* (Baltimore: Johns Hopkins University Press, 2014); Mario T. García, *Católicos: Resistance and Affirmation in Chicano Catholic History* (Austin: University of Texas Press, 2008); Anne M. Martínez, *Catholic Borderlands: Mapping Catholicism onto American Empire, 1905–1935* (Lincoln: University of Nebraska Press, 2014).

50. For critical race studies in general, see Richard Delgado and Jean Stefancic, *Critical Race Theory: An Introduction*, 2nd ed. (New York: New York University Press, 2012); Ian F. Haney-López, *White by Law: The Legal Construction of Race* (New York: New York University Press, 1996). For whiteness studies that significantly discuss Mexican Americans, see Neil Foley, *The White Scourge: Mexicans, Blacks, and Poor Whites in Texas Cotton Culture* (Berkeley: University of California Press, 1997); Gómez, *Manifest Destinies*; Neil Foley, *Quest for Equality: The Failed Promise of Black-Brown Solidarity* (Cambridge, MA: Harvard University Press, 2010); Brian D. Behnken, *Fighting Their Own Battles: Mexican Americans, African Americans, and the Struggle for Civil Rights in Texas* (Chapel Hill: University of North Carolina Press, 2011); Ian F. Haney-López, *Racism on Trial: The Chicano Fight for Justice* (Cambridge, MA: Harvard University Press, 2003); Thomas A. Guglielmo, "Fighting for Caucasian Rights: Mexicans, Mexican Americans, and the Transnational Struggle for Civil Rights in World War II Texas," *Journal of American History* 92, no. 4 (March 2006): 1212–1237; Ariela J. Gross, *What Blood Won't Tell: A History of Race on Trial in America* (Cambridge, MA: Harvard University Press, 2008).

51. Michael A. Olivas, ed., *"Colored Men" and "Hombres Aquí": Hernandez v. Texas and the Emergence of Mexican American Lawyering* (Houston: Arte Público Press, 2006); Linda Gordon, *The Great Arizona Orphan Abduction* (Cambridge, MA: Harvard University Press, 2001); Ignacio M. García, *White but Not Equal: Mexican Americans, Jury Discrimination, and the Supreme Court* (Tucson: University of Arizona Press, 2009); Carlos Kevin Blanton, "George I. Sánchez, Ideology, and Whiteness in the Making of the Mexican American Civil Rights Movement, 1930–1960," *Journal of Southern History* 72, no. 3 (August 2006): 569–604; Max Krochmal, "Chicano Labor and Multiracial Politics in Post-World War II Texas: Two Case Studies," in *Life and Labor in the New New South*, ed. Robert H. Zieger (Gainesville: University Press of Florida, 2012), 133–176; Benjamin H. Johnson, "The Cosmic Race in Texas: Racial Fusion, White Supremacy, and Civil Rights Politics," *Journal of American History* 98, no. 2 (September 2011): 404–419; Julie M. Weise, "Mexican Nationalisms, Southern Racisms: Mexicans and Mexican Americans in the US South, 1908–1939," *American Quarterly* 60, no. 3 (September 2008): 749–777; Blanton, *George I. Sánchez*; Arnoldo De León, *Racial Frontiers: Africans, Chinese, and Mexicans in Western Amer-*

ica, 1848–1890 (Albuquerque: University of New Mexico Press, 2002); Martha Menchaca, *Recovering History, Constructing Race: The Indian, Black, and White Roots of Mexican Americans* (Austin: University of Texas Press, 2001); Gordon Keith Mantler, *Power to the Poor: Black-Brown Coalition and the Fight for Economic Justice, 1960–1974* (Chapel Hill: University of North Carolina Press, 2013); Shana Bernstein, *Bridges of Reform: Interracial Civil Rights Activism in Twentieth-Century Los Angeles* (New York: Oxford University Press, 2011); María Josefina Saldaña-Portillo, "'How Many Mexicans [Is] a Horse Worth?': The League of United Latin American Citizens, Desegregation Cases, and Chicano Historiography," *South Atlantic Quarterly* 107, no. 4 (Fall 2008): 809–831.

52. Cynthia E. Orozco, *No Mexicans, Women, or Dogs Allowed: The Rise of the Mexican American Civil Rights Movement* (Austin: University of Texas Press, 2009); Ignacio M. García, *Viva Kennedy: Mexican Americans in Search of Camelot* (College Station: Texas A&M University Press, 2000); Craig A. Kaplowitz, *LULAC: Mexican Americans and National Policy* (College Station: Texas A&M University Press, 2005); Emilio Zamora, *Claiming Rights and Righting Wrongs in Texas: Mexican Workers and Job Politics during World War II* (College Station: Texas A&M University Press, 2009); Benjamin Márquez, *Democratizing Texas Politics: Race, Identity, and Mexican American Empowerment, 1945–2002* (Austin: University of Texas Press, 2014); Roy Lujan, "Dennis Chavez and the National Agenda: 1933–1946," *New Mexico Historical Review* 74, no. 1 (January 1999): 55–74; Rosina A. Lozano, "Managing the 'Priceless Gift': Debating Spanish Language Instruction in New Mexico and Puerto Rico, 1930–1950," *Western Historical Quarterly* 44, no. 3 (Autumn 2013): 271–293.

53. Blackwell, *¡Chicana Power!*; Orozco, *No Mexicans, Women, or Dogs Allowed*; Pérez, *The Decolonial Imaginary*; Catherine S. Ramirez, *The Woman in the Zoot Suit: Gender, Nationalism, and the Politics of Cultural Memory* (Durham, NC: Duke University Press, 2009); Vicki L. Ruiz, *From Out of the Shadows: Mexican Women in Twentieth-Century America* (New York: Oxford University Press, 1998); Deena J. González, *Refusing the Favor: The Spanish-Mexican Women of Santa Fe, 1820–1880* (New York: Oxford University Press, 1999); Elizabeth R. Escobedo, *From Coveralls to Zoot Suits: The Lives of Mexican American Women on the World War II Home Front* (Chapel Hill: University of North Carolina Press, 2013); Miroslava Chávez-García, *Negotiating Conquest: Gender and Power in California, 1770s to 1880s* (Tucson: University of Arizona Press, 2004); Lori A. Flores, "An Unladylike Strike Fashionably Clothed: Mexicana and Anglo Women Garment Workers against Tex-Son, 1959–1963," *Pacific Historical Review* 78, no. 3 (August 2009): 367–402; Ana Elizabeth Rosas, "Breaking the Silence: Mexican Children and Women's Confrontation of Bracero Family Separation, 1942–1964," *Gender and History* 23, no. 2 (August 2011): 382–400; Miroslava Chávez-García, "The Interdisciplinary Project of Chicana History: Looking Back, Moving Forward," *Pacific Historical Review* 82, no. 4 (November 2013): 542–565; Cynthia E. Orozco, "Regionalism, Politics, and Gender in Southwest History: The League of United Latin American Citizens' Expansion into New Mexico from Texas, 1929–1945," *Western Historical Quarterly* 29, no. 4 (Winter 1998): 459–483; Richard T. Rodríguez, *Next of Kin: The Family in Chicano/a Cultural Politics* (Durham, NC: Duke University Press, 2009); Freder-

ick Luis Aldama, *Brown on Brown: Chicano/a Representations of Gender, Sexuality, and Ethnicity* (Austin: University of Texas Press, 2005); Elizabeth R. Escobedo, "The Pachuca Panic: Sexual and Cultural Battlegrounds in World War II," *Western Historical Quarterly* 38, no. 2 (Summer 2007): 133–156; Ernesto Chávez, "'Ramón Is Not One of These': Race and Sexuality in the Construction of Silent Actor Ramón Novarro's Star Image," *Journal of the History of Sexuality* 20 (2011): 520–544.

54. Stephen J. Pitti, *The Devil in Silicon Valley: Northern California, Race, and Mexican Americans* (Princeton, NJ: Princeton University Press, 2003); Matt García, *A World of Its Own: Race, Labor, and Citrus in the Making of Greater Los Angeles, 1900–1970* (Chapel Hill: University of North Carolina Press, 2001); Anthony Quiroz, *Claiming Citizenship: Mexican Americans in Victoria, Texas* (College Station: Texas A&M University Press, 2005); Raúl A. Ramos, *Beyond the Alamo: Forging Mexican Ethnicity in San Antonio, 1821–1861* (Chapel Hill: University of North Carolina Press, 2008); Edward J. Escobar, *Race, Police, and the Making of a Political Identity: Mexican Americans and the Los Angeles Police Department, 1900–1945* (Berkeley: University of California Press, 1999); Eduardo Obregón Pagán, *Murder at the Sleepy Lagoon: Zoot Suits, Race, and Riot in Wartime LA* (Chapel Hill: University of North Carolina Press, 2003); Guadalupe San Miguel Jr., *Tejano Proud: Tex-Mex Music in the Twentieth Century* (College Station: Texas A&M University Press, 2002); Armando C. Alonzo, *Tejano Legacy: Rancheros and Settlers in South Texas, 1734–1900* (Albuquerque: University of New Mexico Press, 1998); José M. Alamillo, *Making Lemonade out of Lemons: Mexican American Labor and Leisure in a California Town, 1880–1960* (Urbana: University of Illinois Press, 2006).

55. Sonia Hernández, *Working Women into the Borderlands* (College Station: Texas A&M University Press, 2014); Anthony P. Mora, *Border Dilemmas: Racial and National Uncertainties in New Mexico, 1848–1912* (Durham, NC: Duke University Press, 2011); José Angel Hernández, *Mexican American Colonization during the Nineteenth Century: A History of the US-Mexico Borderlands* (New York: Cambridge University Press, 2012); Geraldo L. Cadava, *Standing on Common Ground: The Making of a Sunbelt Borderland* (Cambridge, MA: Harvard University Press, 2013); Andrés Reséndez, *Changing National Identities at the Frontier: Texas and New Mexico, 1800–1850* (New York: Cambridge University Press, 2005); John McKiernan-González, *Fevered Measures: Public Health and Race at the Texas-Mexico Border, 1848–1942* (Durham, NC: Duke University Press, 2012); Miguel Antonio Levario, *Militarizing the Border: When Mexicans Became the Enemy* (College Station: Texas A&M University Press, 2012); Omar S. Valerio-Jiménez, *River of Hope: Forging Identity and Nation in the Rio Grande Borderlands* (Durham, NC: Duke University Press, 2013); Kelly Lytle Hernández, *Migra! A History of the US Border Patrol* (Berkeley: University of California Press, 2010); Gilbert G. Gonzalez, *Mexican Consuls and Labor Organizing: Imperial Politics in the American Southwest* (Austin: University of Texas Press, 1999); G. Gonzalez, *Culture of Empire: American Writers, Mexico, and Mexican Immigrants, 1880–1930* (Austin: University of Texas Press, 2004); Ruben Flores, *Backroads Pragmatists: Mexico's Melting Pot and Civil Rights in the United States* (Philadelphia: University of Pennsylvania Press, 2014).

56. James F. Brooks, *Captives and Cousins: Slavery, Kinship, and Community in the Southwest Borderlands* (Chapel Hill: University of North Carolina Press, 2002); Juliana Barr, *Peace Came in the Form of a Woman: Indians and Spaniards in the Texas Borderlands* (Chapel Hill: University of North Carolina Press, 2007); Nicole M. Guidotti-Hernández, *Unspeakable Violence: Remapping US and Mexican National Imaginaries* (Durham, NC: Duke University Press, 2011); James A. Sandos, *Converting California: Indians and Franciscans in the Missions* (New Haven, CT: Yale University Press, 2004); Grace Peña Delgado, *Making the Chinese Mexican: Global Migration, Localism, and Exclusion in the US-Mexico Borderlands* (Stanford, CA: Stanford University Press, 2012); Julia María Schiavone Camacho, *Chinese Mexicans: Transpacific Migration and the Search for a Homeland, 1910–1960* (Chapel Hill: University of North Carolina Press, 2012); Robert Chao Romero, *The Chinese in Mexico, 1882–1940* (Tucson: University of Arizona Press, 2012).

57. Gabriela F. Arredondo, *Mexican Chicago: Race, Identity, and Nation, 1916–1939* (Urbana: University of Illinois Press, 2008); Lilia Fernández, *Brown in the Windy City: Mexicans and Puerto Ricans in Postwar Chicago* (Chicago: University of Chicago Press, 2012); Michael Innis-Jiménez, *Steel Barrio: The Great Mexican Migration to South Chicago, 1915–1940* (New York: New York University Press, 2013); Marc Simon Rodriguez, *The Tejano Diaspora: Mexican Americanism and Ethnic Politics in Texas and Wisconsin* (Chapel Hill: University of North Carolina Press, 2011).

58. Leon Fink, *The Maya of Morganton: Work and Community in the Nuevo New South* (Chapel Hill: University of North Carolina Press, 2007); Perla M. Guerrero, *Latinas/os and Asians Remaking Arkansas: Race, Labor, Place, and Community* (book manuscript in progress); Julie Wiese, *Corazon de Dixie: Mexico and Mexicans in the US South since 1910* (Chapel Hill: University of North Carolina Press, 2015).

59. Chávez, *"¡Mi Raza Primero!"*; Blackwell, *¡Chicana Power!*; Lorena Oropeza, *¡Raza Si! ¡Guerra No! Chicano Protest and Patriotism during the Vietnam War Era* (Berkeley: University of California Press, 2005); Laura Pulido, *Black, Brown, Yellow, and Left: Radical Activism in Los Angeles* (Berkeley: University of California Press, 2006); David Montejano, *Quixote's Soldiers: A Local History of the Chicano Movement, 1966–1981* (Austin: University of Texas Press, 2010); Guadalupe San Miguel Jr., *Brown, not White: School Integration and the Chicano Movement in Houston* (College Station: Texas A&M University Press, 2001); George Mariscal, *Brown-Eyed Children of the Sun: Lessons from the Chicano Movement, 1965–1975* (Albuquerque: University of New Mexico Press, 2005); Matt García, *From the Jaws of Victory: The Triumph and Tragedy of Cesar Chavez and the Farm Worker Movement* (Berkeley: University of California Press, 2012); Guadalupe San Miguel Jr., *Chicana/o Struggles for Education: Activism in the Community* (College Station: Texas A&M University Press, 2013); Mario T. García, ed., *The Chicano Movement: Perspectives from the Twenty-First Century* (New York: Routledge, 2014); Lorena Oropeza, "The Heart of Chicano History: Reies López Tijerina as a Memory Entrepreneur," *The Sixties* 1, no. 1 (2008): 49–67.

60. Ontiveros, *In the Spirit of a New People*, quotation on p. 31; Felipe Hino-

josa, *"¡Medicina Sí Muerte No!* Race, Public Health, and the 'Long War on Poverty' in Mathis, Texas, 1948–1971," *Western Historical Quarterly* 44, no. 4 (Winter 2013): 437–458, quotation on p. 458.

61. Mariscal, *Brown-Eyed Children of the Sun*, 268–273; Ignacio M. García, "Juncture in the Road: Chicano Studies since 'El Plan de Santa Bárbara,'" in *Chicanas/Chicanos at the Crossroads: Social, Economic, and Political Change*, ed. David R. Maciel and Isidro D. Ortiz (Tucson: University of Arizona Press, 1996), 181–203; Rodolfo F. Acuña, "Truth and Objectivity in Chicano History," in Rochín and Valdés, *Voices of a New Chicano History*, 23–50.

62. Pérez, *The Decolonial Imaginary*; Gutiérrez, "Internal Colonialism"; Vicki L. Ruiz with Leisa D. Meyer, "Ongoing Missionary Labor: Building, Maintaining, and Expanding Chicana Studies/History (An Interview with Vicki L. Ruiz)," *Feminist Studies* 34, nos. 1–2 (Spring/Summer 2008): 1–14; Soldatenko, *Chicano Studies*; Bebout, *Mythohistorical Interventions*; Ontiveros, *In the Spirit of a New People*; García, ed., *The Chicano Movement*. See also the outstanding *Pacific Historical Review* special issue of November 2013, "Chicano/a History: Looking Forward After 40 Years," and the essays by its contributors, Albert M. Camarillo, Ernesto Chávez, Natalia Molina, Miroslava Chávez-García, Raúl A. Ramos, and Alexandra Minna Stern.

63. Natalia Molina, "Examining Chicana/o History through a Relational Lens," *Pacific Historical Review* 82, no. 4 (November 2013): 520–541; Vicki L. Ruiz, "Neustra America: Latino History as United States History," *Journal of American History* 93, no. 3 (December 2006): 655–672; Sánchez, *Becoming Mexican American*; Pulido, *Black, Brown, Yellow, and Left*; Luis Alvarez, *The Power of the Zoot: Youth Culture and Resistance during World War II* (Berkeley: University of California Press, 2008); Al Camarillo, "Navigating Segregated Life in America's Racial Border Hoods, 1910s–1950s," *Journal of American History* 100, no. 3 (December 2013): 645–662; Luis Alvarez and Daniel Widener, "A History of Black and Brown: Chicana/o-African American Cultural and Political Relations," *Aztlán* 33, no. 1 (Spring 2008): 143–154.

64. Mariscal, *Brown-Eyed Children of the Sun*, 270–273, quotation on p. 270. Mariscal's apparent desire for a unity of research and activism in his excellent study represents what I would call a traditional outlook. Unfortunately, his insertion of age in a pejorative fashion does little to further understanding in the field. It is an example of the kind of generational ad hominem characterization this chapter hopes to avoid.

65. Ontiveros, *In the Spirit of a New People*, 36–38.

CHAPTER TWO

The Accidental Historian; or,
How I Found My Groove in Legal History

MICHAEL A. OLIVAS

Some scholars are hedgehogs, rooting around in the same small niche of the panopticon universe, while others are foxes, less focused and more eclectic, roaming over large and often unrelated terrains. Neither extreme is attractive to me, although a review of my own work since 1974, when I published my first article, on John Updike, in *Modern Fiction Studies*, and 1975, when I published my first book, also on John Updike, shows how far to the fox end of the spectrum I have been.[1] To be sure, there are areas where I have dug intensely and hedgehogly, such as college residency requirements, minorities in higher education, and Section 529 prepaid savings plans; in these areas I have regularly maintained long and deep attention.[2] But it is surely a fair assessment to say that I have had more of a punctuated equilibrium, to borrow and adapt Stephen J. Gould's extraordinary term for a form of evolution, manifesting itself intermittently over the arc of my career.[3] I am sixty-three as I write this, and have hit my stride, so I hope that there will be other, later chapters, but more importantly, I realize how lucky I have been and how many of the fates that befell me or presented themselves without notice were largely forces for good. I certainly do not believe I am a good example for any such career trajectories, and many people have had exceptional careers without any of the *Sturm und Drang* or dark moments I have encountered—or, for that matter, without my many exhilarating moments. Each of us carves out our own solitary climbing path along the mountain. But I do believe that many Chicano and Chicana scholars, especially prolific and productive ones, have encountered a version of the same scholarly drift and flow that I have encountered, even without leading the examined life, as this essay has given me such an occasion.

If there were ever an example of my punctuated equilibrium style, it is my uneven and intermittent movement across these boundaries/*fronteras* rather than the straight and linear course that seems to me more historian-like and hedgehog-like. As an example of this trait, I recall trying to involve historians in my own conferences or book projects, only to hear that they already have a project on which they are working. (To protect the busy innocents, I will not identify several who have stiff-armed me with this excuse.) I mean no disrespect—indeed, the opposite, as I always admire people who function so differently—when I write that it takes such a focused turn of mind and serial projects to be a successful history scholar. I have seen this trait in my own historian brother, Professor Richard Olivas—who earned his doctorate in religious history at the University of California, Los Angeles with Gary Nash—and have come to believe through my observations of a number of successful historians, some of whom I have known since elementary and secondary school, that successful historian work habits derive from the near-universal requirement at many universities that they publish their dissertation with a university press to achieve tenure. In today's competitive environment and with the shrinking universe of university presses, this necessitates a laser-like focus to get over that hump. And perhaps this is changing. Narrow field and disciplinary boundaries have melted away in recent decades in Chicana/o history and throughout the history profession, a point made by Carlos Blanton in his chapter in this collection as well as having recently appeared in the pages of the *Chronicle of Higher Education*.[4]

Over the short haul, this exacting process favors the hedgehogs, and successful repeat behavior is necessary for promotion to full professor. In a historian's scholarly lifetime there is still room for more fox-like behavior, a broader approach, and wider peripheral vision, but old habits, especially successful ones that were efficacious, die hard. As a corollary, many successful historians find small niches or gold mines where they labor for long periods of time as they work their patient way through archives and library collections. While there are legal historians who work in the same fashion, I think it is fair to say that a large number of law scholars tend to have more catholic, policy-oriented interests. I have been struck by how many talented young law scholars ask me about emerging topics and subjects in need of study; no historian would ever seek such advice, if my characterizations are accurate. It is not yet clear whether the hiring of nonlawyers on law faculties or teachers with dual degrees has affected traditional law scholarship, or the reverse. That jury is still out.

As I have become aware of being an Accidental Historian, I note that the evidence of my own scholarly punctuated equilibrium is that I have now come and gone on several history pathways, ones that have evident connective tissue. For example, I am interested in the organizational histories of certain civil rights groups (ranging from the Mexican American Legal Defense and Educational Fund [MALDEF] to the Alliance Defending Freedom); the legislative history of both higher education and immigration statutes and implementation regimes, such as the state and federal DREAM Acts (Development, Relief, and Education for Alien Minors); and most formally, the litigation history of certain cases, the organizational forces that flow into them, and the effect they have upon the polity (such as *Plyler v. Doe* and *Hernández v. Texas*). So though I am not in a history department, I am very much a historian or at least engaged in the unauthorized practice of history.

Most of my work, upon my own recent reflection, falls into these forms. The "accidental" dimension of this work is not so much that I was never formally trained in history, although that is accurate, but rather that my true and genuine long-standing interests veer in this direction, in ways completely unknown to me, for I have never before looked back in any deep, systematic, or introspective way. Thus, my growing sense of the development of this scholarly focus is more about the synonyms of the research direction being *unexpected*, *involuntary*, and *unconscious*, not the more *haphazard*, *unexpected*, or *random* nuances of the word. Just as one makes one's own luck and also improves upon the chance of being fortunate, one can be serendipitous and improve upon the likelihood of that serendipity taking root or making a difference. By subscribing to and reading a number of historical journals, books, and resources, I have doubtlessly improved my exposure to historical method and my appreciation of its scholarly and rhetorical argot.

In the beginning, I had to find my personal niche, a search that was made more prolonged by my childhood commitment to study for the Catholic priesthood, which took eight years of seminary high school and college to work through my plans. This experience was incredible and formative. I agree with Felipe Hinojosa's chapter in this collection that histories often ignore the role of faith and religion. For me, attending and then leaving seminary and theological studies was the best vocational decision I ever made. It turned out that I was much better at afflicting the comfortable than I ever was at the requisite comforting the afflicted. After I left my college seminary, I loved being a graduate student in American literature. I was deeply drawn to the textual exegesis of manuscripts such as textual analysis of the Nathaniel Hawthorne papers, housed at Ohio State for the Modern Language Association editions. I also anticipated additional studies in folklore, then becoming a strong emphasis at Ohio State. Folklore always seemed of interest to me in my studies, where the combination of reading and actually finding the reading materials from informants or other sources seemed to play to my academic strengths. I also believed that down the road, returning to my native New Mexico would allow me to collect *dichos, corridos, cuentos*, and other stories that were the stuff of folklore studies. It was not to be.

My formal post-baccalaureate studies in English were altered when the job market took a serious nosedive—a development known to most academic historians—and when two of my advisers at Ohio State died in my short time there, one a suicide, I took it as a sign of one sort or another. After 1974, when I received my master's degree, I left the field, although I became the editor of the *John Updike Newsletter*, which I continued to do as a labor of love for several more years. I then turned to the formal study of higher education—a field of study I had not even known existed—and completed my doctoral studies at Ohio State in 1977, writing a dissertation on the political history of the Ohio Board of Regents.[5] Well, everyone needs a topic, after all. Looking back on it, I suppose the history seeds were planted then, although I did not consciously nourish them. I loved the archival and detective work that went into library scholarship, and fondly recall my dissertation research, especially plowing through many old documents, records, minutes, newspaper archives, and various private and public studies that helped me find the narrative arc of the real story. Of all the various intellectual seeds that sprouted in me, it was undoubtedly these unlikely sources that served as the provenance of my curiosity and vectors of my history scholarship.

In an attempt to situate my efforts in legal history, I will dissect four projects in my chapter: my legal history of the *Plyler v. Doe* decision, leading to larger research, service, and advocacy efforts. These include *Plyler*, from its inception through its role in the history of deferred action, when President Obama adopted the policy for undocumented college students/DREAMers in 2012. I then examine a trilogy of Texas Latino legal events from 1925 to the present, including Alonso S. Perales (an early Tejano lawyer), the post–World War II Macario Garcia matter, and the 1954 *Hernández v. Texas* Supreme Court case. I will go quickly through *Plyler*, as I have discussed its significance at book length.[6] I will explain the Texas trilogy of earlier cases in chronological manner, even though—perhaps as an example of my own odd and punctuated equilibrium—I undertook them in reverse order, moving from *Hernández* in 1954 to Macario Garcia in 1945 and then finally to 1925 when Alonso Perales was admitted into the Texas Bar, only the third Mexican American to practice in the state.[7]

Plyler

My research on *Plyler*'s legal history includes several law review articles, two book chapters (one of which is actually point zero in this narrative), and a full-length book on the case, the first full-length single-authored book on the case, *No Undocumented Child Left Behind: Plyler v. Doe and the Education of Undocumented Schoolchildren*, which I published in 2012, thirty years after the 1982 US Supreme Court decision and thirty-seven years after the original 1975 Texas state tuition legislation that gave rise to the case.[8] I first wrote about the case when I held my first IHELG conference at the University of Houston on the implications of the case, papers for which were published in a special issue of the *Journal of Law and Education* in 1986.[9] At first I carefully laid out the holding of the case, straightforwardly and with more attention to how the school law holding might be extended to the higher education setting. Relatively few scholars had paid attention to *Plyler*, and it was widely considered—to the extent that it was considered at all—as an anomalous outlier, wrongly decided and unlikely to have any genuine doctrinal significance or constitutional impact. Ironically, its holding probably helped the 1986 passage of the Immigration Reform and Control Act (IRCA). These are the twin high-water marks of immigrant rights in this country: *Plyler* allowing the children to stay in school, and IRCA providing generous amnesty and legalization pathways, in exchange for the imposition of employer sanctions.

In 2003 or so, I was asked by immigration law professors David Martin of the University of Virginia and Peter Schuck of Yale University to participate in writing a series of law readers that were surfacing in legal education. These new readers are designed to serve as supplemental texts to the more traditional casebooks, which edit and strip down cases to their quintessence, often sacrificing the blood and sinew of a dispute or contest for considerations of length and convenience. Therefore, the series editors were soliciting authors to write the backstories for classic immigration cases (such readers for Constitutional Law, Tort Law, Tax

Law, and the basic building blocks courses were already emerging, so the publishers were branching out into other discrete areas with identifiable bodies of cases). Professor Schuck called and asked me to write about another case, and I was so pleased to have been invited to the party that I agreed. But after thinking about it for a bit, I contacted him and said I would rather take *Plyler*, inasmuch as it was a Houston and Texas case and I had access to the newly available archival MALDEF materials at Stanford's rare book library, where I happened to know the lead archivist, Roberto Trujillo, a fellow New Mexican who had acquired and maintained the MALDEF files and published a helpful finding tool. I had acquired a copy of this concordance earlier, but I filed it away, pending my next unrelated trip to Stanford, where I had a niece enrolled at the time. Peter demurred, saying that *Plyler* was the case he wanted to write about for his own book. But when I laid out the preliminary homework I had already done and conveyed my enthusiasm, he relented. It also helped that I had already written carefully about the actual details of the case without using the Stanford archival materials. I therefore had a framework for the historical research and provenance of the case. I had not even known much about the original case I was assigned for the book project and it was not one that I had taught over the years; it also did not involve my educational law interests. I would have gladly undertaken the project, but *Plyler* seemed so much better, all things considered.

Dispatched to write the definitive legal history of the case, I was again reminded of how much luck counts, but also how one can improve the trajectory of luck. With the assistance of Roberto and his staff, I was able to arrange all the relevant MALDEF archives for my basic research. I was able to take all my basic notes within the three days I had cobbled together for the trip. I found exceptional materials, trial preparation memos, letters of support and crucial correspondence, and even some references to me, from my having chaired the Hispanic Higher Education Coalition, a DC-based consortium designed to involve Latinos in the reauthorization of the Higher Education Act. It was the good, bad, and ugly of MALDEF's generous gift to Stanford and to scholars generally. It turned out that I was the first person to have used the archives, and the papers were waiting there for me when I arrived. Also waiting for me was a note from a Columbia PhD student in history, Lisa Y. Ramos, who said she had seen the stack with my name on it and wanted to know if we could meet while I was there. I invited her to my *Hernández v. Texas* project the next year, where she served as a conference research assistant. She wrote her dissertation on *Hernández* and it figures prominently in her scholarship.[10] One makes one's own luck with new colleagues as well.

After writing the chapter for the *Immigration Law Stories* reader, I used the materials to prepare for the Ernesto Galarza Distinguished Lecture at Stanford, as befitted a project derived from that university's archives.[11] I also undertook a volume in the same Foundation Press series, which resulted in *Education Law Stories*; a collaborator and I chose a dozen key higher education and K–12 Supreme Court cases and co-wrote the introduction to the volume.[12] Once again I had created the venue and facilitated my own work and that of others in a project that was greater than the sum of its individual parts. I also harvested the chapter as the foundation of my book on *Plyler*, which was greatly improved through its iterations and the feedback I received from readers, including several historians and political scientists. I also benefited from people peripherally involved in the case, including some of the undocumented children who were plaintiffs, and especially from my main informant, the MALDEF attorney Peter Roos, who gave generously of his time and with whom I collaborated on subsequent postsecondary *Plyler* cases. As recently as 2013 I served on a commemorative panel on the case with him at an academic conference, and it was deeply satisfying to have gotten it right by his high measure.

My experience over the years reading every word written on the *Plyler* case has led me to believe that many professional bibliographies or reviews of literature across fields are so narrowly focused in their own discipline that they are amazingly incomplete. For example, I have run across many dozens of articles on *Plyler*, some quite nuanced and sophisticated, whose authors seem completely unaware of legal scholarship in the case, if citations are any indication. While I have not been very systematic about this, I would only note that in my rough count, sociologists, political scientists, economists, and historians are the worst offenders at citing only from their own scholarly domains. This is another manifestation of the fox and hedgehog metaphor. When I see major mistakes that might have been avoided had the authors read more widely, I can only rejoice at interdisciplinary work drawn from many sources and rhetorical traditions. As just one example, many nonlegal readers (and, to be sure, some lawyers) completely misunderstand the interplay of federal and state law in the governance of residence requirements, particularly the complicated relationship among the many provisions in federal immigration statutes. I understand when a restrictionist

lawyer might get it wrong to score a client point, but I do not understand why historians, policy scholars, or sociologists, or for that matter admissions officials or state legislators, would willingly get it wrong
by not doing their homework. In fairness, the appeals court in *Martinez
v. UC Regents* badly misread the California statute, and it took a unani-
mous state supreme court verdict to right that ship and uphold the residency statute, A.B. 540.

That said, I have probably extracted the best minerals possible from
Plyler and am moving on to mine other locations. Of course, the case is
never far from my mind or conference talks, especially as comprehensive immigration reform will reiterate its importance in the education
polity for both K–12 and higher education. And as my fellow contributors to this collection Perla M. Guerrero and Carlos Blanton demonstrate, the issues of immigrant rights, schools, and DREAMers are not
far away from historians and the history they write. For my part, there
will be other applications of the case to different settings such as professional licensing, or other domains that will draw my attention, and it
will never be far under the surface of my imagination.

Hernández v. Texas

While my *Plyler* work evolved out of the many influences I have outlined, it was current and even contemporaneous legal history. My work
on the *Hernández* case was even more surprising and unexpected. The
case stemmed from one Mexican shooting to death another Mexican in
a Texas cantina in 1951, the year I was born. My interest grew out of my
love and affection for a personal hero, US federal judge James DeAnda.
I had known Judge DeAnda for a number of years, and we had a personal relationship as well, having vacationed and traveled together with
our spouses, including travel to Mexico. At some point, someone asked
me if he were THE James DeAnda, and I was not certain how to answer the loaded question, which included reference to *Hernández*, one
of his cases that went to the Supreme Court. I had no clue and spent a
fruitful few days digging into his past record, which I had only known
sparingly, and which had almost always referenced his work as an enor-
mously successful trial attorney, especially a personal injury lawyer. As
I read *Hernández*, noting it was the case in the 1954 US Reporter that
immediately preceded *Brown v. Board*, I not only noted his participation
but also recognized the significance of the case itself:

The petitioner's initial burden in substantiating his charge of group discrimination was to prove that persons of Mexican descent constitute a separate class in Jackson County, distinct from "whites." . . . The testimony of responsible officials and citizens contained the admission that residents of the community distinguished between "white" and "Mexican." . . .

Children of Mexican descent were required to attend a segregated school for the first four grades. At least one restaurant in town prominently displayed a sign announcing "No Mexicans Served." On the courthouse grounds at the time of the hearing, there were two men's toilets, one unmarked, and the other marked "Colored Men" and "Hombres Aquí" ("Men Here"). . . .

The judgment of conviction must be reversed. . . . His only claim is the right to be indicted and tried by juries from which all members of his class are not systematically excluded.[13]

I was astounded that as a law student, a legal scholar, and a Chicano, I had never heard of the case or of Judge DeAnda's part in it. I took him to lunch to debrief him about the case. He was simply so modest and self-effacing that I had to practically pry out the story. He put me onto earlier versions of the case that he and his then-law partner John Herrera had tried. I was mesmerized. I hired a research assistant to help me track down the case materials and the sparse literature *Hernández* had generated. When I asked colleagues, especially more senior Chicano Texas lawyers, about the Judge, a more fulsome picture emerged. For example, it appeared, as best as I could tell, that this had been the first Supreme Court case argued by Mexican Americans and the first application of the Equal Protection doctrine to Mexican Americans, within weeks of the doctrine's apex, the more broadly known *Brown* case.[14]

By a complete and karmic fluke of timing, the fiftieth anniversary of *Brown* was coming up, and as I and others were becoming involved in important commemorations and (mostly) celebrations, I looked in vain for similar appraisals of its companion case, *Hernández*. There were none, even in Texas or by criminal law and civil rights scholars, those most likely to know of the case. Even MALDEF, formed a dozen years after the decision, was having none of it. So, in the best Mickey Rooney movie tradition, I decided to put on my own conference, the papers for which led to *"Colored Men" and "Hombres Aquí": Hernández v. Texas and the Emergence of Mexican-American Lawyering*, a volume of papers I contributed to and edited.[15] I was able to solicit papers from legal scholars, sociologists, historians, and others. I also attracted several papers from a national call. In addition, the gathering provided PBS filmmaker Carlos Sandoval with a platform to conduct interviews for what became his moving documentary on the case, *A Class Apart*. In an act of recycling, I arranged for the papers to appear as a special issue of the UCLA *Chicano-Latino Law Review*, and then in the Arte Público Press Civil Rights Series, which had published many important books on Chicano figures, such as Dr. Hector P. Garcia (a close friend of Judge DeAnda, who arranged to bring him to Corpus Christi after the 1954 case), Reies Lopez Tijerina, José Angel Gutiérrez, and others. Although I had edited many previous works, including special issues of journals and other books, this was the first time I had worked with a law review and a commercial university publisher on the same body of work.

As important as this project was to the history of Chicanas/os, the law, and the nation, finding publishers was frustratingly difficult. When dozens of law reviews declined to publish the papers, including the *Houston Law Review*, I settled scores in a subsequent piece, "Reflections on Academic Merit Badges and Becoming an Eagle Scout," about how diffident and resistant mainstream journals, across disciplines, are to minority topics and participants.[16] It might not be too surprising to know that this theme of double standards when applied to Chicanos and Chicanas has guided many of my own decisions about whether or not to chase a fire engine out of the firehouse and involve myself in a dispute, or to shrink from a fight. *Hernández* was one of the most important court fights over the important issue of how Mexican Americans were to be legally accommodated in post–World War II Jaime Crow Texas. This was my first history project where raising general consciousness was the motivation, as well as squaring up the record with these remarkable Chicano lawyers whose courage was tested regularly. They could not even stay in the town's hotel, which refused to rent rooms to them. And in the courtroom they were required to reinvent the Equal Protection doctrine for their criminal client, pre-*Brown* (more accurately, exactly at the same time as *Brown*) and at the apogee of the black-white binary, which occasioned no consideration of their unique racial and legal status. I excavated this subject again for a collaborative piece with Latino legal scholar Ian Haney López when we worked together on an expanded chapter that was commissioned for yet another Foundation Press stories series volume, *Race Law Stories*.[17]

The final *Hernández* scorecard: one edited special-issue law review, one full-length edited book, one coauthored chapter in another book, and a PBS documentary in which I appeared. While I have not pursued it further, almost no month goes by when I do not get drawn back into the case, by serving as a book reviewer, an evaluator for scholarly press acquisitions, or as a consultant to Latinos who are trying to make a full-length feature film on the case, one that I always thought had a great dramatic backstory and thematic resonance. I might add that I lectured extensively on the book and the case, ranging from several endowed lectures and a number of banquets to a small library in rural Texas, where I spoke in Spanish to four elderly Mexican American women, one of whom had helped raise funds for the case by tamale sales when she was a small girl. I value that evening more than almost all the others, including one where I autographed and sold three hundred copies of the book at UT-Brownsville with an overflow crowd.

Macario Garcia and the Oasis Café

Following on the cinematic theme, my project "The 'Trial of the Century' that Never Was: Staff Sgt. Macario Garcia, the Congressional Medal of Honor, and the Oasis Café" in 2008 grew out of two intertwined events: one an error by a young historian and the other a key scene in an important movie, *Giant*.[18] I came upon the story of this restaurant incident through several means, including driving on Macario Garcia Boulevard in Mexican East Houston, near the University of Houston and where we lived at the time. I learned through local lore that the street was named after a local World War II hero of the same name and that he had been refused service in 1945 in a redneck restaurant near Houston. Knowing that such discrimination was widespread, I thought nothing more of it until I saw a news reference to the incident in a thread that I was following about Gus Garcia, one of the lawyers involved in *Hernández*, who had led a fascinating life and was a close friend of James DeAnda. That thread was a short and cryptic reference in an online historical resource that averred Gus Garcia and John Herrera had worked together on the Macario Garcia case and had won it: "After a trial in which he was defended by Gustavo (Gus) Garcia and John J. Herrera, [Macario] Garcia was acquitted."[19]

I just knew that was incorrect, as I had examined the Gus Garcia and John Herrera materials quite thoroughly for my *Hernández* project. I was intrigued, however, by this reference to Gus Garcia and Herrera's collaboration, which would have foreshadowed their *Hernández v. Texas* litigation several years later, and I tried to find the evidence. It turns out that in all the files I consulted there is no reference of Gus Garcia having ever been Macario Garcia's lawyer. What is more, there was actually no trial and, hence, no acquittal. Though the other material in this online resource provided by María-Cristina García, a well-respected Cornell University historian of Cuban and Central American immigration to the United States, was accurate and useful, these two references appeared to be inaccurate. When I spoke with Professor Garcia by phone about the matter, she was very gracious and conceded the mistake in the material, which she had written in the late 1970s, when she was a graduate student. Not surprisingly, she had no records of that long-ago project that we might have used to double back and see where she had gotten that idea. I knew, of course, that DeAnda and Herrera had tried many cases together and, as a separate matter, that Gus Garcia and Carlos Cadena had tried *Delgado v. Bastrop*, an important desegregation case. Nonetheless, error or not, it was a ship that sailed my way. It was impossible to prove that there had been no trial, as I explain in the law review article, so I checked every trial record in the venue for a case with this name, up until Macario Garcia's death, and obtained an affidavit from the district attorney's office that there was no such case title.

The trial of the century that never was (a title suggested by my extensive discussions with Judge DeAnda, who was not involved in the case but who soon after partnered with John Herrera in the Houston law practice) was about the much-decorated *veterano* who was refused service in a local restaurant just after returning from VE Day and having been recognized as a war hero by the Sugar Land, Texas, city government:

> The day after his public welcoming, Staff Sgt. Garcia was refused service [while in his military uniform] in Richmond's Oasis Cafe. This September 10, 1945, refusal of service is what triggered the "Macario Garcia incident." While Garcia always denied that he had committed any violence, he was refused service by the owner of the Oasis Cafe, Mrs. Donna Lower Andrews, and beaten with a baseball bat by her son. Because no independent witnesses actually surfaced, the best telling of the tale is that of the weekly local paper, the *Texas Coaster*. It is the "best" version not because it is the most complete or accurate, but because the September 27, 1945, version unwittingly reveals a number of issues that depict the developing public version of the incident.[20]

I applied my graduate-school training in the textual exegesis of primary documents in detective-like fashion and found virtually no accurate fact in the article. In the rest of the law review article, I created a parallel universe in which Sergeant Garcia was partially used by Mexican American political interests who cleverly widened the small incident to a national matter that could draw attention to the unfair and discriminatory treatment that average *veteranos* were receiving. They pushed the argument that if this war hero could be refused public accommodations and even be bloodied and arrested in the matter, then how much more vulnerable were other, less visible *veteranos* with less access to legal counsel? And they employed prominent lawyers (including an Anglo former federal judge and Texas governor) to defend him, to seek delays while the incident was splashed across local and regional papers, and to get the government to drop the charges. Most importantly, Herrera got word to jingoistic national columnist Walter Winchell, who embarrassed the Texas officials bringing assault charges against Garcia; Winchell was particularly supportive of military personnel, so he opined that the town of Sugar Land was hateful toward military heroes. The misspelled name in the local paper, also (mis)used by Winchell (they wrote Marcario rather than Macario), shows the extent to which John Herrera had suggested the broader stage and bigger audience. Ultimately this dispute had just petered out rather than extending the embarrassment of the white politicians and court officials, who delayed the trial several times in the hopes it would never actually materialize.

That these indignities were visited upon returning *veteranos* was not lost on the local Mexican American politicos and lawyers, and with the widespread nature of such incidents elsewhere in Texas, this was a reasonable concern. In the 1948 Alonso Perales book *Are We Good Neighbors?* over a dozen such incidents of Mexican American veterans not receiving services, veterans benefits, or other programs to which they were entitled were notarized and detailed as having occurred in Texas towns.[21]

The next notorious matter of discrimination against a Mexican American veteran in Texas began when the remains of Felix Longoria, a soldier who had been killed in action in 1945 in the Philippines, were returned to Three Rivers, Texas, for burial. The Three Rivers cemetery had a "Mexican-only" section, separated from the Anglo cemetery by strung barbed wire. The funeral director refused to allow the Longoria family to use the cemetery chapel because a previous Latino funeral had been said to be disruptive and because the "whites would not like it." Dr. Hector P. Garcia, a Corpus Christi physician and one of the few Mexican Americans with a medical degree in the state, organized the American GI Forum (AGIF) as a protest against the widespread disrespect accorded veterans, including the high-profile Macario Garcia incident. Garcia realized the potential of the Felix Longoria incident immediately after attempting to mediate between the funeral director and Longoria's distraught widow.[22]

These LULAC (League of United Latin American Citizens) and AGIF members had seen the efficacy of raising public awareness regarding incidents of disrespect, and the Felix Longoria incident became another example of successful exploitation of the media and behind-the-scenes political maneuvering. In this incident, Lyndon B. Johnson, then a Texas senator, saw the larger political value in championing Longoria's cause and arranged for him to be buried in 1949 at Arlington National Cemetery with the full support of President Truman and other national politicians. By 1948, additional cases were being taken up in which Texas attorneys began to question and strike down the segregation of Texas schools, beginning with the *Delgado v. Bastrop* case in 1948, argued by Gus Garcia and Carlos Cadena. In 1954 Cadena became the first Mexican American law professor, joining the St. Mary's law faculty. Garcia, DeAnda, and Herrera went on to their practices, and both DeAnda and Garcia at one time in the 1950s practiced in Houston with Herrera. In 1955 DeAnda moved his practice to Corpus Christi, where he later undertook desegregation litigation, leading to significant cases such as *Cisneros v. Corpus Christi Independent School District* and *Hernández v. Driscoll Consolidated Independent School District*. In 1979 he was named to the federal bench for the Southern District of Texas, becoming only the second Mexican American federal judge in US history.[23] He stepped down in 1992, and in 2014 Houston was still without a Mexican American Article III judge on permanent assignment.[24]

When one looks at these incidents leading to Mexican American organizing efforts and political solidarity, all of which were undertaken in the face of extraordinary hostility, one cannot help but be struck by the courage shown by these lawyers and community activists. While it is true that the Macario Garcia and Felix Longoria matters were eventually satisfactorily resolved in favor of the aggrieved veterans, enormous forces were arrayed against them. All the media outlets, governmental entities, and political establishment in these contexts were directed and dominated by Anglos. In Fort Bend County, the Jaybird Party had successfully cleaved racial divisions into the electoral process, notwithstanding the substantial African American and Mexican American voting age populations. There were very few Mexican American licensed professionals to deliver medical care or provide legal services, and few successful businessmen to finance organizational efforts. LULAC and the AGIF were nascent, decentralized, and underfunded organizations, without larger philanthropic or religious underwriting. MALDEF would not be founded by DeAnda and other southwestern lawyers until 1967–1968. The exclusion of *Mexicanos* from public discourse, political life, and community leadership was nearly total, even in those areas of southern Texas and the Gulf coast with large populations of urbanizing agricultural workers and laborers. Jaime Crow Texas was a caste system almost organic in its near-total control of Mexican American life and opportunity after World War II. Edna, the town where *Hernández v. Texas* was contested in 1951 and 1952, was so dangerous that the lawyers could not safely spend the night there or rent a hotel room. As a result, Cadena and Garcia would drive in each day from San Antonio, while DeAnda and Herrera would drive the hour and a half from Houston. In the very courthouse where the state of Texas was arguing that an all-Anglo jury was a jury of Pete Hernández's peers—in essence arguing that Mexicans were legally white—the official men's bathrooms were reserved for Anglo men while a separate one existed in the basement marked "Colored Men" and "Hombres Aqui." Justice Warren was so struck by the revelatory punch of this signage that he even mentioned it in the *Hernández* opinion as evidence that Edna separated the Anglo and Mexican races as clearly as it did the white and black races.

The Macario Garcia case had cultural significance as well, as it likely influenced Edna Ferber, the author of the best-selling 1952 novel *Giant*, which in 1956 was made into a successful movie of the same name. As I researched the Sugar Land matter, I was struck by the eerie resemblance to the final scenes in the movie, and by the quotidian details being recorded by Alonso Perales, who pursued and recorded so many similar incidents. I just did not know how to connect these hidden matters (that is, hidden to the larger society) to the urbane writer. "How could she have known?" would be the question any cinema historian (or ersatz, unauthorized, accidental historian) would ask. The novel and movie, set in a fictional Texas border county where cattle and oil were king, is one of the few of its time that portrayed Mexican Americans sympathetically. One of the ranch's boys of Mexican origin (Angel Obregon II) goes off to war and is killed. The influential Anglo family intermarries, leaving the Anglo patron to fight on behalf of his Mexican American daughter-in-law and half-Mexican grandchild after they are disrespected by a redneck in an area restaurant. While a number of books about Ferber, the novel, and the movie note the author's unexpectedly positive treatment of the Texas Mexicans, no scholar had noted that the Macario Garcia incident was the likely inspiration for this concluding scene of racial solidarity. Living in New York at the time, Ferber could have read the Walter Winchell columns about the Oasis Café matter, or the March 27, 1951, story in the nationally popular *Look* magazine, which featured searing pictures of impoverished Mexican American families, noting, "The truth is simply this: Nowhere else in America is a group of people so downtrodden and defenseless, and nowhere are human dignity and life held in such low regard." In the movie the remains of the young *veterano* Obregon (portrayed by the pan-ethnic Sal Mineo) are turned away by the local mortician. So the Anglo patron arranges an honored burial on the ranch, mimicking the Felix Longoria incident at Three Rivers, Texas, and Lyndon B. Johnson's intervention.

I found my answer in her biography. Ferber mentioned taking a train trip through Texas to carry out research. After commenting upon the high-end stores in Dallas, she recorded that she "moved on to the less effete regions. Houston. Galveston. San Antonio. Even Brownsville on the Mexican border. It was rather hard going, especially in various smaller towns in between." One of the smaller towns was Corpus Christi, where she met for an extended period with Dr. Hector P. Garcia, "following him on his rounds, listening to and being impressed by his description of conditions under which Texas Mexicans had to live in south Texas."[25] Popular culture, whether film or television or music, vitally informs our perceptions not just of reality, but of the past. Edna Ferber's blurring of fact and fiction calls to mind Luis Alvarez's chapter later in this collection on popular culture and imaginaries in the construction of culture. It is difficult to envision Ferber's imagination conjuring these specific historical references, even in guised and fictional form, had she not spent those three weeks with Dr. Garcia, who founded the American GI Forum and spent his life advocating for Mexican American civil rights, particularly for *veteranos*. Along with his good friend DeAnda, "Dr. Hector" proved to be a thorn in the side of local politicians. These incidents were two small milestones in Mexican American postwar Jaime Crow life that loomed symbolically larger as successes born out of sheer prejudice and racial exclusion. They provided small victories that encouraged the emerging community leaders and that paved the way for more permanent change, a process that is still unfolding half a century later. Looking back on this history, it is clearer now than it must have been at the time that the incidents were significant beyond their small scope, and that Mexican Americans would not merely endure, but prevail.

Alonso S. Perales

There is a whiff of *deus ex machina* about my most recent legal historical project, which culminated in the edited volume *"In Defense of My People": Alonso S. Perales and the Development of Mexican-American Public Intellectuals*, for which I wrote the introduction and a chapter, "The Legal Career of Alonso S. Perales."[26] This time I did not have to fly out to Stanford, Austin, Santa Barbara, and elsewhere for the archival materials; the extensive paper collection came to me. In 2011 the University of Houston's Arte Público Press announced through the Recovering the US Hispanic Literary Heritage Program, its Special Collections Department of the M.D. Anderson Library, and its Law Center that the papers of early Tejano lawyer Alonso S. Perales had been acquired from his family and were available for scholarly examination. Perales (1898–1960) was among the most important organizational figures and public intellectuals of his time. He was instrumental in early and mid-twentieth-century Mexican American political development in Texas. Perales graduated from George Washington University School of Law in 1925, making him one of the earliest Mexican American attorneys to practice law in Texas. Over time he not only developed a successful law practice but also helped found LULAC, served his country in several diplomatic capacities, and was a prolific writer and public figure who employed all the discursive avenues available to him.

Fortunately for scholars, Perales was an inveterate pack rat, producing many files and evidently never throwing away anything. Through an unparalleled opportunity, then-graduate history student Cynthia Orozco had earlier acquired some access to the files when they were squirreled away in the Perales home and garage. She used them to publish her extraordinary *No Mexicans, Women, or Dogs Allowed: The Rise of the Mexican American Civil Rights Movement* in 2009.[27] In that towering work, Orozco determined that Mexican American political organizing and social consciousness arose much earlier than has been generally credited in the work of most historians, political scientists, and other scholars. Whereas many scholars had placed these origins in the late 1920s, especially with the events leading up to the 1929 founding of LULAC in Corpus Christi, the Perales papers and materials reveal roots to predecessor groups and to events from the end of the dictatorship of Porfirio Díaz, the Mexican Revolution, and the early 1920s. These family-held papers, now available in the original and digital formats at UH Special Collections, promise to fill out the record on the structured role of Mexican American men and women in mutual aid societies and civic organizations, as well as the behind-the-scenes role of lawyers—in this instance, not primarily as litigators, but as civic leaders and elected officials. Perales also carried on an extraordinary correspondence with many Latino and Latina and other political figures, revealing wide and deep contacts and affiliations. (Examples of his contacts include Adela Sloss-Vento, George I. Sánchez, Archbishop Robert Lucey, and Anastasio Somoza.) In addition, he carried on a remarkable correspondence with ordinary Mexican American citizens and *Mejicanos de afuera* (Mexican nationals residing in the United States) on a variety of cultural and religious topics ranging from marital counseling, Catholic pieties, and other affirmations of the race, all designed to share his views and expertise widely and deeply. There is virtually no other parallel to the significant and fascinating materials now archived and ripe for examination.

Arte Público Press publisher Nicolas Kanellos approached me to ascertain my interest in doing for these archives what I had done with the *Hernández* conference. Primed by the glimpses I had seen of Perales's work in my earlier research, especially that on the post–World War II *testimonios*, I was ready to plunge in all over again. I knew Perales had collected the stories in his book, and I knew his role in the founding of LULAC (having worked for the organization when I was in law school in Washington, DC), but I had underestimated his actual significance. Perales and the others carried on extraordinary careers, given the enormous odds against them. Racist headwinds often blew against their efforts, especially their civil rights and community work, as hostile legislators, judges, and public officials sought to subordinate Mexican Americans, especially in Texas, which was long considered the equivalent of Mississippi for Chicanos. There is a surprisingly robust scholarly literature on early Texas legal cases, particularly those having to do with education, including authoritative works by Guadalupe San Miguel (1987), George Martinez (1994), Richard Valencia (2008), Carlos Blanton (2006), and other historians and scholars from other disciplines.[28] There has begun a small fleshing-out of World War II–era cases, following the *testimonio* lead of *Are We Good Neighbors?* This extraordinary work—extraordinary in the sense that there are very few such works in this genre, evidence of his lawyerly instincts—was compiled by Perales in 1948 to record the extensive Jaime Crow practices in Texas. Perales provides the anthropological and sociological details of public housing denials, public accommodation exclusionary practices, and employment discrimination, all made known in the public record by Texas lawyers such as Perales and his contemporaries: J. T. Canales, Gus Garcia, Carlos Cadena, John Herrera, Manuel C. Gonzales, Ed Idar Jr., James DeAnda, Alex Armendariz, and others, including nonlawyers such as physician Dr. Héctor P. García, labor organizer Emma Tenayuca, and educators George I. Sánchez, Carlos Castañeda, and José de la Luz Sáenz.

Due to his founding of LULAC, Perales has been cited by many Chicano and Chicana scholars and especially historians, so he is no stranger to Texas history and historiography. He attended high school and Draughn's Business College in Corpus Christi, where he learned to take shorthand and became a stenographer, which later came in handy when he was taking *testimonios* for *Are We Good Neighbors?* Interestingly, he did not graduate from high school. This was consistent with the widespread practice of Mexican schooling in Texas, which rarely extended to finishing high school. He worked in San Antonio as a company clerk and was drafted at the end of World War I. After completing a year of military service, he received an honorable discharge in 1920 and, rather than return to Texas immediately, he obtained civil service positions with the Department of Commerce and the Department of State. Perales served on over a dozen missions to the Dominican Republic, Cuba, Nicaragua, Mexico, Chile, and the West Indies. I agree with Sonia Hernández's chapter later in this collection that argues these earlier generations of Mexican American community activists were far more cosmopolitan and globally connected than previous historians realized. Perales certainly is far more than simply a "local" figure from south Texas.[29]

Simultaneously, he began legal studies at Georgetown in 1922–1923 and then spent a year at National University, which later merged with George Washington University to become its school of law, and was awarded his LLB degree. Before becoming a licensed lawyer, Perales returned to Texas in 1924, worked with a law firm, continued his study of law, and crisscrossed the state to stitch together the mutual aid societies that formally became consolidated into LULAC in 1929. In 1925 Perales passed the Texas bar exam. (He completed additional law studies after being admitted into the bar, and later petitioned GWU to receive his LLB, even though he was not required to have the degree.) Perales then decided to move to McAllen, taking out a full-page advertisement in a Spanish-language newspaper—whose owner he would later represent in a complex and internecine dispute over a Mexican community hospital—and in several other Valley newspapers announcing the July 15, 1927, opening of law offices in McAllen and Rio Grande City, in the South Rio Grande Valley of Texas. In his ad, he indicated that he would also deliver lectures "on behalf of our Race," which he had been doing intermittently in his barnstorming efforts across Texas since 1924. In 1931 he played a supporting role in the appeal of the important *Salvatierra v. Del Rio ISD* school desegregation case, the only time he joined J. T. Canales and M. C. Gonzales, the first two Tejano lawyers, in litigation. He returned to San Antonio in 1933 to open his general practice law office in affiliation with the firm of Still, Wright & Davis, and began doing legal work for the Bexar County Attorney's Office in 1934. He engaged in the private practice of law in one form or another from 1925 until his death in 1960.

The Perales papers project involved many significant scholars across disciplines, including the erstwhile Cynthia Orozco, who refined her own estimation of Perales based upon her improved access to the documents, which had been in cartons and shoeboxes in the Perales family garage when she employed them for her earlier work. They are now digitized and indexed so that scholars can access them more easily and efficaciously. I wrote the detailed chapter on Perales's litigation and lawyering career, apparently the first time anyone had done so.[30] I came to admire him and his worldview, and was struck by how we are now able to get the fuller measure of the man in his various capacities: civil rights lawyer, general practice and appellate lawyer, advice columnist, scholar who tracked unfair practices as a prelude to legislation, advocate, community organizer, Catholic activist, and perhaps above all correspondent with hundreds of different figures, across all walks of life.

I regret concluding this essay, as doing so suggests a finality or thoughtful gathering of learned experiences. Each of these projects has arisen from my restless agenda and short attention span, and by complete and unalloyed fortune, even when I improved the soil by preparing myself to recognize fortune when it appeared. Seizing the opportunities when they presented themselves has been a thread through each one of these projects and the dozen others I could have emphasized. I have had broad as well as deep subject-matter commitments, have evolved a writing style that works well for me (rewriting, rewriting, rewriting), and have improved my learning curve by being more aware of what works for me and what does not. I try to have a number of projects going at once to facilitate the work product and to space out writing times. I try to write every day, and to guard such periods so that I can be better at my craft. I was once asked to ruminate upon what drives me to write, and I recycle a small piece of that essay here.[31] I do so to situate the psychosocial wellsprings of writing, which I find to be the most satisfying dimension of my complex act of being a law professor:

> I write because I like to read and because I am regularly called upon to write and express my views. I carry on regular correspondence with many persons, in law and other fields, both epistolary and through exchange of manuscripts and articles, and each week's mail or e-mail brings me interesting things to read and invitations to write. . . . In short, I also write because I am invited and encouraged to do so and for the academic equivalent of why George Mallory climbed Mt. Everest: because the forum was there.

> I suspect this explanation is what motivates many scholars, and it is a perfectly acceptable reason for taking on the public task of personal revelation. We write to influence, to redirect, to frame, to provoke, to give more precise form to our thinking, to correct the record, and to establish the record. There is a monastic or Talmudic basis to this aspect of our profession—scholars not as scriveners simply transcribing works but rather scholars as commentators and shapers of a synoptic text.[32]

I write because I read, and because no day goes by where I do not mine my experiences and reading to produce scholarship. I have always been a very lucky boy, and being able to write and convey my thoughts is the glory of my being a professor and author. The day that this source dries up, like the water in *Manon of the Spring/Manon des Sources*, is the day I will step down, because the light from my star will have moved on. I will say this, fully appreciating the apparent insincerity, which is anything but insincere: some of my best friends are historians, including art historians and dual-degree historians whose fox-like abilities are increasingly recognized in the history profession today.[33] I admire your hedgehog nature and that, by definition, you are in it for the long haul. I have learned much from your life's work, and appreciate the courtesy and hospitality you have shown me while I happily have sat by your side, as an accidental historian.

Notes

1. Arlen Meyer and Michael A. Olivas, "John Updike, A Selected Checklist," *Modern Fiction Studies* 20 (1974): 121–133; Michael A. Olivas, *An Annotated Bibliography of John Updike Criticism* (New York: Garland Press, 1975).

2. Michael A. Olivas, *Minorities in Two-Year Colleges: A Report and Recommendations for Change* (Washington, DC: Howard University Press, 1979); Olivas, *The Dilemma of Access: Minorities in Two-Year Colleges* (Washington, DC: Howard University Press, 1979); Olivas, "Information Access Inequities in Voucher Plans," *Journal of Law and Education* 10 (1981): 441–465; Olivas, "Indian, Chicano, and Puerto Rican Colleges," *Bilingual Review/Revista Bilingüe* 9 (1982): 36–58; Olivas, "The Tribally Controlled Community College Assistance Act of 1978: The Failure of Federal Indian Higher Education Policy," *American Indian Law Review* 9 (1982): 219–252; Olivas, "State Residency Requirements: Postsecondary Authorization and Regulation," *College Law Digest* 13 (1983): 157–176; Olivas, "Postsecondary Residency Requirements: Empowering Statutes, Governing Types, and Exemptions," *College Law Digest* 16 (1986): 268–299; Olivas, "Lawmakers Gone Wild? College Residency and the Response to Professor Kobach," *SMU Law Review* 61 (2008): 99–132.

3. Stephen J. Gould and Niles Eldredge, "Punctuated Equilibria: The Tempo and Mode of Evolution Reconsidered," *Paleobiology* 3 (1977): 115–151; Stephen Jay Gould, *Punctuated Equilibrium* (Cambridge, MA: Harvard University Press, 2007).

4. Merlin Chowkwanyun and Karen M. Tani, "Training Historians and the Dual Degree," *Chronicle of Higher Education*, January 28, 2014, accessed August 18, 2014, http://chronicle.com/article/Training-Historiansthe/144245/.

5. Michael A. Olivas, "Public Policy Dimensions of Statewide Coordination of Higher Education: Agenda Building and the Establishment of the Ohio Board of Regents" (PhD diss., Ohio State University, 1977); Olivas, "A Legislative History of the Ohio Board of Regents," *Capital University Law Review* 19 (1990): 81–140.

6. Michael A. Olivas, *No Undocumented Child Left Behind: Plyler v. Doe and the Education of Undocumented Schoolchildren* (New York: New York University Press, 2012).

7. As I think more on it, if the standard definition of punctuated equilibrium is that it is a theory of biological evolution in which there is stability in the structure of an organism punctuated by intermittent changes that appear and alter the organism's basic form, then perhaps I have shown a punctuated *dis*equilibrium.

8. For publications on the *Plyler* case and undocumented students and the schools cited in this chapter, see Michael A. Olivas, "Storytelling out of School: Undocumented College Residency, Race, and Reaction," *Hastings Constitutional Law Quarterly* 22 (1995): 1019–1086; Olivas, "IIRIRA, the DREAM Act,

and Undocumented College Student Residency," *Journal of College and University Law* 30 (2004): 435–464; Olivas, "Immigration-Related State Statutes and Local Ordinances: Preemption, Prejudice, and the Proper Role for Enforcement," *University of Chicago Legal Forum* (2007): 27–56; Olivas, "The Political Economy of the DREAM Act and the Legislative Process," *Wayne Law Review* 55 (2009): 1757–1810; Olivas, "Undocumented College Students, Taxation, Financial Aid: A Technical Note," *Review of Higher Education* 32 (2009): 407–416; Olivas and Kristi L. Bowman, "Plyler's Legacy: Immigration and Higher Education in the 21st Century," *Michigan State Law Review* (2011): 261–273; Olivas, "Dreams Deferred: Deferred Action, Discretion, and the Vexing Case(s) of DREAM Act Students," *William & Mary Bill of Rights Journal* 21 (2012): 463–547; Olivas, "From a 'Legal Organization of Militants' into a 'Law Firm for the Latino Community': MALDEF and the Purposive Cases of Keyes, Rodriguez, and Plyler," *Denver Law Review* 90 (2013): 1–58.

9. Michael A. Olivas, "*Doe v. Plyler* and Postsecondary Admissions: Undocumented Adults and 'Enduring Disability,'" *Journal of Law and Education* 15 (1986): 19–55.

10. Lisa Y. Ramos, "Not Similar Enough: Mexican American and African American Civil Rights Struggles in the 1940s," in *The Struggle in Black and Brown: African American and Mexican American Relations during the Civil Rights Era*, ed. Brian D. Behnken (Lincoln: University of Nebraska Press, 2012), 19–48.

11. Michael A. Olivas, "The Story of *Plyler v. Doe*, the Education of Undocumented Children, and the Polity," in *Immigration Law Stories*, ed. David A. Martin and Peter H. Schuck (New York: Foundation Press, 2005), 197–220.

12. Michael A. Olivas and R. G. Schneider, eds., *Education Law Stories* (New York: Foundation Press, 2007); Olivas and Schneider, "Education Law Stories: Law and Society in the Classroom," in *Education Law Stories*, 1–17.

13. *Hernández v. Texas*, 347 U.S. 475 (1954), 248–250.

14. Through complete happenstance, at the dedication of the DeAnda Elementary School, a family member told me the story that DeAnda had actually been offered a federal judgeship by president-elect John F. Kennedy on Thanksgiving Day 1960, but he declined, indicating that he did not think himself qualified, and suggested Reynaldo Garza, a more experienced Texas lawyer. Eventually, it was President Carter who appointed DeAnda to the federal bench. See also Michael A. Olivas, "The First and Last Mexican American Federal Judge in Houston: The Unknown History of James DeAnda and JFK," *Historia Chicana* 20 (March 2012), accessed August 18, 2014, http://xa.yimg.com/kq/groups/13699726/1028938620/name/Michael+A.+Olivas+l+The+First+%26+Last+Mexican+American+Federal+Judge+in+Houston+l+3.19.12.pdf.

15. Michael A. Olivas, ed., *"Colored Men" and "Hombres Aquí": Hernandez v. Texas and the Emergence of Mexican American Lawyering* (Houston: Arte Público Press, 2006).

16. Michael A. Olivas, "Reflections on Academic Merit Badges and Becoming an Eagle Scout," *Houston Law Review* 43 (2006): 81–124, and especially 108–113.

17. Ian Haney Lopez and Michael A. Olivas, "*Hernandez v. Texas*: Jim Crow,

Mexican Americans, and the Anti-Subordination Constitution," in *Race and Law Stories*, ed. Rachel Moran and Devon Carbado (New York: Foundation Press, 2008), 269–306.

18. Michael A. Olivas, "The 'Trial of the Century' that Never Was: Staff Sgt. Macario Garcia, the Congressional Medal of Honor, and the Oasis Café," *Indiana Law Journal* 83 (2008): 1391–1403. In turn, after I finished the project, I was more intrigued by a bit player, Alonso Perales, who grew into a major legal history obsession. The theme here is that no good deed or connection goes unnoticed in historical research.

19. Maria-Cristina Garcia, "Macario Garcia," *The Handbook of Texas Online*, 1977. The online article, essentially an encyclopedia entry, was updated in 2010. The modified version, which deletes the error, was most recently accessed on August 18, 2014. See https://www.tshaonline.org/handbook/online /articles/fga76.

20. Olivas, "The 'Trial of the Century' that Never Was," 1391–1403.

21. Alonso S. Perales, *Are We Good Neighbors?* (North Stratford, NH: Ayers Book Co., 1948; repr., 1974). This book led me to engage in my later work on Perales.

22. For more on this incident see Patrick J. Carroll, *Felix Longoria's Wake: Bereavement, Racism, and the Rise of Mexican American Activism* (Austin: University of Texas Press, 2003).

23. Michael A. Olivas, "The First and Last Mexican American Federal Judge in Houston: The Unknown History of James DeAnda and JFK," *Historia Chicana* 20 (March 2012), accessed August 18, 2014, http://xa.yimg.com/kq /groups/13699726/1028938620/name/Michael+A.+Olivas+l+The+First+%26 +Last+Mexican+American+Federal+Judge+in+Houston+l+3.19.12.pdf.

24. This classification indicates federal judges whose offices are established by Article III of the US Constitution, including judges on the US Supreme Court, the federal courts of appeals and district courts, and the US Court of International Trade.

25. Julie Gilbert, *Ferber: Edna Ferber and Her Circle: A Biography* (New York: Applause Books, 1999), 176.

26. Michael A. Olivas, ed., *"In Defense of My People": Alonso S. Perales and the Development of Mexican-American Public Intellectuals* (Houston: Arte Público Press, 2012); Olivas, "Introduction," in ibid., ix–xxxii.

27. Cynthia E. Orozco, *No Mexicans, Women, or Dogs Allowed: The Rise of the Mexican American Civil Rights Movement* (Austin: University of Texas Press, 2009).

28. Guadalupe San Miguel Jr., *"Let All of Them Take Heed:" Mexican Americans and the Campaign for Educational Equality in Texas, 1910–1981* (Austin: University of Texas Press, 1987); George A. Martinez, "Legal Indeterminacy, Judicial Discretion and the Mexican-American Litigation Experience: 1930–1980," *UC Davis Law Review* 27 (1994): 555–618; Richard R. Valencia, *Chicano Students and the Courts: The Mexican American Legal Struggle for Educational Equality* (New York: New York University Press, 2008); Carlos Kevin Blanton, "George I. Sánchez, Ideology, and Whiteness in the Making of the Mexican American Civil Rights Movement, 1930–1960," *Journal of Southern History* 72, no. 3 (2006): 569–604.

29. For more on Perales and his early life see Olivas, *"In Defense of My People."*

30. Olivas, "The Legal Career of Alonso S. Perales," in *In Defense of My People*, 315–343.

31. Michael A. Olivas, "Immigration Law Teaching and Scholarship in the Ivory Tower: A Response to 'Race Matters,'" *University of Illinois Law Review* (2000): 613–638.

32. Ibid., 619 (first quotation), 620 (second quotation).

33. Chowkwanyun and Tani, "Training Historians and the Dual Degree."

CHAPTER THREE

Moving beyond Aztlán: Disrupting Nationalism and Geographic Essentialism in Chicana/o History

LILIA FERNÁNDEZ

In February 1954 a flyer circulated in Chicago inviting Spanish-speaking people to attend an important meeting at Hull House, the famous social settlement founded by Jane Addams in the city's Near West Side neighborhood. The flyer announced,

> The Mexican American Council of Chicago, Inc., in cooperation with the Office of Labor [*sic*], Commonwealth of Puerto Rico in Chicago welcomes YOU to this city-wide meeting, the first of its kind in the history of the city of Chicago, in which representatives from Spanish-speaking groups have gathered to consider and take action on current social and economic problems affecting the entire community, in particular, persons of Mexican descent and Puerto Ricans who represent the majority of Spanish-speaking people in Chicago.[1]

The meeting was to be held on the afternoon of Sunday, February 21, with an agenda that included remarks by Rubin Torres and Martin Ortíz from the Mexican American Council; Anthony Vega of the Puerto Rico Department of Labor, Migration Division Office; and Luis Carlos Uribe, a local Spanish-language radio announcer, among others. This unprecedented gathering of Mexican and Puerto Rican leaders and community members signaled a historic moment and the first formalized attempt at interethnic collaboration between Mexicans and Puerto Ricans in the city.

During World War II and in the years that followed, Chicago began receiving significant numbers of Mexican migrants—braceros, authorized, and unauthorized immigrants—as well as Mexican Americans from Texas and Puerto Ricans from the island. All came in search of jobs, lured by the prospect of higher wages than those in Puerto Rico, Mexico, or Texas. This was in fact the second wave of Mexican immigration to Chicago, as an earlier population had settled in the city during World War I and the 1920s. With the increased industrial and agricultural production of the Second World War, however, Mexican immigration had surged once more, largely as a result of the bracero program. This time, however, Mexicans were accompanied by Mexican American and Puerto Rican migrants as well. Though to outsiders Mexicans and Puerto Ricans may have appeared indistinguishable, in reality they had differences in linguistic and cultural practices, racial heritage, and at times citizenship status. Puerto Ricans brought with them American citizenship and had the advocacy and support of the local office of the Puerto Rico Department of Labor's Migration Division, which organized their migration to the mainland. Mexican immigrants, particularly braceros and the undocumented, had a more precarious status, although they could rely on Mexican residents who had established themselves in the city three decades earlier. While most Mexican newcomers were foreign-born and citizens of Mexico, they could turn to their more experienced coethnics as they adapted and assimilated to their new environment.

The hostile sociopolitical climate that both ethnic Mexicans and Puerto Ricans faced in early 1954, however, prompted the call for the meeting at Hull House. While most employers took advantage of the new labor force that had arrived at their doorstep, a brief economic recession in 1953–1954 brought both groups under increased public scrutiny. Moreover, not all Chicagoans welcomed the recent arrivals. Puerto Ricans were finding it increasingly difficult to find work and had drawn the unwanted attention of local welfare officials who raised alarms about the population's growing unemployment rates. Some officials had even begun encouraging migrants to "repatriate" to their island and hoped to discourage other potential migrants from setting out for the city in the future. At the same time, unauthorized Mexican immigrants, whose numbers had grown during the bracero program, were becoming the targets of public hysteria and more aggressive deportation raids. The INS had been deporting unauthorized migrants from Chicago, including those who overstayed bracero contracts, for several years, but 1954 marked the beginning of "Operation Wetback," a massive deportation campaign meant to rid the country of unauthorized Mexican immigrants. Thus, both Puerto Ricans and Mexicans were feeling unwelcomed in the city and experiencing heightened policing and harassment.

The situation was apparent in the pages of a local newspaper on February 2. The conservative *Chicago Tribune* carried separate stories that day on both the Puerto Rican welfare "menace" and the Mexican "hordes" invading the border.² One headline warned, "Puerto Ricans Pour into City and Ask Dole," while the other declared, "Mexican Horde Repulsed by Border Patrol." Despite the fact that these distinctive populations came from disparate origins, had followed separate migration routes, and held different immigration statuses, both found themselves under attack and saw their circumstances as similar enough to warrant a collective gathering.

This episode signaled a moment of recognition and the beginning of formal efforts at panethnic coalition building. Mexicans and Puerto Ricans frequently came into contact with one another in Chicago in the postwar years. They often worked in the same factories, frequented the same movie theaters, churches, and night clubs, listened to the same Spanish-language radio broadcasts, and had children attending the same schools. Interactions were unavoidable, and these encounters across ethnic lines demanded efforts to understand each other. Bringing Mexicans and Puerto Ricans in conversation around the precarious conditions that both groups faced in the city enabled them to articulate a biethnic (and later panethnic) "Spanish-speaking" identity.³ Although not all members of the two groups may have advocated alliances with one another, community leaders and others believed that these Spanish-speaking migrants had at least some concerns in common that could be addressed more strategically if they worked together.

How do we interpret this historical encounter between ethnic Mexicans and Puerto Ricans in the urban Midwest through a Chicano history lens? Can such a framework be useful in analyzing this moment, this place, and these populations? Or does the geography of this story and the presence of other Latinos/as move it outside the scope of the field?

As someone trained primarily by Chicana/o historians, I frame my work through a field that has documented the history of ethnic Mexican people in the United States for the past four decades. I have great respect for the germinal work of earlier generations. Still, as a scholar who writes about Mexicans in Chicago, and particularly in relation to a significant Puerto Rican population, my claim to the field might be viewed by purists as tenuous and perhaps contestable. Does research on Mexicans and Puerto Ricans in Chicago count as "Chicano/a history"? What are the criteria for inclusion? Geography? A nationalist framework? A class analysis? An exclusive focus on Mexican Americans? Or does any history that focuses on people of Mexican descent qualify? Nicholas De Genova's definition might be useful:

> What may vitally be considered Chicano studies scholarship is not merely research concerned with Mexicans (or Chicanos) but rather scholarship that (a) takes as a fundamental premise that the U.S. colonization of Mexican territory and the subsequent legacy of racial oppression have an enduring relevance for the experiences of *all* Mexicans in the United States, and (b) self-consciously posits its intellectual enterprise as one that is politically committed to one or another project of radical social critique.[4]

Other Chicano/a scholars of the Midwest, like Dennis Valdes, have grappled with the epistemological question of how the region fits into the field(s) of Chicano/a History and Chicano/a Studies.[5] In his study of Mexicans in Chicago, De Genova concludes that "conceptualizing the ways in which Chicago might be figured as a *theoretical* (and not merely empirical question) for Chicano studies has remained a complicated proposition." As a historian who does comparative, interethnic work on the Midwest, I argue for an expansion of the field's intellectual boundaries and a more geographically fluid approach to the Chicano/a historical imagination.

Since the era of the Chicano Movement, the US Southwest and the overlapping concept of Aztlán have held a central place in the imagined geography of Chicano/a people. Few, however, think of the Midwest, or any other region for that matter, as a "homeland" for Chicanos. In the years of the Movement, most Americans, including Chicanas/os and Latinas/os themselves, had little awareness of the long-standing historical presence of Mexican Americans in the Midwest. The famed Chicano poet Alurista recalled in an interview that when he attended Corky Gonzales's 1969 Chicano Youth Liberation Conference in Denver, he met Mexicans from other southwestern states for the very first time. He continued, "And then there were Mexicans from Chicago . . . Kansas. I didn't know there were Mexicans in Kansas!"[6] He was likely not the only one encountering Mexicans from the Midwest for the first time. The engagement with fellow Mexicans from other parts of the country evoked a shared sense of belonging and consciousness as a people, "La Raza." Perhaps most unexpected, and little remarked by Chicano/a activists, however, was that there were contingents of Puerto Ricans at the conference as well, including some from Chicago and others from New York City. Could they too be part of "la raza"? Did places like Kansas and Chicago fit into the imagined homeland of Aztlán? The presence of these groups from unfamiliar backgrounds and surprising places challenged the boundaries of a Chicano "imagined community."

The lack of knowledge about Mexicans (or Latinos/as of any ethnic origin) in the Midwest persisted in subsequent decades even while journalists like Rubén Martínez documented recent Mexican immigration in the 1990s to such unlikely locations as Garden City, Kansas, the St. Louis metropolitan area, and small towns in Wisconsin.[7] In the twenty-first century, although many scholars recognize that there are sizable Mexican, Puerto Rican, Central American, and South American populations in the middle of the country, the Midwest continues to be overlooked, understudied, and simply unexamined by many scholars.[8] Whether intentional or not, this neglect of the region is no longer acceptable for a field that seeks to capture the rich historical experiences of Mexican Americans throughout the United States.[9]

The bicoastal geographic hegemony on knowledge about Latinos/as has focused our analytical attention on Puerto Rican and other Caribbean populations in the Northeast and Mexican Americans in the Southwest. Researchers in the main have continued to fix these ethnic groups to these regions, concluding that they have been historically isolated from one another and have developed distinct and separate identities. Consequently, scholars have argued, the construction of "Hispanics" or "Latinos/as" has been a bureaucratic or mainstream activist fabrication rather than an organic social formation emerging from people's lived and shared experiences, something the opening vignette clearly disproves. This argument assumes Mexicans, Puerto Ricans, and other Latinos/as simply have not encountered one another until recently.[10] One can only reach these conclusions, however, by conspicuously overlooking the Midwest, a region where diverse "Spanish-speaking" groups have had rich interactions since at least the mid-twentieth century. Moreover, closer analysis of moments or places that we have assumed to be ethnically homogeneous may reveal surprising heterogeneity.

The Denver Youth Conference, for example, points to two interventions I aim to make in this chapter. The first is to rupture the geographical essentialism of the field of Chicano/a history that has kept it focused so exclusively on the Southwest and to make the case for greater attention to other regions, especially the US Midwest. Second, I challenge the rather outdated nationalist impulse of studying Mexican Americans in isolation from other Latino/a ethnic groups. These two limitations of the discipline are mutually constitutive and emerge out of an interdependent relationship. The geographical focus on the Southwest has resulted in a narrow focus strictly on ethnic Mexicans, while the interest in studying Mexicans alone has led many historians to the Southwest.[11] The remedy to these limitations, however, reveals itself if we extend our gaze beyond Aztlán. Due to its demographic significance and diversity, the Midwest lends itself readily to doing comparative, interethnic histories of Chicanos/as and other Latinos/as. While I do not wish to make an argument for midwestern exceptionalism, I maintain that the region and its historically diverse Latino/a populations produced a unique history that has not been replicated in many other parts of the country and that does not easily fit into the current parameters of Chicano history, unless we take a more inclusive approach. The Midwest and its Latino/a population offers an alternative to the geographic essentialism and nationalism of the field.[12]

My second intervention is not simply one of adding other Latinos/as into the Chicana/o history narrative, but of loosening the field's boundaries to more flexibly and creatively capture ethnic Mexicans' lived experiences. As I discuss below, Chicanos/as or Mexican Americans have not lived in isolation from other Spanish speakers. Mexican Americans, particularly in the Midwest, but increasingly in other parts of the country, have encountered, lived among, and interacted with other Latino/a groups for decades. Studying Mexicans exclusively in early twentieth-century Los Angeles or San Antonio might make sense: they were the dominant (and perhaps only) Spanish-speaking group in these locations. Yet even these locations reveal unexpected non-Mexican actors. The first Hispanic-owned, Spanish-language newspaper in San Antonio, for example, was *El Ranchero* in 1856, a collaboration between Mexican American businessman Narciso Leal and Cuban poet José Agustín Quintero.[13]

Quintessential moments in Chicano/a history, such as the *Mendez v. Westminster* case (1947), bear the signs of inter-Latino/a mixing as well. Felicita Mendez, the mother of the Mendez children whose exclusion from the "white" Westminster Elementary School inspired the anti-segregation lawsuit, was Puerto Rican.[14] In Chicano/a labor history, another iconic figure defies simplistic nationalist assertions. Luisa Moreno, the famed labor leader who organized and fought alongside Mexican workers, hailed from an elite Guatemalan family, not from working-class Mexican origins as some might assume.[15] Other examples abound. As Luis Alvarez maintains in his chapter in this collection, Chicano/a culture and identity has been shaped historically by Chicanos/as as well as non-Chicanos/as. We must account for these influences, intersections, and intermingling.

There is evidence as well that Chicanos or Mexican Americans have been present in moments or movements that have been interpreted as strictly Puerto Rican. The lionized Young Lords Organization (YLO) of Chicago, for example, which gave birth to the more widely known Young Lords Party in New York City, has long been considered by many to be a Puerto Rican nationalist organization. Yet the Chicago chapter actually had an interethnic membership, reflecting the presence of Mexican Americans in the diverse community where the YLO originated. The presence of Mexican Americans within the Puerto Rican enclave in the Lincoln Park neighborhood tempered strict nationalism and necessitated more inclusive political expressions. Thus, the Young Lords called for the liberation of all Latinos in their thirteen-point platform, at the same time that they declared their motto *"Tengo [a] Puerto Rico en Mi Corazon"* (Puerto Rico Is in My Heart). Even more ironically, perhaps, the young man who developed the group's emblem—a raised fist holding a rifle over the silhouette of the island inscribed with the motto—was actually Mexican American. When the radical youth group took over and occupied the Armitage Methodist Church, renaming it the People's Church, as Felipe Hinojosa cites elsewhere in this volume, the murals they painted on the walls included work by the Chicana artist Felicita Nuñez and featured images of Emiliano Zapata and other Chicano/a icons.[16] The YLO's newspaper regularly had images of Zapata emblazoned on its masthead and frequent coverage of Chicano struggles in the Southwest.[17]

This interethnic solidarity and exchange should come as no surprise, particularly in the political sphere, given the Chicano left's adoration of Argentinian-born martyr of the Cuban Revolution Che Guevara, whose ubiquitous image graced countless murals, protest signs, and publications during the Chicano Movement and since. Chicanos/as have a long history of influencing and being influenced by other Latin Americans in social movements, political struggles, and popular culture. Scholars of social movements and of Latina/o history must uncover a much more nuanced, complex interweaving of social relations that shaped organizations we have come to understand as strictly nationalist or monolithic in their ethnic/racial makeup.

What do these examples mean for Chicano/a history, given that they disrupt what Carlos Blanton identifies as traditional interpretations in the field? They suggest that Chicano/a history must expand its boundaries to make it more reflective of lived experiences in the past as well as contemporary demographic realities. Mexican Americans continue to be the largest Latino/a ethnic group in the United States and likely will remain so for decades to come. As the largest Spanish-speaking nation in Latin America and our closest neighbor, Mexico continues to send the greatest number of migrants to this country. Mexicans have also had the longest territorial history in the United States as a result of the land that was seized at the end of the US-Mexico War in 1848. Thus, Mexican Americans have a primacy and numerical dominance among Latinos/as in the United States that is not likely to change any time soon. In 2015, Chicana/o history has matured sufficiently as a field that studying Mexican Americans in relation to other Latinos/as should not cause concern that such comparative and relational work somehow will dilute the specificities of ethnic Mexican history. On the contrary, the interethnic encounters that Mexican Americans have had with other groups are a part of Chicano/a history that has been understudied and a story that has gone largely untold. Exploring those interactions enriches and animates the historical narrative considerably.

Nationalist Origins and Early Paradigms

Emerging as the scholarly arm of the Chicano Movement, the discipline of Chicana/o studies and the field of Chicano/a history have focused on the Chicana/o "nation" and the geographical territory where Mexicans have had the longest history—the US Southwest. Indeed, early Chicano/a history did the important political work (whether intentional or not) of reclaiming the region as the rightful homeland of people of Mexican descent, particularly in the sociopolitical context of anti-Mexican sentiment in the 1970s and 1980s. Chicano/a historians asserted the right of Mexican Americans to be present and active participants in what was originally their ancestral homeland and part of the former nation-state of Mexico, thus challenging Anglo characterizations of ethnic Mexicans as foreign, undesirable interlopers. As the famous Chicano/a adage goes, "We didn't cross the border, the border crossed us." Leftist sociologists and historians advanced the position that Chicanos were a colonized people whose territory had been wrongfully occupied and stolen by Anglo Americans during the height of nineteenth-century "Manifest Destiny" and its resulting unjust US-Mexican War.[18]

These political assertions established a rather narrow geographical scope, however. What about Mexican Americans in other parts of the country? What claims of belonging could they make? While Aztlán or the southwestern homeland has taken geographical priority in this narrative, such an essentialist rendering of Chicano/a ethnic origins—whether those of our indigenous ancestors or our Spanish colonial forebears—limits our genealogy considerably. If indeed Chicanos/as need to make territorial claims to assert their legitimacy in the United States, can we expand our geography? After all, Spanish colonial explorers such as the conquistador Francisco Vasquez de Coronado traveled as far as Kansas in the early sixteenth century in search of the fabled Seven Cities of Gold. While this left an admittedly faint trace on the midwestern landscape, the Spanish had a presence there nonetheless. Hernando de Soto and Alvar Nuñez Cabeza de Vaca, two other famed Spanish conquistadors, traveled throughout the present-day US Southeast even earlier, though these explorations in the region are seldom acknowledged in US history textbooks. If we want to claim "Chicano/a" territorial origins, can we include Spanish travels through these regions?[19]

Considering our indigenous ancestors alternatively, it is worth remembering that the ancient inhabitants of the Southwest and Mexico did not observe an impassable border once they reached the present-day American Midwest. On the contrary, the remains of the ancient city of Cahokia near present-day St. Louis, for example, reveal remarkably similar architectural design and spiritual purposes as the city of Teotihuacan outside of Mexico City.[20] Each society probably influenced the other, engaged in trade, and perhaps even exchanged inhabitants. Material artifacts from faraway locations (i.e., seashells, minerals) provide archaeological evidence of some form of contact. The incredible earthworks found in Central Ohio, believed to be sites of ancient pilgrimage, provide further evidence of their connections to indigenous people in precolonial Mexico and Latin America.[21] Ancient peoples, in other words, traveled far and wide for trade and even spiritual renewal. If we want to lay claim to Chicano/a "origins" by excavating historical experiences, can we include inhabitants in the Midwest who migrated, traveled, and interacted throughout modern-day Latin America? Recent scientific exploration and interdisciplinary research—in archaeology, biology, anthropology, and other fields—has produced new evidence and theories about the ancient inhabitants of the Americas. As the technology available for such inquiries expands, we will certainly make more surprising and unexpected discoveries that connect indigenous people throughout the hemisphere.

Beyond this, however, the presence of Mexico or Mexican things dots the midwestern landscape and inhabits the region's imaginary in other, perhaps less noticeable ways. For example, towns with Spanish names—often those of cities or places in Mexico, Spain, or Latin America—exist throughout the region. Many of these places are likely remnants of the US-Mexican War, the legacy of returning soldiers who were rewarded by the US government with plots of land that they then named after the places they had seen or where they did battle.[22] Regardless of how seriously we take these tenuous connections, they are worthy of consideration and would broaden the territory (real or imagined) that Chicanas/os claim as "home."

At the same time that Chicano/a scholars outlined the parameters of Chicano/a studies and Chicano/a history, scholars of Puerto Rican history were busy documenting the history of Puerto Ricans—their migration from the island to the mainland, their labor, and their community activism. While Chicano/a historians traced the historical presence of Mexican people to Aztlán, Puerto Rican scholars mapped out the Puerto Rican diaspora, one originating in the Caribbean but anchoring itself on the US mainland, primarily in New York City.[23] Puerto Rican studies crafted a nationalist narrative that pointed to the colonized island and emphasized transnational movement, circular migration, cultural politics, and anticolonial resistance.[24] Like Chicano/a studies, Puerto Rican studies did the political work of claiming the right of Puerto Ricans to belong in the United States and of critiquing American imperialism and colonialism.

Early Chicano and Puerto Rican historians produced important work that illuminated our heretofore limited understanding of Mexican Americans and Puerto Ricans. In their eagerness to document these populations, they described them discretely and separately from other Spanish-speaking or Latin American people.[25] The historical reality of Mexicans and Puerto Ricans, however, has proved much more complex, messy, and fraught with tensions. In the last two decades these fields have had to consider difficult questions: Where do Dominicans, Central Americans, and other Latinos/as fit within these nationalist paradigms? How do we account for the historical presence and experiences of other Latinos/as, some of whom have been present in the mainland United States in small numbers for as long as Mexican Americans or Puerto Ricans, while others are more recent migrants who have become part of diverse Latino/a communities throughout the country? Studying individual ethnic groups is much easier to do than documenting overlapping and sometimes divergent ethnic histories and accounting for relations, solidarities, and conflicts between various Latino/a populations. Yet this intermingling has occurred for decades. It has long awaited historians' interpretations.

The Midwest, Comparative Analysis, and Latino/a Panethnicity

The Midwest has always been a unique meeting place when it comes to the history of Chicanos/as and Latinos/as in the United States. As the largest city and the unofficial capital of the region, Chicago was the destination of choice for most of these migrants. Perhaps nowhere else, except San Francisco, did Mexicans mingle so extensively among Puerto Ricans and other Spanish-speaking people in the mid-twentieth century.[26] Their numbers in Chicago, however, were much larger than in San Francisco. Moreover, the migration patterns of these two cities differed significantly. While the Bay Area received a small number of Puerto Ricans in the early twentieth century and a smattering of Central Americans in the 1910s and 1920s as a result of transnational trade and commerce with Central America, Chicago received sizable numbers of Mexicans during the Mexican Revolution and both Mexican and Puerto Rican labor migrants during and after World War II.[27] In terms of the ethnic mix of Spanish speakers and the timing of their migration, then, Chicago stands out as a distinctive site of Latino/a settlement.[28]

The interethnic exchange between Mexican Americans and other Latino/a national origin groups in Chicago dates back to the first wave of Mexican migration in the 1920s. Mexican immigrants sought services from, lived among, or interacted with diverse Latin American businesspeople, professionals, and elites.[29] Two decades later, Mexican immigrants, particularly the ubiquitous *solos*, or unaccompanied male migrants, sought out companionship and romantic partnerships with Puerto Rican and European immigrant women.[30] In the 1950s and 1960s, Mexicans intermarried with Puerto Ricans and other ethnic groups with growing frequency. Mexican Americans, to state the obvious, have never lived entirely in isolation from other Latino/a groups, or from non-Latino/a ethnic groups for that matter.[31]

In 1973 the *Pacific Historical Review* (*PHR*) published a special issue on Chicano/a history. Surprising to some perhaps, the journal included an essay on Chicanos/as in the Midwest, a study of the repatriation of Mexican steel and rail workers and their families in Gary, Indiana, during the Great Depression.[32] This attention to the Midwest did not end there. Three years later, the Chicana/o studies journal, *Aztlán*, devoted a special issue to "Chicanos in the Midwest," complete with articles on the history of Mexicans in Chicago and Indiana's steel mill communities as well as analyses of 1970 census data on the Spanish-speaking population in the region. That year as well, Louise Año Nuevo Kerr completed her groundbreaking dissertation, "The Chicano Experience in Chicago: 1920–1970," which stood for over three decades as the only historical study of Mexicans in the city. Chicana/o scholars in the Midwest called upon their colleagues in the Southwest to acknowledge and bear witness to the significant Chicana/o population in the middle of the country.[33]

Scholars like Año Nuevo Kerr, those who published in the special issue of *Aztlán*, and various other researchers who prepared reports and papers throughout the 1970s stressed three very important points about Mexican Americans in the Midwest. First, they had a historical presence in the region that dated back at least to World War I. Indeed, the first significant wave of Mexican migration to the area occurred during the war and the great labor strikes of 1919. Second, the Spanish-speaking population in the Midwest, estimated at 1.2 million in 1973, was noteworthy and deserving of attention from not only academics but all levels of government, employers, educators, and social service providers. The Spanish speakers were a sizable group. Yet they had little official representation or political power locally or on the national scene. Third, Mexicans were not the only Spanish-speaking people in the region (especially not in urban areas) but lived among a large population of Puerto Ricans, as well as Cubans, Central Americans, and South Americans.[34] While Mexicans continued to migrate to the Midwest in the 1970s and later, they were increasingly accompanied by migrants from the Caribbean and other parts of Latin America.

Chicago had the largest concentration of Spanish-speaking people in the Midwest and perhaps the most diverse such population in the country. A 1973 report, which signaled City Hall's long-overdue recognition of the population, noted, "Chicago is unique in that it is the only major city in the U.S. with substantial percentages of all the major ethnic groups constituting the Spanish-speaking population of the nation."[35] The 1970 census had officially counted 247,343 Spanish-speaking persons in the city, of which Mexicans were the largest group—106,000, or 43 percent of Latinos/as. Puerto Ricans were the next largest, believed to number 78,000, or 32 percent. Cubans, Central Americans, and South Americans made up the remaining 25 percent. Researchers and community leaders estimated that this was a severe undercount, however, especially of recent Mexican immigrants, and particularly the undocumented. They argued that it was much more likely that nearly half a million Latinos/as lived in the city by the late 1970s. If we accept this assertion, then Latinos/as were a much larger population than official numbers indicated, and Mexicans were the majority of the city's Spanish-speaking people.[36]

With a population concentrated in Chicago and in its surrounding suburbs, the state of Illinois had the most Spanish-speaking residents in the Midwest—an estimated 686,700 people in 1973.[37] This figure far exceeded the estimated numbers of the Spanish-surnamed in better-recognized states of Mexican American settlement such as Arizona (357,000), Colorado (272,500), or New Mexico (387,000).[38] Why was Illinois, a state with almost twice as many Spanish-speaking residents as Arizona or New Mexico, and far more than double the number of Colorado, less visible than those states on the national stage and in the Chicano/a imaginary? The answer had to do with the ethnic politics emanating from the Southwest and the political power that southwestern leaders were able to wield on a national scale. The Midwest had few visible Chicano/a or Latino/a leaders. Even intellectually, however, although Chicano/a scholars were aware in the 1970s of the Mexican presence in the Midwest, most scholarship emanated from the Southwest and focused on the populations of the five southwestern states. Midwestern Chicanos/as were at best an afterthought in conversations about the nation's Mexican Americans, and at worst entirely overlooked.

Chicana/o researchers in the Midwest lamented that *Raza* in the region were so neglected: hardly anyone during this time studied them, wrote their history, or addressed their needs. Consequently, Spanish-speaking people in the region lagged behind southwesterners in acquiring meaningful political power and resources. Midwestern scholars stressed the importance of examining the specificities of the region:

> Simple generalizations from the case of various Chicano communities in the Southwest or about the experience of Puerto Ricans in New York or on the island cannot adequately explain the situation or problems of *La Raza* in the Midwest. The causes of internal differentiation and heterogeneity within *Raza* communities as well as those that lead toward

greater consciousness and greater solidarity, . . . while comparable to such factors in the Southwest or Puerto Rico, nonetheless, merit separate consideration. The problems related to migration and settlement, . . . while being traceable to larger social processes and . . . comparable to the earlier experiences of Chicanos in the Southwest or Puerto Ricans in New York, are, nevertheless, somewhat distinctive and perhaps unique, if not in magnitude at least in form.[39]

This ethnically diverse Latino/a demographic did not fit easily into bicoastal paradigms of conquest, migration, racialization, or identity formation. The Midwest begged to be studied on its own terms and in all its particularities. Still, Chicano/a scholars who called for greater attention to Mexicans in the Midwest in the 1970s were so immersed in an essentialized southwestern kind of geographical imagination that they insisted on calling Mexicans in the Midwest "*los desarraigados*," or the uprooted ones, who had been torn from their homelands and journeyed not to the more *culturally familiar* southwestern states (Aztlán), but to the more distant, foreign, and inhospitable middle of the country.[40]

In the decades since *Aztlán*'s and *PHR*'s special issues, only a handful of historians took up the call to research and publish on Mexican Americans in the Midwest. Juan R. Garcia, Zaragosa Vargas, and Dionicio Valdés produced monographs on Mexican immigration to the region, Mexican industrial labor in Detroit, and Mexican and Puerto Rican agricultural workers in Michigan.[41] The sociologist Felix Padilla produced a groundbreaking and now classic study of Latino/a panethnicity, attesting to the uniqueness of Chicago's Latino/a ethnic composition. Padilla traced the formation of "situational Latino ethnic consciousness" within Mexican American and Puerto Rican coalitions, arguing that the two ethnic groups came together as "Latinos" for specific and targeted political goals, such as fighting employment discrimination against Spanish-speaking workers.[42] Padilla's sociological analysis has stood as a critical source for historians in subsequent decades. These few studies in the late 1980s and early 1990s barely began to document these communities but left many other topics ripe for investigation.

Beginning in the twenty-first century, Puerto Rican scholars turned their attention to the Midwest as well, specifically to Chicago. Elena Padilla's master's thesis in anthropology at the University of Chicago had documented the beginnings of Puerto Rican migration to the city in the 1940s and for decades remained the only study of this population in the middle of the country. By the mid-1980s, Felix Padilla's *Puerto Ri-*

can Chicago extended the documentation of Puerto Rican migration and settlement through the mid-twentieth century. In the early twenty-first century, however, anthropologists and sociologists took a renewed interest in this topic, issuing a number of books and articles on the islanders in the Windy City that explored themes of transnationalism, circular migration, nationalist politics, gender, and identity.[43] Simultaneously, historical attention to Mexican Americans in the region began to grow as well, as demonstrated by the work of Marc Rodriguez, Gabriela Arredondo, Nicholas De Genova, Michael Innis-Jiménez, and my own work.[44] While most Chicano/a historians continue to hail from the Southwest and/or their analytical gaze has remained focused on that region, a growing number of younger scholars have begun exploring the Midwest in greater detail and are discovering the region to be rich in potential for fascinating inter- and intra-ethnic work.

Still missing in this new body of historical scholarship, however, is a comparative approach to analyzing distinct Latino/a communities. Studying Mexicans or Puerto Ricans in isolation from one another, as if they occupied discrete, insular spheres, may be adequate in some rural communities, or earlier in the twentieth century. Yet in the postwar era and in urban areas, limiting our historical focus to *one* ethnic or national group elides the ways in which different national-origin groups have lived among one another, intermarried, and also experienced conflict and contention.

In recent years, the emerging field of Latina/o history has developed as a pedagogical tool, if not yet a clearly defined field of study, to document distinct group histories. Courses on Latino/a history are in high demand as the Latino/a population continues to diversify beyond predominantly Mexican or Puerto Rican in many parts of the country and as growing numbers of diverse Latino/a students enter colleges and universities. The subject area makes sense as an educational imperative, whether for students hoping to learn about their own heritage, those who want to meet college general-education "diversity" requirements, those who wish to work with Latina/o populations in their chosen professions, or those who simply want to know more about the largest "minority" group in the country. As a scholarly field, however, Latino/a history has not yet come of age. While we may gather the aggregate of Chicano/a, Puerto Rican, Cuban, Salvadoran, and Ecuadorean history all together under the umbrella of "Latino/a history," we have not yet figured out how to do comparative, relational, interethnic, and integrated work that examines more than one of these groups at a time. The challenge in the future will be to find a way to examine Mexican Americans in relation to Guatemalans, Hondurans in relation to Nicaraguans, or Colombians in relation to Dominicans. For those who identify intellectually as Chicano/a historians, this seems an area primed for exploration. Were the field to embrace more comparative work (not only within Latino/a communities but across other nonwhite racial and ethnic groups), it would engage a generation of students and scholars who are eager for this kind of interethnic analysis.[45]

The call for doing comparative, interethnic historical scholarship must be distinguished, however, from a focus on panethnicity—the construction of a sociopolitical identity that crosses ethnic lines and builds upon perceived common interests or values. To be sure, (im)migrants arriving from other countries of origin usually do not see themselves as part of larger panethnic flows of migration. Indeed, most see themselves in local, regional, or sometimes national terms. Panethnic affinities and expressions are contingent upon the social environments in which people find themselves and the identities that become most valuable in those contexts. For a Salvadoran immigrant living in a diverse Latin American immigrant community, for example, asserting her ethnic distinctiveness may be most salient in her environment. Alternately, expressing solidarity and affinities with fellow immigrants from other countries may offer other benefits in her community (social or otherwise). The choices people make about ethnic identification are complex, personal, and often contextually dependent.[46]

The debate over a shared or distinctive identity and racialization among different Latinos/as has intrigued researchers in recent years. Social scientists are studying the extent to which different Latino/a ethnic groups find solidarity with one another, identify as "Latino/a," or insist on a single ethnic identification (e.g., Dominican, Chilean, Bolivian). Nicholas De Genova and Ana Ramos-Zayas, for example, challenged Felix Padilla's assertions about Mexican and Puerto Rican panethnicity, concluding that Mexicans and Puerto Ricans actually find little in common with one another and in fact see each other as rivals. While this is the result of the way in which US capitalism disciplines domestic and immigrant labor, it makes the prospect of panethnic identification and political alliances seem very unlikely.[47] Cristina Beltran argues that the notion of a "Latino/a electorate" or voting demographic is problematic and misleading in that it assumes political unity across Latino/a ethnic groups. The value of Latino/a panethnicity, in her opinion, is questionable. G. Cristina Mora furthers the claim that the panethnic term "Hispanic" emerged out of official government channels and the work of political elites, thus casting suspicion on the authenticity of such social formations at the grassroots level.[48] Yet again, the history of Latinos/as in the Midwest, including the opening vignette, challenges these conclusions. In her study of Mexicans and Puerto Ricans in Grand Rapids, Michigan, for example, Delia Fernandez demonstrates that through their shared experiences as Spanish-speaking newcomers in a predominantly white city, Mexicans and Puerto Ricans sought each other out for leisure and recreation, to baptize one another's children, as marriage partners, and as allies in struggles for economic opportunity. Fernandez offers us a view into the intimate sociality of *Latinidad* and how populations cultivate panethnic alliances and affiliations in often unexamined spaces—churches, families, athletic leagues, and community organizations—and as a precursor to the more explicit political mobilization that Felix Padilla documents.[49] Still, other scholars have emphasized the shared racialization that both groups experience, highlighting the possibilities for a shared *Latinidad*.[50] Historians must engage in these discussions alongside social scientists.

On social media and in hallway conversations at national conferences, some Chicano (and Puerto Rican) scholars lament the dilution of Chicano (and Puerto Rican) history and their potential displacement by the more diversified panethnic field of Latino/a history. Indeed, die-hard nationalists bristle at the field of "Latino/a Studies" and the concept of *Latinidad* as just the latest commodified intellectual trend, which fails to pay homage to the Chicano/a and Puerto Rican activism and scholarship that first opened the doors to the academy for Latinos/as decades ago. Some worry that this popular new formulation will replace traditional Chicano/a and Boricua Studies intellectual frameworks and departments that have had to fight for their legitimacy in the academy. These programs have endured repeated attacks and constant threats of dismantling, especially in moments of budget cuts or political backlash. We can understand the impulse to defend and preserve these traditional programs, many of which were established through the great sacrifice of students and other activists. Yet the increasing diversity of the nation's Latino/a population, interethnic subjectivity, and the question of *Latinidad* are a demographic reality for many young people in the United States today. As Latinos/as continue to intermarry across ethnic lines, the model of studying single national origin groups to the exclusion of others is becoming increasingly outdated and unsustainable.

I have not made the case here for completely discarding Chicano/a history in favor of a multiethnic Latino/a history model. Rather, in addressing Chicano/a historians and students of the field, I propose instead that in order to keep Chicano/a history intellectually viable and relevant, (1) we look more carefully at the historical reality that Mexican Americans have lived in the United States to find moments of cross-ethnic interactions, (2) we extend the boundaries of the field to make room for those inter-Latino/a encounters and for doing comparative work, and finally (3) we move beyond the usual and well-worn sites of inquiry to explore Mexican Americans in places like Indiana, Wisconsin, Iowa, and Ohio, to name but a few. As the Latino/a population in the United States continues to grow and diversify, especially in new and unexpected places, it is inevitable that historical scholarship will have to catch up. Chicano/a historians will need to write the story of the late twentieth and early twenty-first centuries with all of the complexities, triumphs, and tragedies of the era. To do this, we will need to shed our traditionalist and nationalist paradigms and move beyond Aztlán.

Notes

1. Flyer, February 1954, folder 4, box 373, Welfare Council of Metropolitan Chicago Papers, Chicago History Museum.

2. "News Summary," *Chicago Tribune*, February 2, 1954.

3. I use the term "Spanish-speaking" to refer to Mexicans and Puerto Ricans collectively—rather than the contemporary label "Latina/o"—to accurately capture the terminology of the time. Although second-generation children of immigrants and Mexican American migrants from Texas may not necessarily have spoken Spanish, the phrase connoted what Mexicans and Puerto Ricans believed they had most in common: a shared Spanish linguistic and colonial heritage.

4. Nicholas De Genova, *Working the Boundaries: Race, Space, and "Illegality" in Mexican Chicago* (Durham, NC: Duke University Press, 2005), 105.

5. See, for example, Dionicio Nodín Valdés, *Barrios Norteños: St. Paul and Midwestern Mexican Communities in the Twentieth Century* (Austin: University of Texas Press, 2000).

6. Galán Productions, Inc., National Latino Communications Center, and KCET–Los Angeles, *Chicano! History of a Mexican American Civil Rights Movement* (Galán Productions, 1996).

7. Rubén Martínez, *Crossing Over: A Mexican Family on the Migrant Trail* (New York: Picador, 2002).

8. As recently as the 2014 inaugural Latino/a Studies Conference, a Chicano scholar featured in the plenary session made dismissive comments about the region, suggesting that the most valuable knowledge about Latinos/as and their experiences could be gleaned from the East Coast or the West Coast. Not

surprisingly, he received vocal criticism from members of the audience who spoke on the significance of the region and the symbolism of this first gathering being held in Chicago, the city with the second-largest Mexican population and third-largest Latino/a population in the country.

9. While I do not want to single out specific scholars and suggest that any of them intentionally ignore the region, a review of Chicano/a historiography reveals the overwhelming bias toward the US Southwest and scant attention to Mexican Americans in the Midwest.

10. Two studies that assert the ethnic isolation paradigm of Mexican Americans and Puerto Ricans, for example, are Suzanne Oboler, *Ethnic Labels, Latino Lives: Identity and the Politics of (Re)Presentation in the United States* (Minneapolis: University of Minnesota Press, 1995); and G. Cristina Mora, *Making Hispanics: How Activists, Bureaucrats, and Media Constructed a New American* (Chicago: University of Chicago Press, 2014).

11. The presence of hundreds of thousands of Central Americans since the 1970s in cities like Los Angeles, for example, has challenged this narrow focus on Chicanos/as. This has manifested itself most visibly in the creation of Central American Studies programs such as the one at California State University's Northridge campus established in 2000.

12. The South also has begun to receive significant attention from scholars, particularly as the Latino/a population has grown dramatically in the 1980s, 1990s, and 2000s. See Perla M. Guerrero's chapter in this volume.

13. Juan González and Joseph Torres, *News for All the People: The Epic Story of Race and the American Media* (New York: Verso, 2011), 85–86.

14. Jennifer McCormick and Cesar Ayala, "Felícita 'La Prieta' Méndez (1916–1998) and the End of Latino School Segregation in California," *Centro Journal* 19, no. 2 (Fall 2007): 12–35.

15. Vicki L. Ruiz, "Of Poetics and Politics: The Border Journeys of Luisa Moreno," in *Women's Labor in the Global Economy: Speaking in Multiple Voices*, ed. Sharon Harley (New Brunswick, NJ: Rutgers University Press, 2007).

16. Other examples of religious activism in the 1960s have often been sites where Mexicans and Puerto Ricans encountered one another and cultivated panethnic sensibilities. See Felipe Hinojosa's chapter in this volume.

17. Fernández, "From Street Gang to Revolutionaries: The Evolution of the Young Lords Organization," in *Brown in the Windy City: Mexicans and Puerto Ricans in Postwar Chicago* (Chicago: University of Chicago Press, 2012), 173–205.

18. Robert Blauner, *Racial Oppression in America* (New York: Harper & Row, 1972); Rodolfo Acuña, *Occupied America: The Chicano's Struggle toward Liberation* (San Francisco: Canfield Press, 1972); David J. Weber, ed., *Foreigners in Their Native Land: Historical Roots of the Mexican Americans* (Albuquerque: University of New Mexico Press, 1973). For early Chicano/a history monographs, see Albert Camarillo, *Chicanos in a Changing Society: From Mexican Pueblos to American Barrios in Santa Barbara and Southern California, 1848–1930* (Cambridge, MA: Harvard University Press, 1979); Mario T. García, *Desert Immigrants: The Mexicans of El Paso, 1880–1920* (New Haven, CT: Yale University Press, 1981); Richard Griswold del Castillo, *The Los Angeles Barrio, 1850–1890: A Social History* (Berkeley: University of California Press, 1979); Ricardo Romo, *East Los*

Angeles: History of a Barrio (Austin: University of Texas Press, 1983); Vicki L. Ruiz, *Cannery Women, Cannery Lives: Mexican Women, Unionization, and the California Food Processing Industry, 1930–1950* (Albuquerque: University of New Mexico Press, 1987). For later monographs, see Edward J. Escobar, *Race, Police, and the Making of a Political Identity: Mexican Americans and the Los Angeles Police Department, 1900–1945* (Berkeley: University of California Press, 1999); Matt Garcia, *A World of Its Own: Race, Labor, and Citrus in the Making of Greater Los Angeles, 1900–1970* (Chapel Hill: University of North Carolina Press, 2001); Deena González, *Refusing the Favor: The Spanish-Mexican Women of Santa Fe, 1820–1880* (New York: Oxford University Press, 1999); Stephen Pitti, *The Devil in Silicon Valley: Northern California, Race, and Mexican Americans* (Princeton, NJ: Princeton University Press, 2003); Zaragosa Vargas, *Labor Rights Are Civil Rights: Mexican American Workers in Twentieth-Century America* (Princeton, NJ: Princeton University Press, 2005).

19. On Spanish exploration of the Southeast and Midwest, see primary sources in Weber, *Foreigners in Their Native Land*; Alvar Núñez Cabeza de Vaca, *Castaways: The Narrative of Alvar Núñez Cabeza De Vaca*, ed. Enrique Pupo-Walker (Berkeley: University of California Press, 1993).

20. See http://cahokiamounds.org/ and http://www.inah.gob.mx/boletines/44-lista-de-zonas-arqueologicas/6036-zona-arqueologica-teotihuacan, both accessed April 19, 2015.

21. Similar earthworks have been found as far south as Bolivia and elsewhere in South America. See, for example, Charles Mann, *1491* (New York: Knopf, 2005).

22. Omar-Valerio Jimenez, Foreword, in Saúl Sánchez, *Rows of Memory: Journeys of a Migrant Sugar-Beet Worker* (Iowa City: University of Iowa Press, 2014).

23. History Task Force Centro de Estudios Puertorriqueños, *Labor Migration under Capitalism: The Puerto Rican Experience* (New York: Research Foundation of the City University of New York, 1979); Juan E. Hernández-Cruz, "A Perspective on Return Migration: The Circulation of Puerto Rican Workers" (PhD diss., New York University, 1982); Frank Bonilla and Ricardo Campos, "A Wealth of Poor: Puerto Ricans in the New Economic Order," *Daedalus* 110, no. 2 (Spring 1981): 133–176; Frank Bonilla and Héctor Colón Jordán, *Puerto Rican Return Migration in the '70s* (New York: Centro de Estudios Puertorriqueños, CUNY, 1979); Edwin Maldonado, "Contract Labor and the Origins of Puerto Rican Communities in the United States," *International Migration Review* 13, no. 1 (Spring 1979): 103–121.

24. See, for example, Virginia Sánchez Korrol, *From Colonia to Community: The History of Puerto Ricans in New York City* (Berkeley: University of California Press, 1994); Andrés Torres and José E. Velásquez, eds., *The Puerto Rican Movement: Voices from the Diaspora* (Philadelphia: Temple University Press, 1998); Carmen Teresa Whalen, *From Puerto Rico to Philadelphia: Puerto Rican Workers and Postwar Economies* (Philadelphia: Temple University Press, 2001); Gina Pérez, *The Near Northwest Side Story: Migration, Displacement, and Puerto Rican Families* (Berkeley: University of California Press, 2004); Carmen Teresa Whalen and Víctor Vázquez-Hernández, *The Puerto Rican Diaspora: Historical Per-*

spectives (Philadelphia: Temple University Press, 2005); Jorge Duany, *The Puerto Rican Nation on the Move: Identities on the Island and in the United States* (Chapel Hill: University of North Carolina Press, 2002).

25. For some early reflections on the intermixing and relations between Chicanos/as and Puerto Ricans, see, for example, Angie Chabram-Dernersesian, "'Chicana! Rican? No, Chicana Riqueña!' Refashioning the Transnational Connection," in *Between Woman and Nation: Nationalisms, Transnational Feminisms, and the State*, ed. Caren Kaplan, Norma Alarcón, and Minoo Moallem (Durham, NC: Duke University Press, 1999), 264–295; J. Jorge Klor de Alva, "Aztlán, Borinquen, and Hispanic Nationalism in the United States" in *Aztlán*, ed. Rudolfo A. Anaya and Francisco A. Lomelí (Albuquerque: Academia/El Norte Publications, 1989), 135–171.

26. Tomás Summers-Sandoval, *Latinos at the Golden Gate: Creating Community and Identity in San Francisco* (Chapel Hill: University of North Carolina Press, 2013); Eduardo Contreras, *Latinos in the Liberal City: From San Francisco's Big Strike to Gay Liberation* (University of Pennsylvania Press, manuscript in progress).

27. Despite the historical presence of Mexicans in Chicago since World War I, histories of immigrants in the city and their labor union activism have overlooked Mexicans. See, for example, Lizabeth Cohen, *Making a New Deal: Industrial Workers in Chicago, 1919–1939* (Cambridge, UK: Cambridge University Press, 1990). Even recent popular narratives of Chicago history persistently recount a black and white story, ignoring the significant influx of Mexicans and Puerto Ricans in the post–World War II era. See Thomas Dyja, *The Third Coast: When Chicago Built the American Dream* (New York: Penguin, 2013).

28. See Fernández, *Brown in the Windy City*, chap. 1.

29. See, for example, Gabriela F. Arredondo, *Mexican Chicago: Race, Identity, and Nation, 1916–39* (Urbana: University of Illinois Press, 2008).

30. Elena Padilla, "Puerto Rican Immigrants in New York and Chicago: A Study in Comparative Assimilation" (master's thesis, University of Chicago, 1947); Arredondo, *Mexican Chicago*.

31. For examples in Los Angeles and New York, see chap. 7 in this volume, as well as George J. Sánchez, "What's Good for Boyle Heights Is Good for the Jews: Creating Multiracialism on the Eastside during the 1950s," *American Quarterly* 56, no. 3 (September 2004): 633–661; Sanchez Korrol, *From Colonia to Community*; Fernández, *Brown in the Windy City*, especially chaps. 2 and 3.

32. Neil Betten and Raymond A. Mohl, "From Discrimination to Repatriation: Mexican Life in Gary, Indiana, during the Great Depression," *Pacific Historical Review* 42, no. 3 (1973): 370–388.

33. Gilbert Cardenas, "Los Desarraigados: Chicanos in the Midwestern Region of the United States," *Aztlán* 7, no. 2 (Summer 1976): 153–186; Juan R. García, "History of Chicanos in Chicago Heights," ibid., 291–306; F. Arturo Rosales, "The Regional Origins of Mexicano Immigrants to Chicago during the 1920s," ibid., 187–202; Louise Año Nuevo Kerr, "The Chicano Experience in Chicago: 1920–1970" (PhD diss., University of Illinois, 1976).

34. See special issue, *Aztlán* 7, no. 2 (Summer 1976); Gilberto Cardenas, Call for Papers, *Aztlán* special issue, "Chicanos in the Mid-West," February 25,

1975, box 9, Gil Cardenas Papers, Institute for Latino Studies Library and Archives, University of Notre Dame; Gilbert Cardenas and Ricardo Parra, "La Raza in the Midwest and Great Lakes Region," University of Notre Dame, Centro de Estudios Chicanos, Institute for Urban Studies, January 1973, 33.

35. City of Chicago, Department of Development and Planning, *Chicago's Spanish Speaking Population: Selected Statistics* (Chicago: author, 1973).

36. Ibid., and John Walton and Luis Salces, "The Political Organization of Chicago's Latino Communities," Center for Urban Affairs, Northwestern University, 1977. Walton and Salces compared census undercount estimates for African Americans, which the Census Bureau calculated at 7.7 percent, and doubled this figure for Latinos, arguing that they had higher mobility rates, language barriers to completing the census, and greater suspicion of the census because of undocumented relatives or other members of their households. These INS estimates of the undocumented may have been inflated, as the perception at the time was that "illegal aliens" were ubiquitous and creating a social crisis in the country. Still, Walton and Salces used the lower of the INS estimates. The Chicago office in fact estimated *as many as* 500,000 illegal aliens in the city.

37. This included hundreds of thousands of Latinos/as in the surrounding Chicago suburbs of Cook, Lake, DuPage, Will, and Kane counties.

38. Walton and Salces, "The Political Organization of Chicago's Latino Communities."

39. Cardenas and Parra, "La Raza in the Midwest and Great Lakes Region," 35.

40. The term "los desarraigados" originally appeared as the title of two Mexican films (one in 1960 and one in 1976) about Mexican immigrants in the United States. Gilberto Cardenas used the term, however, in his essay about Chicanos in the Midwest, "Los Desarraigados: Chicanos in the Midwestern Region of the United States," *Aztlán* 7, no. 2 (Summer 1976): 153–186. The Midwest Council of La Raza, based at the University of Notre Dame in the 1970s and which Cardenas participated in, named its regular newsletter *Los Desarraigados* as well. Leticia Wiggins, "Institutionalizing Activism, Deconstructing Borderlands: La Raza in the Midwest, 1970–1978" (unpublished master's paper, Ohio State University, 2012).

41. Juan R. García, ed., *Perspectives in Mexican American Studies: Mexicans in the Midwest*, vol. 2 (Tucson: University of Arizona Press, 1989); García, *Mexicans in the Midwest, 1900–1932* (Tucson: University of Arizona Press, 1996); Dennis Nodín Valdés, *Al Norte: Agricultural Workers in the Great Lakes Region, 1917–1970* (Austin: University of Texas Press, 1991); Zaragosa Vargas, *Proletarians of the North: A History of Mexican Industrial Workers in Detroit and the Midwest, 1917–1933* (Berkeley: University of California Press, 1993).

42. Felix Padilla, *Latino Ethnic Consciousness: The Case of Mexican Americans and Puerto Ricans in Chicago* (Notre Dame, IN: University of Notre Dame Press, 1985).

43. Felix Padilla, *Puerto Rican Chicago* (Notre Dame, IN: University of Notre Dame Press, 1987); Ana Y. Ramos-Zayas, *National Performances: The Politics of Class, Race, and Space in Puerto Rican Chicago* (Chicago: University of Chicago

Press, 2003); Pérez, *The Near Northwest Side Story*; Mérida Rúa, *A Grounded Identidad: Making New Lives in Chicago's Puerto Rican Neighborhoods* (New York: Oxford University Press, 2012); Maura Toro-Morn, "Gender, Class, Family, and Migration: Puerto Rican Women in Chicago," *Gender and Society* 9 (1995): 712–726. See also a special issue in *Centro Journal* 13, no. 2 (Fall 2001).

44. Marc S. Rodriguez, *The Tejano Diaspora: Mexican Americanism and Ethnic Politics in Texas and Wisconsin* (Chapel Hill: University of North Carolina Press, 2011); De Genova, *Working the Boundaries*; Arredondo, *Mexican Chicago*; Michael Innis-Jiménez, *Steel Barrio: The Great Mexican Migration to South Chicago, 1915–1940* (New York: New York University Press, 2013); Fernández, *Brown in the Windy City*; Fernández, "From the Near West Side to 18th Street: Un/Making Latina/o Barrios in Postwar Chicago," in *Beyond El Barrio: Everyday Life in Latina/o America*, ed. Gina Pérez, Frank Guridy, and Adrian Burgos (New York: New York University Press, 2010), 233–252.

45. Natalia Molina's *Fit to Be Citizens?* is a good example of Chicano/a history that incorporates a comparative analysis of the racialization of several nonwhite ethnic groups, namely Mexican, Chinese, and Japanese Americans. Molina, *Fit to Be Citizens? Public Health and Race in Los Angeles, 1879–1939* (Berkeley: University of California Press, 2006).

46. See, for example Michael Rodriguez-Muñiz, "Grappling with Latinidad: Puerto Rican Activism in Chicago's Pro-Immigrant Rights Movement," in *Marcha! Latino Chicago and the Immigrant Rights Movement*, ed. Amalia Pallares and Nilda Flores-González (Urbana: University of Illinois Press, 2010), 237–258; Mérida Rúa, "Colao Subjectivities: Portomex and MexiRican Perspectives on Language and Identity," *Centro Journal* 13, no. 2 (Fall 2001): 117–133; Frances Aparicio, "Jennifer as Selena: Rethinking Latinidad in Media and Popular Culture," *Latino Studies Journal* 1, no. 1 (2003): 90–105.

47. Nicholas De Genova and Ana Y. Ramos-Zayas, *Latino Crossings: Mexicans, Puerto Ricans, and the Politics of Race and Citizenship* (New York: Routledge, 2003).

48. Cristina Beltrán, *The Trouble with Unity: Latino Politics and the Creation of Identity* (New York: Oxford University Press, 2010); Mora, *Making Hispanics*.

49. Delia Fernandez, "Becoming Latino: Mexican and Puerto Rican Community Formation in Grand Rapids, Michigan, 1926–1964," *Michigan Historical Review* 39, no. 1 (Spring 2013): 71–100.

50. Rodriguez-Muñiz, "Grappling with Latinidad"; Lilia Fernández, "Of Migrants and Immigrants: Mexican and Puerto Rican Labor Migration in Comparative Perspective, 1942–1964," *Journal of American Ethnic History* 29, no. 3 (Spring 2010): 6–39; Victor Rodriguez-Dominguez, "The Racialization of Mexican Americans and Puerto Ricans: 1890s-1930s," *Centro Journal* 17, no. 1 (2005): 71–105.

CHAPTER FOUR

Chicana/o History as Southern History: Race, Place, and the US South

PERLA M. GUERRERO

I was born in Guanajuato, Mexico. At the age of five I immigrated with my family to southern California. When I was sixteen we migrated to Arkansas. When I was twenty-two I moved back to Los Angeles. And at thirty-one I relocated to Washington, DC. As a kid growing up in a pre-dominantly Mexican American suburb on Los Angeles's east side I was told the term *Chicana/o* meant "the US-born child of Mexican parents" or "Mexican American," and so as an immigrant, I believed the term did not apply to me.[1] When I moved to Los Angeles to pursue my graduate education, I learned about the Chicana/o Movement and what the term *Chicana/o* means to some of the people that use it—struggle, empowerment, an assertion of ethnic identity, and political consciousness.

I never embraced the term in my personal life for two reasons. The first, and most frivolous, is that in some segments of LA's Chicana/o community there is a lot of performativity and use of aesthetics based on or inspired by indigenous groups. This plays out in a variety of ways, from clothing to hairstyles to tattoos or other body modifications. In other words, if I did not wear a *huipil*, somehow I was not really Chicana.[2] The notion of cultural authenticity, as indicated by Luis Alvarez in his chapter in this collection, is far more complicated than such simplistic appropriations. The second and more significant reason is that I have always grown up with other immigrants who were not Mexicans. My family's closest friends in Los Angeles were Salvadorans and Peruvians, and in Arkansas my closest friends were Vietnamese, Laotian, Chinese, and white. In DC all of my neighbors are black and my friends are Filipina/o, South Asian, African American, African, and Latina/o. In this part of the East Coast, ethnic Mexicans are a minority among Latin Americans, the largest community being Central Americans, particularly Salvadorans, and the term Chicana/o does not resonate.

Having lived in three distinct US regions, I have experienced what many studies have argued—place makes race. In California people saw me as Mexican; in northwest Arkansas they initially thought I was Vietnamese; in central Arkansas I was for a time perceived as white; in DC I am assumed to be Central American. In Arkansas I also experienced the shift from being an exotic other to being an "illegal alien." Such definitions constitute processes of interpellation, whereby individuals are turned into subjects, with ideological structures and power bearing down on them in ways that nurture life or foster death. As the South continues to diversify, new groups of people are forging paths that converge, diverge, or parallel well-known patterns. The ways in which new southerners negotiate and alter social relations will not be uniform across the region; they will be unique to each place given the articulation of its social formation. However, in order for Chicana/o history to remain at the forefront of nuanced knowledge production, the field needs to engage with Latina/o southerners as well as with southern history.

Broadly speaking, Chicana/o history chronicles Mexican American lives and Latina/o history addresses the lives of what two authors have called "the other Latinos."[3] The other Latinos are, in essence, everyone who is not Mexican or Mexican American. There was and is a need to distinguish between groups because imperialism, colonialism, and empire occurred differently across the globe, with important consequences for the different Latin American communities that would go to the United States.[4] The trajectories of immigrants to the United States from Mexico, Cuba, Guatemala, El Salvador, and Chile can be quite different, from the reasons for leaving, to the resources a person brings with her, to the adaptation that happens in the new country. Earlier Chicana/o studies were based on necessity. Mexican American history had to be built—documents collected, interviews conducted, archives established—to begin to excavate the rich history of ethnic Mexicans in the United States.[5] Today, however, the moment has arrived to expand the boundaries of Chicana/o history to get a more nuanced and textured sense of people's experiences and realities. The artificial division between Chicana/o and Latina/o history obfuscates a much richer and complex reality: Chicanas/os and Latinas/os do not live in a vacuum, isolated from each other or from other ethnic and racial groups, as demonstrated in the previous chapter by Lilia Fernández. The communities and histories of Latinas/os, Asian Americans, African Americans, and Native Americans have always been intertwined.

In 2013, Albert Camarillo, a founding scholar of Chicana/o history, wrote that the question, "What is Chicano history?" is irrelevant because of the growth of the field. He felt that the days when "traditional U.S. historians either devalued or invalidated the work" are now gone.[6] This was no easy feat and should be celebrated. However, I believe that Chicana/o history is experiencing a crisis. What does Chicana/o history do with diverse communities? In other words, who and what does Chicana/o history study? And where does it take place? I agree with Carlos Blanton that debating these questions within the field will make us better scholars who produce more nuanced work that more accurately captures people's realities and lived experiences.[7]

Diversifying the US South: Immigration, Migration, Labor, and Racialization

Let me draw from my own work on Arkansas to illustrate what I mean. Latinas/os, primarily ethnic Mexicans, began migrating in large numbers to the US South in the 1990s. For some, Arkansas was a second or third site of settlement; they had moved there after years, even decades, of living in more traditional states of immigrant settlement such as California and Texas. They were working-class people who thought they had found their US homes, only to realize that their livelihoods were threatened or eliminated in the 1990s recession, which hit California particularly hard. Other factors facilitated the migration and settlement of these new southerners, but as Steve Striffler argues, "the role of chicken cannot be underestimated."[8] In the 1990s the poultry industry, searching for low-wage workers who were more exploitable, offered year-round employment and lax enforcement of employment verification restrictions on immigrants; meanwhile the state's low cost of living provided Latinas/os with opportunities of upward mobility and home-ownership unavailable in traditional states of immigrant reception and settlement.[9]

I have traced Latina/o migrants to northwest Arkansas beginning in the late 1980s. After enormous increases in the 1990s the Latina/o population (the majority of whom are ethnic Mexicans) had grown to more than 186,000 by 2010, or 6.4 percent of the state's inhabitants—dramatic growth for a state that, according to the 1980 and 1990 census, had held fewer than 20,000 Latinas/os.[10] At the beginning of the twenty-first century Latinas/os accounted for 41 percent of the over-

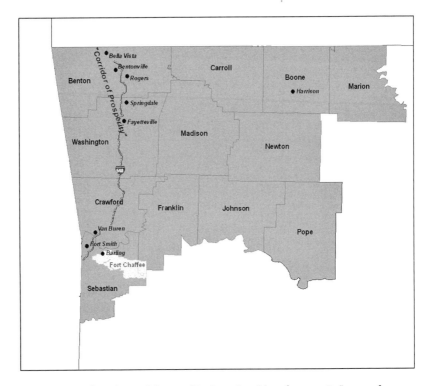

Figure 1. Map of northwest Arkansas. The term "corridor of prosperity" comes from Brooks Blevins's *Hill Folks: A History of Arkansas Ozarkers and Their Image* (University of North Carolina Press, 2002).

all population growth in Arkansas. They also tended to settle in northwest Arkansas, an overwhelmingly white area for most of the twentieth century.[11] Today there are towns, cities, and districts with a substantial Latina/o community such as Senate District 7 in Washington County, where they made up almost one-third of the population.[12] In the small city of Springdale they made up more than 35 percent, making them by far the largest group after white people.[13]

Attention to place at the level of counties or towns demonstrates the importance of focusing on how regions are shaped by specific communities that, though close in proximity, may differ in significant ways. Brooks Blevins argues that the African American community of the Ozarks "was never more than minuscule."[14] That is not quite accurate since slaves constituted 25 percent of the population in Washington County, Arkansas, in 1840. However, the county differed in that regard from most of its neighbors. It contained towns with black residents in numbers larger than the state average, which influenced the development of the area in important ways. In 1870, Harrison in neighboring Boone County had 115 people, 8 percent of whom were African Americans.[15] Jacqueline Froelich and David Zimmermann cite white attendance at black community fund-raisers as evidence of a more malleable color line in Boone County and in this part of Arkansas than in the Black Belt. However, much of their other research demonstrates the contrary, that the color line was rigidly drawn.

In 1905, white people exploded in mass violence toward their African American neighbors. In September of that year a black man from outside the community sought shelter from the cold and entered a white man's house; he was arrested and two days later an angry mob pulled him from jail and terrorized the black neighborhood by tying men and women to trees and whipping them, drowning them, and burning several of their houses with the demand that they leave town.[16] Some African American families returned to Harrison after a prudent period. But in 1909, after a local young black man was accused of rape and rumors spread that the alleged victim was near death, the white townspeople once again erupted in mob violence. All but one of the black Harrisonians then left the community for good; Alecta Caledonia Melvina Smith remained with the family she worked for and lived with.[17]

Several factors led to this episode of anti-black racist terror. The arrival of unemployed, single African American men from outside of the community at the end of their work on a railroad project raised white people's fears because they were strangers and had no one in the local community to vouch for them. At that time, there was also an escalation of racial radicalism facilitated by the tenure of a strongly racist governor, Jeff Davis, which added to a long tradition of "public displays of punitive aggression" even within the white community.[18] The impact of these events spread beyond the town as the African American populations of two adjoining counties dropped dramatically between 1900 and 1910.[19] By 1930 there were fewer than a thousand black people in the Ozarks; 80 percent lived in Izard, Van Buren, or Washington counties, and seven counties had no black farm families. By 1969 there were only three black farm families in a fifteen-county region.[20] In short, this section of Arkansas had a history of racial terror directed at African Americans that would be critical in the future with regard to dealing with racial difference and fundamental to the way the place was constructed as a "White Man's Heaven."[21]

The demographic and economic shifts that brought the poultry industry to Arkansas and the South and eventually caused it to rely on an immigrant, mainly Latina/o workforce had roots in the 1940s. The poultry industry began in the US Northeast, but was effectively moved to the South during World War II when the federal government contracted all the production from the Delmarva Peninsula (Delaware, Maryland, and Virginia), then the national center for poultry production, and entrepreneurs like John Tyson used the opportunity to expand their businesses. The federal government also encouraged American consumers to eat more chicken so that soldiers could be ensured a steady supply of red meat. This policy dramatically changed domestic consumption patterns of poultry and laid the groundwork for it to become the nation's most preferred source of meat.

But raising and producing young chickens, or broilers, was not a lucrative endeavor, and companies and farmers struggled to increase their profits. The industry responded by vertically integrating as well as developing "further-processed" or "value-added" poultry products. Vertical integration resulted in further concentration of production in the South, where processing plants could be located close to key resources like feed mills and chicken farms, and where labor costs were reduced by the region's historically low wages and antipathy toward labor unions. With Tyson often leading the way, the industry began developing additional products, selling parts of the bird as opposed to the whole, creating boneless breasts and tenders that led to a deskilling of labor but an increase in line speeds and repetitive motions, which made working conditions worse.[22]

The increased demand for chicken in the second half of the twentieth century coincided with a regional boom in the South and the rise of what is often called the Sunbelt based on industrial growth in a variety of sectors, from the military industrial complex to aeronautics to technology and jobs in the service sector, construction, and manufacturing. These endeavors created middle-class employment opportunities for some southerners, mainly white men, who often relocated to urban areas from their rural homes, and less profitable work for working-class and working-poor laborers willing to do the strenuous jobs at poultry plants. Nationally, from 1980 to 2000, the white workforce in the poultry industry dropped from nearly 70 percent of the total to just over 30 percent, while black workers increased from 30 to 50 percent and Latina/o laborers from 1 to 17 percent. During the same period, the number of workers in the industry more than doubled.[23] By the 1990s, Latinas/os had migrated in significant numbers to the South to work in poultry plants, and the industry saw a variety of benefits when they hired them, especially undocumented people: they were eager to work, did not complain about working conditions, and rarely filed worker's compensation claims.

The Latinas/os who arrived in Fort Smith, Arkansas, in the 1990s were documented and undocumented immigrants; the latter in particular moved for employment opportunities since social and immigrant networks were reporting that *polleras*, as many Spanish-speakers refer to the poultry industry, *"no checan papeles"* ("they don't check papers," i.e., work authorization documents). This meant the real possibility of steady employment and a weekly paycheck regardless of legal status, something that was increasingly difficult to attain in areas like Los Angeles, where some families had previously lived for years or even decades.[24] Sometimes companies hired recruiters to bring in laborers from Texas, California, or even from south of the border. But my research shows that in northwest Arkansas the laborers acted as recruiters and coaxed others to make the trip.

Immigrants were not the only ones talking about what was happening in Arkansas—southerners, state newspapers, and federal agencies began to take note of the changing demographics. In 1993 state newspapers began reporting that northwest Arkansas was becoming home to large numbers of "illegal aliens." According to Border Patrol agent Jessee F. Tabor, "illegal aliens" were increasingly a "very significant" part of the poultry industry for at least two reasons: the 3 percent unemployment rate and a high turnover rate.[25]

Given the concerns over the growing "illegal alien" population, the federal government coordinated with southern state agencies in 1995 and launched Operation SouthPAW, a multi-agency task force that raided worksites throughout the region. In September the task force raided more than two dozen food processing (mainly poultry) and light manufacturing plants in Arkansas and caught about six hundred undocumented workers. The poultry industry, however, said there were already jobs available beforehand. A Tyson spokesman said, "The suggestion that any of these Hispanic workers are taking jobs away from Americans is absolutely nonsense." A Simmons Foods spokesman said, "There's a very tight labor market in this area. There is not an easy answer. Jobs are available, and we're looking for workers currently. But we had jobs available before Wednesday. I'm not going to blame INS or say INS is causing us a problem, but this is something we've got to work through."[26]

State and federal officials frequently praised Arkansas employers for doing a good job of checking that applicants had the correct documentation. None of the Arkansas plants received fines for hiring undocumented workers as a result of Operation SouthPAW.[27] According to an INS spokesman, the difficulty is that federal authorities "have to prove they [employers] knowingly hired illegal workers. If the illegal workers present fraudulent documents—unless the fraudulent documents were given to them by the employers—it's difficult to prove the employer knowingly hired undocumented workers. . . . There is a lot of document fraud out there."[28] This reasoning portrayed Latinas/os as experts in deception, criminals who took advantage of naive and unsuspecting employers. If Latinas/os were undocumented, then they had to purchase documents to present to employers, and maybe the latter truly had no idea that some of the credentials were counterfeit.

However, that argument no longer held when businesses began accepting new documents from workers that had been deported only days before. Reporter Don Johnson cited an instance where a man was deported after a raid but was able to get back in a few days. He then showed up at his old worksite with new documentation and a different name and was rehired. When Johnson asked him why company officials were not curious about his new name, he smiled and said, "They know." Another INS agent also voiced doubts: "What I find hard to believe is a personnel office where they hire umpteen thousand people and they see a good Social Security card and good green card, and they accept some of the other cards as being good as well. I find it difficult to believe that they believe these people aren't illegal aliens."[29]

Historically, many northwest Arkansans worked intermittently in poultry plants because of their working-class backgrounds. White laborers left the poultry processing plants during the industry's 1990s economic boom, however, and when they ceased being the majority of those toiling on the poultry lines, the labor became racialized as "Mexican" work. By 2005, Latinas/os constituted a major percentage of the industry's workforce. In some plants in northwest Arkansas their numbers reached into the seventieth percentile.[30] The region's ideas about whiteness and race changed as the poultry industry's workforce became majority Latina/o and the work was racialized specifically as "Mexican."

Steve Striffler conducted field work in 2000 by working in one of Tyson Food's poultry processing plants in northwest Arkansas. He found that Latinas/os were well aware of their exploitation. Moreover, they had a keen understanding of the way that race and labor were intertwined. "We're all Mexican here [in the plant]. Screwed-over Mexicans," claimed Alejandro, a Mexican man, because all of them were forced to work harder and faster as managers sped up the lines. Alejandro understood that inside of the workplace they were exploited, whether they were white, Latina/o, or otherwise. When Striffler asked them how everyone was understood outside of the plant, Alejandro explained that Striffler was a "gringo," white "from here," an insider; but Mexicans were seen as foreigners, as outsiders and, poignantly, as not belonging. Alejandro elaborated, "At least here in the plant we belong even if we are exploited."[31] Inside the plant, Alejandro understood that Mexicans' acceptance was premised on the labor they provided, while outside in the community their subjecthood was constructed in very different ways.

But the panorama in northwest Arkansas was even more complex because the Latina/o migrants and immigrants of the 1990s were preceded by refugees from Southeast Asia (largely Vietnamese) in 1975 and Cubans from Mariel in 1980. The Vietnamese and Cubans were fleeing Communist regimes, but each group was received and racialized differently, so that by the 1990s Southeast Asians had made Arkansas home while very few Cubans stayed in the state.[32] After 2000, Marshallese immigrants came to the area and joined Latinas/os on the poultry line. Today, Springdale is home to the largest Marshallese community outside of the Marshall Islands.[33] Striffler estimated that when he conducted his ethnography, the workforce in the poultry processing plant was 75 percent Latina/o, while Southeast Asians and Marshallese accounted for most of the rest, with only a few white people on the lines, though management was overwhelmingly white.[34]

In order to write a thorough account of the history of Mexican immigrants and Mexican Americans in Arkansas, I have to engage with the histories of the communities that preceded or followed them because they share neighborhoods, often work at the same plants, and send their children to the same public schools. As does Luis Alvarez in his chapter for this collection, I privilege the relational over static conceptions of what groups are or are not. This is a more nuanced way to situate race and place. Yet each of these groups also differs in the legal status they have within the United States. Some Mexican immigrants are undocumented, while others are permanent residents or naturalized citizens; many Southeast Asians entered as refugees and have naturalized; Marshallese are non-immigrants who can work and study in the United States but are not lawful permanent residents who are allowed to naturalize. Their children are native-born US citizens, southerners, Chicanas/os, and people of color, and they are negotiating what each of those categories means independently, in relationship to each other, and within the region.

In the public schools, educators formed opinions about these students and the ethnic and racial groups they represented. I interviewed a variety of people to get a more complete picture of the changes that occurred over the past thirty years. A comment from Anna, a white educator in Fort Smith (in a larger city that historically has had an established and significant African American community constituting about 16 percent of its population), lays bare the processes at play and how students were racialized in relationship to each other. Anna worked in the local public schools for most of her career and had seen and experienced the demographic changes in the area.

> The one thing that I noticed immediately when we began to enroll what I would call "the wave" of Hispanics was that they were the easiest of all the races to talk to or to get information from. They didn't have the reticent or the reserved nature of the Asians nor did they have any chip on their shoulders as the Blacks. The one thing that I remember specifically is that they all seemed very glad to be here. And they seemed to be very grateful to be here. . . . They were all cooperative. The Asians were all cooperative if you exclude the Laotian males which can be very uncooperative or some of the Laotian females that could be very uncooperative.[35]

There are at least three issues here. First, the racialization of Latinas/os is grounded in local and state histories that are specific to place. Anna "triangulated" the position of Latinas/os in relationship to Southeast Asians and African Americans, two groups of color that preceded them in the school district.[36] She also engaged in what Natalia Molina calls "racial scripts," a term that "emphasize[s] the ways in which we think, talk about, and act toward one racialized group based on our experiences with other groups whose race differs from our own."[37] Anna made sense of Latinas/os and their behaviors based on her experiences with Asian and black students, even though the latter are not an immigrant group who are learning a foreign language or adapting to a new place. In this case, the behavior of Latinas/os was a welcomed difference from that of Asian refugees or African Americans.

Anna also shared that in the 1970s many of the teachers and students had cultural misunderstandings because Vietnamese and Laotian students would not look at the teacher when he or she was speaking, a behavior Arkansas educators believed was disrespectful. Eventually, a cultural translator explained that the opposite was true—Southeast Asian students were showing deference precisely by not making eye contact with their teachers—and eventually students understood how teachers wanted them to behave. But not all Asians occupied the same racial terrain, since she distinguished between what she believed to be Laotians' difficult behavior in contrast to that of more pleasant Asian students (there were also Hmong, Thai, Cambodian, and Chinese immigrants, but in much smaller numbers).

The second issue is about whiteness as the unmarked but always looming category against which Latina/o students, as well as Asians and African Americans, are judged. In this quote, indeed in our lengthy conversation, Anna did not explicitly compare students of color to white students, yet they needed to be sufficiently cooperative, grateful, and pleasant in order to achieve some level of inclusion or assimilation. She simultaneously reinscribed the idea that black students were resentful without sufficient cause instead of acknowledging their experiences with systemic racism and prejudice. Anna singled out Laotians, male and female, for their allegedly "uncooperative" bravado and in doing so racialized them more akin to black students. Unlike meek Vietnamese, difficult Laotians, or resentful black students, she saw Latinas/os as very happy, cooperative, and compliant, and in this way perhaps racialized them as more similar to white students, at least in the early stages of demographic change. The racialized position of Latinas/os in the public schools can only be understood by accounting for the positions of the other racial and ethnic groups.

The third issue is the labyrinthine setting in the school system that favored some students but negatively impacted others. The ways in which Chicanas/os and other students of color were racialized helped to contour their experiences at school and with school officials. In essence, students could find some level of inclusion if they were communicative, cooperative, and grateful. Otherwise they were seen as less than desirable students. This meant there were internal fissures such as legality, language proficiency, and comportment that were exacerbated by school officials seeking out "exceptional" students with whom they were willing to invest extra time and effort. I returned to Arkansas in the summer of 2012 to conduct more interviews, and during that visit several recent high school Latina/o graduates from multiple school districts told me that they sought information about college admissions and finances on their own—even though the flagship campus of the University of Arkansas was just forty-five minutes away. Moreover, many of them were not encouraged to pursue a college education, but were instead expected to drop out of high school or simply graduate.

These issues have historical similitude with the well-documented experiences of Chicanas/os in the Southwest during earlier time periods.[38] Public school officials have rarely encouraged Chicana/o students to pursue higher education, and when they do, it is often single students they determine are gifted enough and worthy of their investment. Those students then receive guidance on how to successfully exit the maze that is often public K–12 education. In short, in schools and in the community, Latinas/os and Chicanas/os have to be the right kind of person, one deemed "good" in order to be granted some semblance of belonging or opportunity to succeed.

New Directions in Chicana/o History: Place, Ethnicity, and the South

As do my fellow essayists Luis Alvarez, Lilia Fernández, and Sonia Hernández, my work challenges and pushes the boundaries of Chicana/o history. I expand Chicana/o history outside of an urban setting in the Southwest. I focus on relational notions of race and ethnicity among Latinas/os and other immigrant groups. And I am attuned to intra-Latina/o relations. In my larger project I draw extensively from geography to grasp how Arkansas came to be a particular kind of place, to understand better the processes that led Latinas/os and Asians to Arkansas, and to explore how this place and its communities reacted to newcomers. I also demonstrate how their presence changes precisely what kind of place Arkansas is.

According to geographers, places are important because people and economics construct them. They are made in particular ways and for specific purposes, from neighborhoods to cities, regions, and nations.[39] Regions are also made up of identities and cultures that are related to the type of work performed and who is doing that labor.[40] Moreover, the culture of a region influences its political controversies and strategies; the more homogenous the culture is, the more unity around a regional disruption. Historically, the South has been the most distinctive region in the United States, and prior to the 1990s northwest Arkansas was overwhelmingly white, in some areas up to 99 percent white, making it one of the nation's most homogenous places at the end of the twentieth century.[41] This history of place mattered in how Latinas/os and Asians were accepted or rejected, how they were understood as people that were neither white nor black, and how they understood themselves in racial and ethnic terms in a diverse social field.

The identity formation of Latinas/os in Arkansas is different from that of their counterparts in states such as California or Texas because the history of those places was vastly different, shaped largely by the Mexican American War and Mexico's massive territorial loss. Mexicans have been in those places for a long time. That history, that presence, matters very much for the regional racial formation of Chicanas/os and for the political struggles and gains achieved since 1848. Moreover, California and Texas in the twentieth century were traditional states of immigrant reception where hundreds of thousands of documented and undocumented Mexican immigrants as well as other Latin Americans arrived in search of better lives.

In contrast, Mexican immigrants and Chicanas/os in the South were often constructing their identities in areas where Mexicans had little history and where racial and ethnic diversity was new and varied. In Arkansas, Chicanas/os learned to negotiate their position in the southern field of social relations, which included relationships not only to Mexican immigrants but also to Salvadorans and Puerto Ricans, to Vietnamese, Laotians, and Cambodians, and to educated and often middle-class Latin American immigrants who increasingly serve as a kind of managerial class or as cultural brokers between Mexican and Chicana/o working-class communities and the established white communities.[42] And, of course, even in areas where the African American community is small or not present, Latinas/os define themselves in relationship to black people and blackness. Though Latinas/os have received the bulk of the attention in terms of the changing South, there are growing Asian immigrant and Asian American communities throughout the region whose experiences also fissure along ethnicity and class.[43]

The heterogeneity of Latina/o immigrants also means that scholars have to be careful not to categorize all Latinas/os as Mexicans or as working-class. When I conducted interviews and oral histories, I often asked Latinas/os about their experiences with racism and prejudice, and at that time I thought they were going to tell me about white or black people behaving in a derogatory manner. Yet I heard instead far more about intra-Latina/o tensions than I anticipated. Several of the people I interviewed talked about the racism and prejudice they experienced from white people, but tended to bring up that issue after they first talked about the difficulties between Mexicans and Salvadorans.

Gretel is a Colombian immigrant who arrived in Northwest Arkansas in the early 1980s and worked for one of the school districts. In an interview, she said:

> Before we were more united, I don't know what's happening right now, there are a lot of people coming that are pushing us off course and we don't know what's happening, but before we were much more united. The second people that started to arrive after Mexicans were the Salvadorians, there's a lot of Salvadorians. It's so much—as a teacher in the public schools—one can see a lot of gangs. We didn't see that seven, eight years ago one didn't see any of those things. Right now there are a lot, a lot of gangs, a lot problems in the public schools between Salvadorians, Mexicans, and Americans; there are many problems right now.[44]

Gretel stopped short of stating that Salvadorans brought gangs with them, though according to her there had been no gangs eight years earlier when the Latina/o population was mostly Mexican. Interviewees often blamed gang activity on Latino youth who had lived in poor neighborhoods of Los Angeles, Dallas, and other metropolitan areas prior to moving to Arkansas. Genoveva, a Mexican immigrant who worked for many years in the school system, elaborated on the phenomenon by drawing on her experiences in the public schools:

> Unfortunately I see a lot of problems with Hispanics among each other when they're not from the same country, which I could never understand. . . . I used to go into the schools and saw Salvadorians fighting with the Mexicans or the Guatemalans fighting with the Salvadorians and Salvadorians and Mexicans are just enemies. "Are you kidding? You're both Hispanic, you both speak the same language, you have to be united, you can't fight, you already have trouble with everybody else hating you for you to hate each other."[45]

In contrast to Striffler's research within poultry processing plants, Latina/o youth were finding it difficult to establish common ground *as* Latinas/os and instead divided along national origins. More research needs to be conducted with youth and in schools to understand if and how a pan-Latina/o identity might evolve.

Moreover, these divisions might indicate a changing field in terms of how racial categories will be understood in the South. Helen B. Marrow argues that there is sufficient preliminary evidence to suggest that the color line in the rural South is moving toward black/nonblack in contrast to white-black.[46] Marrow is careful to locate her argument within a rural setting. Indeed, in other places in the South, the argument might not hold up. Southeast Arkansas, part of the Black Belt, is quite different from northwest Arkansas because their economies have been different for decades; the southeast remains heavily African American, while the northwest's racial and ethnic diversity is increasing because of Asian and Latina/o newcomers. The histories, specificities, and nuances of place need to be central to studies that seek to document and analyze this changing region.

There is not enough research on Latina/o communities in the South, but there is an extensive historiography on labor, cultural production, social relations, and black and white communities in *some* southern places. New Orleans has been a focus of such studies due to its location and its importance in trade for the region, the nation, and the hemisphere. This plethora of research allows scholars to analyze how hiring Latina/o workers, some of them undocumented, to work on cleanup and construction crews after Hurricane Katrina fits in with a long history of racial exploitation and simultaneously serves to reinscribe the idea that African Americans are inadequate workers. The hiring of Latina/o workers occurred at the same time that many displaced black people with roots in the area extending back hundreds of years could not return or were essentially prohibited from returning to post-Katrina New Orleans. This knowledge provides a great entry point for rich in-depth studies of Asians and Latinas/os in New Orleans that will be impossible to match for understudied southern places. Extensive research needs to be conducted, because studies of a few southern places cannot accurately reflect the variety of ways that social relations are negotiated in the region and or suggest how they will change in this century.

I am not proposing that there is only one way to study the Latina/o South, but I would argue that local history and political economy offer important starting points for nuanced analyses of race and ethnicity, immigration and migration, labor and class, as well as gender. I believe Chicana/o history is uniquely able to produce some of the most nuanced studies.

The Future of Chicana/o History:
Political Economy and the Nuevo South

If the future of Chicana/o history is in the South but Chicana/o historians do not recognize these communities as Chicana/o, then how is the region and its people going to be studied? Who will make sense of the multiplicity of issues occurring? Scholars and experts in fields as diverse as demography, anthropology, sociology, political science, and geography can contribute, but I believe only Chicana/o historians can do justice to these communities by placing their histories along studies that exist about Mexican Americans in the Southwest and, increasingly, the Midwest.[47]

The US South has experienced dynamic growth since the 1990s, and by 2011 seven of the ten US counties with the fastest Latina/o growth rate (over 75 percent) were in the South.[48] Chicana/o historians should also go back and embrace the field's roots in political economy to better comprehend the dynamics driving the diversification of the US South at the end of the twentieth and the beginning of the twenty-first centuries, and to understand how the political and economic arenas have changed over time in response to the growth of Latinas/os in the region, or how development efforts are largely responsible for initially drawing migrants and immigrants. Albert Camarillo, David Montejano, Neil Foley, and Tomás Almaguer are just a few of the scholars who have written on the importance of land and land loss, economics, labor, and policy for Mexican Americans.[49] The histories of the South and Southwest and their places are different, and historians need to reckon with those legacies. Mexicans were once frequently declared "the negro problem" of the Southwest, but what happens when these two so-called problems coalesce in once place?[50] What happens when Latinas/os make lives in a region where African Americans toiled for centuries, where systems of oppression were constructed to deal with and exploit them, and where black people fought back through rebellions, marches, and cultural production?

Clyde Woods argues that the blues is a theory of social and economic development and change. It critiques plantation social relations and their extension while expressing the desire for communities to be independent of the plantation monopoly. He theorized that the plantation bloc had been in power since the Trail of Tears and continued until the present, constantly adjusting by building new alliances that always work to keep black people and poor white people at the bottom of economic development. The plantation bloc enacted what he called Mississippi Plans, characterized by a cycle of economic and social crises, a shift in the form of social exploitation, and a new and stable regime of accumulation. Within the plantation complex, "slavery, sharecropping, mechanization, and prison, wage and migratory labor are just a few of the permutations possible."[51] Focusing on the production of culture captures the workings of economic, political, and ideological power in the US South as they impact Latinas/os, just as it does for East LA in Luis Alvarez's chapter in this collection. Using a framework such as this one allows historians to explore the extent to which political, economic, and social dynamics have changed with the arrival of new groups of people. A focus on political economy allows us to see that many Latinas/os in the South are immigrants who moved to the region to work in meat-processing plants. In 2006 William Kandel found that "rapid Hispanic growth counties correspond[ed] to high-poultry production counties."[52] Consider that Tyson Foods, the world's largest meat producer, is based in northwest Arkansas and that the industry as a whole has undergone enormous growth that coincides with the migration of Latinas/os and Asians. In other words, immigrants provided the inexpensive labor necessary for the poultry industry to grow quickly and profitably as a new plantation regime.

The works coming out about Latinas/os in the South that have a serious engagement with place and race demonstrate the extent to which every place is unique, with different racial histories and experiences with work and labor. Angela C. Stuesse and Laura E. Helton write about how the poultry processing industry in central Mississippi recruited workers from south Texas in direct response to the labor organizing efforts of black workers. Consequently, ethnic Mexicans moved to an area with a majority African American population undergoing a fight about exploitation and fair pay that extends back to the post–Civil War period.[53] In contrast, my research demonstrates that it was a sojourner working in a northwest Arkansas poultry processing plant who told his social network in California and Mexico about the opportunities available. In this case ethnic Mexican workers moved to an overwhelmingly white area where there was no battle over fair pay and labor rights. What these two studies demonstrate is that place (race, political economy, and history) is of the utmost importance for a nuanced study of the processes that drive migration and the changes that occur when a community begins to grow in a different direction.

Today there is a growing field of interdisciplinary study often called the "Nuevo South" or the "Nuevo New South" that assesses the growth of Latinas/os in the region within a broader "geographic diversification of American immigration," explores "the structure and dynamics of Mexican migration to new destinations in the United States," and views the migration within the national trend of moving out of metropolitan areas.[54] Scholars have also studied the crucial role of social networks in the migration, the "pull" factors like the restructuring of poultry, beef, and construction industries, and the trend to locate production plants in areas with lower wage rates like the South.[55] There has also been much documentation of the responses of local school districts to the arrival of Latinas/os. Most of the time districts are unprepared, overwhelmed, and underfunded to deal with the sheer growth of school-age children and to accommodate Spanish-speaking students.[56]

The research has provided vital demographic information on Latinas/os in some parts of the US South, mainly in rural areas, but has until now lacked a keen focus on issues of race or place. Jamie Winders points out that most studies note Latinas/os are moving to an area that has historically been defined by its black and white racial divisions, yet researchers have had an "overall failure to engage two topics: the geographic and place specificity of arguments about Latino migration to the South and the impacts of Latino migration on racial formations and politics in southern communities."[57] Moreover, despite describing simultaneous economic integration and social isolation, scholars have not "analyzed the practices that place Latinos outside the boundaries of community."[58]

In many instances the term "Nuevo South" is used as if it were self-explanatory, or, in some of the more egregious cases, the word "nuevo" is used simply in an exoticizing manner—Latinas/os are moving to the South and Latinas/os speak Spanish, so we can now refer to the South as the "Nuevo South." Felipe Hinojosa writes elsewhere in this collection of confronting lazy stereotypes from scholars with little understanding of Chicana/o history. The field of Latinas/os in the US South is similar. In this case, the term "Nuevo South" is vapid because the authors never define "Nuevo South" or how using it will provide insight into the way ideas of race, labor, and belonging are reshuffled and rearticulated in the region. Scholars who write about the "Nuevo South" have often missed an opportunity to engage with the field of history where the term "New South" has been constructed, defined, argued against, and defended—all productive activities that have contributed some level of clarity to understandings of the region and its places.

The literature about the New South, historiographically anchored by W. E. B. Du Bois's *Black Reconstruction* and C. Vann Woodward's *Origins of the New South*, demonstrates that the post-Reconstruction South was marketed as having reinvented the ideology of the New South in order to produce a business-friendly and not (as) racist region capable of securing northern investment.[59] New South leaders adjusted their regime of accumulation and used new labor forces in a manner most financially beneficial for them, yet did little to disrupt the socioeconomic and political landscape. In my book project, *Nuevo South: Latinas/os, Asians, and the Remaking of Place*, I work toward a framework that scrutinizes the legacies of southern history in terms of dealing with racial difference and driving economic development. I take into account political and social factors, considering how refugees and immigrants negotiate these dynamics in their daily lives and interactions. The book moves beyond "Nuevo South" as a mere catchphrase and gives it the rigor necessary to explore how and to what extent difference is reformulated to serve business leaders in exploiting the region for material gain.

The historian Raymond Mohl was one of the first scholars to publish articles about "Latinization in the Heart of Dixie" and what he called the *"Nuevo* New South." He connected the migration of Latinas/os to new global trends of deindustrialization and free trade.[60] One of the shortcomings of that early work, however, was that he suggested Latinas/os were adapting and thriving despite describing resentments held by white people and to a lesser extent by African Americans. In part, Mohl argued that white people were moving out of jobs they had held for years, black people were moving up in employment, and Latinas/os were moving into the state for those less desirable jobs. More than a decade later, however, the notion that everyone benefited, and especially that Latinas/os did not face a severe backlash, has not panned out. By 2011 Alabama had passed one of the most stringent anti-immigrant and anti-Latina/o laws in the country.[61] Nevertheless, the strength of Mohl's work lies in its focus on the state's political economy in relationship to regional, national, and global trends. In a similar vein, another early work on Latinas/os in the South, Leon Fink's study of Guatemalan Maya immigrants in Morganton, North Carolina, was particularly strong due to its focus on the local, regional, and hemispheric labor and social issues that were driving factors in establishing a new migration stream and ultimately a new community in the state. Fink focuses on the specificities of Morganton as they relate to labor, union organizing efforts, and issues of community for longtime residents and newcomers alike.[62]

The historians James C. Cobb and William Stueck contribute an edited collection about globalization and the American South. Their book was one of the first that had a regional political economic focus. Its chapters dealt with specific places (the Sun Belt South, Atlanta, and Spartanburg, South Carolina), the immigrant groups that were reshaping the region (Latinas/os and Asians), and the role of various industries in the ongoing changes (economic globalization in general and foreign corporations in particular).[63] The authors, however, did not believe that globalization had negative effects nationally or that it exacerbated inequality because some evidence suggested "a nation's global economic involvement correlates positively with a rise from day-to-day subsistence to a more stable and secure existence for many of its people."[64]

A few years later, Fran Ansley and Jon Shefner, respectively professors of law and sociology, edited a book that also focused on the relationship between the global and the local. But they and the contributing authors reached a different conclusion than Cobb and Stueck. They argued that despite aggregate economic growth in some Latin American countries, inequality was increasing; they also argued that while US worker salaries stagnated, workers lost jobs only to replace them with lower-paying ones.[65] Ansley and Shefner's book demonstrates that scholars can focus on global forces yet remain grounded in the specificities of place. The book is an important contribution to the literature about the Nuevo South because it showcases how the same factors played out differently across the region for various Latina/o communities.

Jamie Winders, a geographer, has more recently published a book focused on Nashville and the ways in which recent immigrants, often Latinas/os but also Asians, have changed the city.[66] Her engagement with place is superbly focused and nuanced. Indeed, she has been one of the few scholars in any discipline who has had a sustained engagement with Latinas/os, the US South, and place.[67] Her work, however, would be improved by engaging with Chicana/o history and Chicana/o studies because many of the issues occurring in the South in the twenty-first century have historical parallels in the Southwest of the nineteenth and twentieth centuries.

James Chaney also writes about Latinas/os in Nashville, but his work falters precisely because he fails to engage a vast and deep literature about ethnic enclave formation. Again, the need for Chicana/o history is striking. For example, a Chicana/o historian would not express surprise that in Nashville Latinas/os have established an ethnic enclave in response to discriminatory public policies, or that this neighborhood is where many of them choose to live and conduct their business as a means of limiting contact with others and avoiding police harassment.[68] Indeed, a Chicana/o scholar might have used the word "barrio" to describe the neighborhood and might have also talked about barrioization and barriology—concepts theorized in relationship to how Chicanas/os use space in a variety of ways.[69] Chicana/o history is replete with studies that painstakingly describe the use of space by Chicanas/os and for Chicanas/os and how it was often a response to structural inequality and discrimination.[70]

Increasingly there are scholars, mainly historians and geographers, who are paying close attention to the issues of place and the specificities of history. George Sánchez, for example, argued in 2007 that it was crucial for immigrant rights issues to be analyzed within the context of the African American experience.[71] In doing so he foreshadowed the framework that DREAMers, undocumented youth seeking to legalize their status, would come to rely so heavily on—that their fight was one which sought social justice and continued the work of the Civil Rights movement, as ably illustrated in Michael Olivas's autobiographical chapter in this collection. Not only do many DREAMers frame their struggles through civil rights discourse, but they have modeled many of their strategies on the black civil rights movement, from sit-ins to freedom rides.[72] And, whether they know it or not, they are also mirroring the Chicana/o Movement. Nevertheless, the crisis of representation in Chicana/o history remains. In 2013 I asked an Arkansas DREAMer whether the term "Chicana" meant anything to her, and she said, "It means Mexican heritage, born in the US. A lot of Latinas I know that were born here use that term."[73] In this brief response, this DREAMer, this Chicana, demonstrates that some Chicanas/os are holding steadfastly to the idea that this group can only be defined by birthright citizenship, even when many immigrant youths are the ones mobilizing for a better future, a more just South. The fissures along nativity are not new to the ethnic Mexican community. They have long resulted in bitter divisiveness and political failure.[74] Yet today we have the benefit of hindsight and the plethora of information that Chicana/o history has to offer.

Any scholar of the Nuevo South should read the vast literature in

Chicana/o history and Chicana/o studies to have a more thorough and nuanced understanding of community and identity formation, the development of ethnic enclaves, English-language acquisition and code switching, racialization, institutionalized discrimination, segregation and self-segregation. The longer Nuevo South scholars wait to engage with Chicana/o history, the longer their studies will lack nuance and the greater disservice they will do to the cause of seeking to understand southern Latina/o communities.

In a similar vein, Chicana/o historians need to pay attention to the Nuevo South, because the region is changing dramatically, often due to the growth of Chicanas/os. In 2010 Latina/o youth (those under eighteen) made up 83 percent of the youth of color in Arkansas—a former Confederate state that is not Texas or Florida.[75] Many of those youths are Chicanas/os, and they deserve to know their history. As scholars, we have to resolve the crisis of representation so that we can provide a framework and a historical backdrop for Chicana/o and Latina/o southerners to better understand the long fight for rights and inclusions without surrendering ethnic identity.

Notes

1. A note on terminology: In this chapter I use the terms "Mexican American" and "Chicana/o" interchangeably to refer to people of Mexican ancestry who were born in the United States or immigrated to the country at a young age because I believe that the experiences that youth have with racialization, particularly in schools, shape their formation in important ways. I use "Latina/o" when speaking about women and men of Latin American descent and "ethnic Mexican" to refer to immigrants and Mexican Americans together. Finally, I use "Chicana" and "Latina" to refer specifically to women and "Chicano" and "Latino" to refer specifically to men.

2. A *huipil* is a tunic worn by many indigenous women whose design and color choices have historically reflected the community of origin. Beyond the aesthetic issues, claiming Chicana/o indigeneity as if it were the same as that of indigenous people in Mexico is a grave disservice to those communities because Chicanas/os in the United States experience exploitation, marginalization, and oppression in different ways than indigenous communities in Latin America. As indigenous immigrants move to the United States, these differences can be exacerbated, since it is much easier—though not always easy—to access Spanish-language translation than it is to access Quechua or Mixtec.

3. José Luis Falconi and José Antonio Mazzotti, eds., *The Other Latinos: Central and South Americans in the United States* (Cambridge, MA: Harvard University Press, 2008).

4. Juan González, *Harvest of Empire: A History of Latinos in America* (New York: Penguin Books, 2000).

5. Rodolfo Acuña, *A Community under Siege: A Chronicle of Chicanos East of the Los Angeles River, 1945–1975* (Los Angeles: UCLA Chicano Studies Research Center, 1984); Acuña, *Occupied America: The Chicano's Struggle toward Liberation*, 1st ed. (San Francisco: Canfield Press, 1972); Albert Camarillo, *Chicanos in a Changing Society: From Mexican Pueblos to American Barrios in Santa Barbara and Southern California, 1848–1930* (Cambridge, MA: Harvard University Press, 1979); Mario T. García, *Desert Immigrants: The Mexicans of El Paso, 1880–1920* (New Haven, CT: Yale University Press, 1981); Mario Barrera, *Race and Class in the Southwest: A Theory of Racial Inequality* (Notre Dame, IN: University of Notre Dame Press, 1979).

6. Albert M. Camarillo, "Looking Back on Chicano History: A Generational Perspective," *Pacific Historical Review* 82, no. 4 (2013): 496–504, quotation on p. 503.

7. I and other scholars such as Julie Weise have begun to document these more complex histories. See Julie Weise, "Mexican Nationalisms, Southern Racisms: Mexicans and Mexican Americans in the US South, 1908–1939," *American Quarterly* 60, no. 3 (2008): 749–777; Perla M. Guerrero, "A Tenuous Welcome for Latinas/os and Asians: States' Rights Discourse in Late 20th Century Arkansas," in *Race and Ethnicity in Arkansas: New Perspectives*, ed. John Kirk (Fayetteville: University of Arkansas Press, 2014), 141–151.

8. Steve Striffler, *Chicken: The Dangerous Transformation of America's Favorite Food* (New Haven, CT: Yale University Press, 2005), 95.

9. Perla M. Guerrero, "Impacting Arkansas: Vietnamese and Cuban Refugees and Latina/o Immigrants in Arkansas, 1975–2005" (PhD diss., University of Southern California, 2010).

10. John Lyon, "Hispanics Have Yet to Make Inroads in Arkansas Politics," *Arkansas News*, January 22, 2012, accessed June 30, 2014, http://pbcommercial.com/sections/news/state/hispanics-have-yet-make-inroads-arkansas-politics.html; US Bureau of the Census, *General Population Characteristics, Arkansas*, prepared by US Department of Commerce, Economics and Statistics Administration (Washington: Bureau of the Census, 1980); US Bureau of the Census, *General Population Characteristics, Arkansas*, prepared by US Department of Commerce, Economics and Statistics Administration (Washington: Bureau of the Census, 1990). The African American population in Arkansas has hovered around 15 percent for most of the twentieth century, with many living in areas where cotton plantations once were located. Plantations were never numerous in northwest Arkansas.

11. Brooks Blevins, *Hill Folks: A History of Arkansas Ozarkers and Their Image* (Chapel Hill: University of North Carolina Press, 2002), 212.

12. Lyon, "Hispanics Have Yet to Make Inroads."

13. US Bureau of the Census, "Springdale, Arkansas," in *State and County Quick Facts*, http://quickfacts.census.gov/qfd/states/05/0566080.html.

14. Blevins, *Hill Folks*, 211.

15. Jacqueline Froelich and David Zimmermann, "Total Eclipse: The Destruction of the African American Community of Harrison, Arkansas in 1905 and 1909," *Arkansas Historical Quarterly* 58, no. 2 (1999): 131.

16. Ibid., 141–145.

17. Ibid., 148–156.

18. Ibid., 139.

19. Gordon Morgan, *Black Hillbillies of the Arkansas Ozarks* (Fayetteville: University of Arkansas, 1973).

20. Blevins, *Hill Folks*, 212.

21. Kimberly Harper, *White Man's Heaven: The Lynching and Expulsion of Blacks in the Southern Ozarks, 1894–1909* (Fayetteville: University of Arkansas Press, 2010).

22. David Griffith, *Jones's Minimal: Low-Wage Labor in the United States* (Albany: State University of New York Press, 1993), 83–114; Donald D. Stull and Michael J. Broadway, *Slaughterhouse Blues: The Meat and Poultry Industry in North America* (Belmont, CA: Wadsworth, 2004), 1–21, 36–51; David Griffith, Michael J. Broadway, and Donald D. Stull, "Introduction: Making Meat," in *Any Way You Cut It: Meat Processing and Small-Town America*, ed. Donald D. Stull, Michael J. Broadway, and David Griffith (Lawrence: University Press of Kansas, 1995), 1–16; David Griffith, "*Hay Trabajo*: Poultry Processing, Rural Industrialization, and the Latinization of Low-Wage Labor," in ibid., 129–151.

23. William Kandel and Emilio Parrado, "Hispanics in the American South and the Transformation of the Poultry Industry," in *Hispanic Spaces, Latino Places: Community and Cultural Diversity in Contemporary America*, ed. Daniel D. Arreola (Austin: University of Texas Press, 2004), 265.

24. Personal interviews and surveys, Fort Smith, Arkansas, August 2004.

25. D. R. Stewart, "Rich in Jobs, Northwest Arkansas Becomes Mecca for Illegal Aliens," *Arkansas Democrat-Gazette*, March 4, 1993.

26. Associated Press, "Poultry Firms: INS Raids Don't Level Field on Jobs," *Arkansas Democrat-Gazette*, September 10, 1995, section B.

27. Don Johnson, "Northwest Passage: Being Illegal—It's a Job," *Arkansas Democrat-Gazette*, March 24, 1997.

28. D. R. Stewart, "Raids Net 350 Illegals at Plants," *Arkansas Democrat-Gazette*, September 9, 1995.

29. Ibid.

30. Brent E. Riffel, "The Feathered Kingdom: Tyson Foods and the Transformation of American Land, Labor, and Law, 1930–2005" (PhD diss., University of Arkansas, 2008), 259. In 2003 a Tyson manager said one-third of their line force was Latina/o, but Human Rights Watch investigators who interviewed Tyson workers in northwest Arkansas suggested a majority of their coworkers were immigrants, and in that area the majority of immigrants would be Latina/o. See Human Rights Watch, *Blood, Sweat, and Fear: Workers' Rights in US Meat and Poultry Plants* (2004), 110.

31. Steve Striffler, "'We're All Mexicans Here': Poultry Processing, Latino Migration, and the Transformation of Class in the South," in *The American South in a Global World*, ed. James L. Peacock, Harry L. Watson, and Carrie R. Matthews (Chapel Hill: University of North Carolina Press, 2005), 152–165, quotation on p. 163.

32. Guerrero, "A Tenuous Welcome for Latinas/os and Asians."

33. Kemba J. Dunham and Kortney Stringer, "Wal-Mart Fosters a Region's Rise, but Not All Benefit," *Wall Street Journal*, February 10, 2005.

34. Striffler, "We're All Mexicans Here," 153–156. In 2005 a special census counted two thousand Marshallese, but other estimates put the number past six thousand. "Film Documents Springdale 'Island,'" *Daily Headlines*, University of Arkansas, May 25, 2006.

35. I use pseudonyms in order to protect interviewees' identities. Personal interview, September 9, 2005.

36. Claire Jean Kim, "The Racial Triangulation of Asian Americans," *Politics and Society* 27, no. 1 (1999): 105–138.

37. Natalia Molina, "The Power of Racial Scripts: What the History of Mexican Immigration to the United States Teaches Us about Relational Notions of Race," *Latino Studies* 8, no. 2 (2010): 157.

38. Intertwined with these issues are those of bilingual education and curriculum. For a discussion of education and Chicana/o history, see Carlos Blanton, *The Strange Career of Bilingual Education in Texas, 1836–1981* (College Station: Texas A&M University Press, 2004); Guadalupe San Miguel, *"Let All of Them Take Heed": Mexican Americans and the Campaign for Educational Equality in Texas, 1910–1981* (Austin: University of Texas Press, 1987).

39. Neil Smith, "Contours of Spatialized Politics: Homeless Vehicles and the Production of Geographical Scale," *Social Text* 33 (1992): 54–81.

40. Ann Markusen, *Regions: The Economics and Politics of Territory* (New York: Rowman & Littlefield, 1987); Neil Smith, *Uneven Development: Nature, Capital, and the Production of Space* (New York: Blackwell, 1984), 73–74.

41. Markusen, *Regions*, 57; Blevins, *Hill Folks*, 212.

42. Guerrero, "Impacting Arkansas."

43. Eric Tang, "A Gulf Unites Us: The Vietnamese Americans of Black New Orleans East," *American Quarterly* 63, no. 1 (2011): 117–149; Khyati Y. Joshi and Jigna Desai, *Asian Americans in Dixie: Race and Migration in the South* (Urbana: University of Illinois Press, 2013).

44. Personal interview, August 5, 2004.

45. Personal interview, August 5, 2004.

46. Helen B. Marrow, "New Immigrant Destinations and the American Colour Line," *Ethnic and Racial Studies* 32, no. 6 (2009): 1037–1057.

47. Gabriela F. Arredondo, *Mexican Chicago: Race, Identity and Nation, 1916–39* (Urbana: University of Illinois Press, 2008); Michael Innis-Jiménez, *Steel Barrio: The Great Mexican Migration to South Chicago, 1915–1940* (New York: New York University Press, 2013); Lilia Fernández, *Brown in the Windy City: Mexicans and Puerto Ricans in Postwar Chicago* (Chicago: University of Chicago Press, 2012).

48. Pew Research, Hispanic Trends, "US Hispanic Population by County, 1980–2011," accessed January 10, 2014, http://www.pewhispanic.org/2013/08/29/u-s-hispanic-population-by-county-1980-2011/.

49. Camarillo, *Chicanos in a Changing Society*; David Montejano, *Anglos and Mexicans in the Making of Texas, 1836–1986* (Austin: University of Texas Press, 1987); Tomás Almaguer, *Racial Fault Lines: The Historical Origins of White Supremacy in California* (Berkeley: University of California Press, 1994); Neil Foley, *The White Scourge: Mexicans, Blacks, and Poor Whites in Texas Cotton Culture* (Berkeley: University of California Press, 1997).

50. For a brief discussion of "the negro problem" of the Southwest, see Molina, "The Power of Racial Scripts," 157, 164–169.

51. Clyde Woods, *Development Arrested: The Blues and Plantation Power in the Mississippi Delta* (New York: Verso, 1998), 6.

52. William Kandel, "Meat-Processing Firms Attract Hispanic Workers to Rural America," accessed January 10, 2014, http://www.ers.usda.gov/amber-waves/2006-june/meat-processing-firms-attract-hispanic-workers-to-rural-america.aspx#.Uwvpa15RHVU.

53. Angela C. Stuesse and Laura E. Helton, "Low-Wage Legacies, Race, and the Golden Chicken in Mississippi: Where Contemporary Immigration Meets African American Labor History," *Southern Spaces*, December 31, 2013, accessed January 10, 2014, southernspaces.org/2013/low-wage-legacies-race-and-golden-chicken-mississippi#sthash.To5sN74e.dpuf.

54. Douglas S. Massey and Chiara Capoferro, "The Geographic Diversification of American Immigration," 25–50; Mark A. Leach and Frank D. Bean, "The Structure and Dynamics of Mexican Migration to New Destinations in the United States," 51–74; and Katharine M. Donato et al., "Changing Faces, Changing Places: The Emergence of New Nonmetropolitan Immigrant Gateways," 75–98; all in *New Faces in New Places: The Changing Geography of American Immigration*, ed. Douglas S. Massey (New York: Russell Sage Foundation, 2008).

55. Charles Hirschman and Douglass S. Massey, "Places and Peoples: The New American Mosaic," in *New Faces in New Places*, 4–10; William Kandel and Emilio A. Parrado, "Industrial Transformation and Hispanic Migration to the American South: The Case of the Poultry Industry," in *Hispanic Spaces, Latino Places: Community and Cultural Diversity in Contemporary America*, ed. Daniel D. Arreola (Austin: University of Texas Press, 2004), 255–276; Striffler, *Chicken*; Michael J. Broadway, "From City to Countryside: Recent Changes in the Structure and Location of the Meat- and Fish-Processing Industries," in Stull et al., *Any Way You Cut It*; Griffith, "*Hay Trabajo*"; Rebecca M. Torres, E. Jeffrey Popke, and Holly M. Hapke, "The South's Silent Bargain: Rural Restructuring, Latino Labor and the Ambiguities of Migrant Experience," in *Latinos in the New South: Transformations of Place*, ed. Heather A. Smith and Owen J. Furuseth (Burlington, VT: Ashgate, 2006), 37–68; James D. Engstrom, "Industry and Immigration in Dalton, Georgia," in *Latino Workers in the Contemporary South*, ed. Arthur D. Murphy, Colleen Blanchard, and Jennifer A. Hill (Athens: University of Georgia Press, 1999), 44–56; Greig Guthey, "Mexican Places in Southern Spaces: Globalization, Work, and Daily Life in and around the North Georgia Poultry Industry," in ibid., 57–67; Emilio A. Parrado and William Kandel, "New Hispanic Migrant Destinations: A Tale of Two Industries," in *New Faces in New Places*, 99–123.

56. Andrew Wainer, "The New Latino South and the Challenge to Public Education: Strategies for Educators and Policymakers in Emerging Immigrant Communities" (University of Southern California: Tomás Rivera Policy Institute, 2004); William A. Kandel and Emilio A. Parrado, "Hispanic Population Growth and Public School Responses in Two New South Immigrant Destinations," in *Latinos in the New South*, 111–134; David Griffith, "New Midwest-

erners, New Southerners: Immigration Experiences in Four Rural American Settings," in *New Faces in New Places*, 179–210; Regina Cortina, "MexAmerica and the Global American South," conference paper presented at Navigating the Globalization of the American South, University of North Carolina-Chapel Hill, 2005.

57. Jamie Winders, "Changing Politics of Race and Region: Latino Migration to the US South," *Progress in Human Geography* 29, no. 6 (2005): 683–699. For some exceptions, see Barbara Ellen Smith, "Across Races and Nations: Social Justice Organizing in the Transnational South," in *Latinos in the New South*, 235–256; Helen B. Marrow, "Hispanic Immigration, Black Population Size, and Intergroup Relations in the Rural and Small-Town South," in *New Faces in New Places*, 211–248; Paula D. McClain et al., "Racial Distancing in a Southern City: Latino Immigrants' Views of Black Americans," *Journal of Politics* 68, no. 3 (2006): 571–584; and Angela Christine Stuesse, "Globalization 'Southern Style': Transnational Migration, the Poultry Industry, and Implications for Organizing Workers across Difference" (PhD diss., University of Texas at Austin, 2008).

58. Winders, "Changing Politics of Race and Region," 689.

59. W. E. B. DuBois, *Black Reconstruction in America, 1860–1880* (1935; New York: Free Press, 1998); C. Vann Woodward, *Origins of the New South, 1877–1913*, 2nd ed. (Baton Rouge: Louisiana State University Press, 1971).

60. Raymond Mohl, "Latinization in the Heart of Dixie: Hispanics in Late-Twentieth-Century Alabama," *Alabama Review* 87, no. 4 (2002): 243–274; Mohl, "The *Nuevo* New South: Hispanic Migration to Alabama," *Migration World Magazine* 30, no. 3 (2002): 14–18.

61. ACLU, "Crisis in Alabama: Immigration Law Causes Chaos," accessed June 30, 2014, https://www.aclu.org/crisis-alabama-immigration-law-causes-chaos.

62. Leon Fink, *The Maya of Morganton: Work and Community in the Nuevo New South* (Chapel Hill: University of North Carolina Press, 2003).

63. James C. Cobb and William Stueck, eds., *Globalization and the American South* (Athens: University of Georgia Press, 2005).

64. Ibid., xv.

65. Fran Ansley and Jon Shefner, eds., *Global Connections and Local Receptions: New Latino Immigration to the Southeastern United States* (Knoxville: University of Tennessee Press, 2009); Jon Shefner and Katie Kirkpatrick, "Introduction: Globalization and the New Destination Immigrant," in ibid., xv–xl.

66. Jamie Winders, *Nashville in the New Millennium: Immigrant Settlement, Urban Transformation, and Social Belonging* (New York: Russell Sage Foundation, 2013).

67. Jamie Winders, "Changing Politics of Race and Region"; Winders, "Bringing Back the (B)order: Post-9/11 Politics of Immigration, Borders, and Belonging in the Contemporary US South," *Antipode* 39 (2007): 920–942; Winders, "New Directions in the Nuevo South," *Southeastern Geographer* 51 (2011): 327–340; Winders, "Re-Placing Southern Geographies: The Role of Latino Migration in Transforming the South, Its Identities, and Its Study," *Southeastern Geographer* 51 (2011): 342–358; Winders, "Representing the Immigrant:

Social Movements, Political Discourse, and Immigration in the US South," *Southeastern Geographer* 51 (2011): 596–614.

68. James Chaney, "The Formation of a Hispanic Enclave in Nashville, Tennessee," *Southeastern Geographer* 50 (2010): 17–38.

69. Raúl Villa, *Barrio-Logos: Space and Place in Urban Chicano Literature and Culture* (Austin: University of Texas Press, 2000).

70. Acuña, *A Community under Siege*; Camarillo, *Chicanos in a Changing Society*; García, *Desert Immigrants*; Barrera, *Race and Class in the Southwest*; Richard Griswold del Castillo, *The Los Angeles Barrio, 1850–1890: A Social History* (Berkeley: University of California Press, 1979); Ricardo Romo, *East Los Angeles: History of a Barrio* (Austin: University of Texas Press, 1983); George Sánchez, *Becoming Mexican American: Ethnicity, Culture, and Identity in Chicano Los Angeles, 1900–1945* (New York: Oxford University Press, 1993); Matt Garcia, *A World of Its Own: Race, Labor, and Citrus in the Making of Greater Los Angeles, 1900–1970* (Chapel Hill: University of North Carolina Press, 2001); Arredondo, *Mexican Chicago*; Fernández, *Brown in the Windy City*; Innis-Jiménez, *Steel Barrio*; Geraldo L. Cadava, *Standing on Common Ground: The Making of a Sunbelt Borderland* (Cambridge, MA: Harvard University Press, 2013).

71. George Sánchez, "Latinos, the American South, and the Future of US Race Relations," *Southern Spaces*, April 26, 2007, accessed June 30, 2014, http://www.southernspaces.org/2007/latinos-american-south-and-future-us-race-relations.

72. Donald Kerwin, "The Freedom Riders and the Dreamers: High Noon in the Immigration Debate," *Huffington Post*, April 3, 2013, accessed June 30, 2014, http://www.huffingtonpost.com/donald-kerwin/the-freedom-riders-and-the-dreamers-high-noon-in-the-immigration-debate_b_3002906.html.

73. Personal correspondence, September 14, 2013.

74. David G. Gutiérrez, *Walls and Mirrors: Mexican Americans, Mexican Immigrants, and the Politics of Ethnicity* (Berkeley: University of California Press, 1995); Gilda L. Ochoa, *Becoming Neighbors in a Mexican American Community: Power, Conflict, and Solidarity* (Austin: University of Texas Press, 2004); Matthew Garcia, *From the Jaws of Victory: The Triumph and Tragedy of Cesar Chavez and the Farm Worker Movement* (Berkeley: University of California Press, 2012).

75. "Univision Insights: Hispanics Show Double Digit Growth in Maryland, Arkansas, Iowa, Indiana and Vermont According to 2010 Census Data," Univision Communications, Inc., February 11, 2011.

CHAPTER FIVE

Sacred Spaces: Race, Resistance, and the Politics of Chicana/o and Latina/o Religious History

FELIPE HINOJOSA

Between May 1969 and March 1970 a religious awakening took over American churches. Not a spiritual reformation or even a Holy Spirit–infused Azusa-type revival.[1] This awakening was about physical occupations, breakfast programs, candlelight vigils, and the clash between the growing cultural nationalism of Chicana/o and Puerto Rican activists and the politics of Catholic and Protestant churches.

The first of these clashes took place in the heart of Chicago's Lincoln Park neighborhood when a multiethnic coalition, led by the predominantly Puerto Rican activist group known as the Young Lords Organization, took over the McCormick Theological Seminary in May 1969. Designed to hold the seminary at least partially responsible for its role in the city's urban renewal push in the neighborhood, the Young Lords occupied it for five days. The following month they occupied the nearby Armitage Methodist Church and transformed the church's basement into a community center where they offered day-care services, a small health clinic, and free breakfast for schoolchildren.[2]

Several months later, in Descanso, California, Chicana/o youth took over a Catholic Church camp and renamed it "Centro Cultural de la Raza" in late November 1969. That move sparked a violent confrontation a month later on the steps of the St. Basil's Catholic Church in Los Angeles. On a cool Christmas Eve, activists from the newly formed group called Católicos Por La Raza (CPLR) clashed with police and church leadership in an effort to get the wealthy St. Basil's Church to respond to what they felt were the dire social and economic needs of the surrounding Mexican American community.

Only days after the conflict at St. Basil's Church, the Young Lords Party took over the First Spanish Methodist Church (FSMC) in New

York City and renamed it "the People's Church." Located in the historic Puerto Rican neighborhood "El Barrio" in East Harlem, the church remained in the control of the Young Lords for two weeks during the last days of 1969 and into 1970. In that time they offered a variety of social services, including a free breakfast program and cultural identity classes. Two months later, in Houston, members of the Mexican American Youth Organization (MAYO) broke a window in an empty Presbyterian Church in the city's Northside neighborhood and took over the space. Like the Young Lords, MAYO activists initiated a number of community service programs throughout the three weeks that they occupied the Presbyterian church building.[3]

More than random acts of protest, these church takeovers evinced a larger shift in the trajectory of Latino religious politics that began in the years after World War II. Increased Latino migration to places in the West and the urban North, along with the "crucial conjunction" of Vatican II and the Civil Rights movement, pressured church leaders to address racial injustice and urban poverty and situated the church as a site of struggle.[4] These grassroots movements bring to light the historic "interactive relationship," as the historian Roberto Treviño argues, that Latinas/os have had with the institutional church. They force us to move beyond the false dichotomy of a "folk versus formal" relationship.[5] In this chapter, I try to make sense of this interactive relationship by arguing that the study of religion, both historical and theological, can pave the way for understanding the multiple formulations and expressions of Chicana/o and Latina/o cultural nationalism during the civil rights era. Whereas previous studies blame "the liberal intelligentsia and Chicano activists" for religion's curious absence in much of Chicana/o scholarship, these church takeovers and demonstrations force us to reconsider this claim. Part of the problem is that these critiques focus solely on an absence of overt religiosity among young radicals and scholars, rather than interrogating how religion might advance our understanding of Chicana/o and Latina/o history.[6]

To be clear, I do not presume that increased attention to religion can magically revolutionize Chicana/o and Latina/o history. But I do believe that integrating religious studies can create exciting possibilities for expanding the thematic boundaries of Chicana/o and Latina/o history. Research in religious archives, as the historian Vicki Ruiz argues, offers multiple "points of departure" that provides scholars with a sense of the decisions that Latinas/os made, their lives as religious people, and the ways in which they resisted and accommodated Americanization efforts.[7] In this chapter, resistance to sacred spaces offers generative possibilities for resituating the Chicano movement within a relational Latino civil rights framework that acknowledges common struggles across space, place, and culture. It opens new avenues for recognizing the political and religious heterogeneity of the Latina/o community and, most importantly, blurs the line between the secular and the sacred. Ultimately, I am invested in narrating a Latina/o history that merges the rich historiographical and literary traditions of Chicana/o and Puerto Rican studies. Religious studies provide an important framework for this.

More than any other institutional space, the church has stood as a marker of colonial expansion, white supremacy, and political apathy. And yet it has also been a space that many Mexican Americans and Puerto Ricans have trusted, visited every Sunday, and given their hopes for a better life. Locating resistance within the space of the church highlights this religious trope even as it reveals the multiple expressions, narratives, and experiences that made churches both contested and sacred spaces in the community. More than filling historiographical gaps, this chapter teases out the limits and possibilities of religious activism in Chicana/o and Puerto Rican communities and the conflicts and dilemmas that arose around the church as a religious institution.[8]

There are two important interdisciplinary interventions I wish to make. The first centers on the fragmented relationship between religious studies, Chicana/o, and Latina/o history. In the last fifteen years, Chicana/o historians (almost exclusively) have come under attack from some religious studies scholars who are critical of the exclusion or misrepresentation of religion in works that were published in the 1960s and 1970s. These religious scholars follow a familiar, almost boilerplate, line of criticism, arguing that the history produced during this era stressed the "victimization" of the Mexican origin population and ignored the important, positive role of religion in people's lives.[9] The representative straw man is Rodolfo Acuña, whose classic work, *Occupied America*, is often cited as the central text of "victimization" history.[10] More than forty years later, works published in the 1970s continue to be cited as key examples of the supposed disdain of Chicano scholars and activists for religion and religious studies. While these are important critiques, they do not go far enough in interrogating the ways in which religion helps us (re)imagine Chicana/o and Latina/o histories.[11]

The second point builds on the first by focusing on the three case studies with which this chapter opens. Examining the revolutionary origins of church clashes in Los Angeles and the takeovers in Houston and

New York blows the whistle on the tired cliché that Latina/o activists did not want to have anything to do with "the church" and other religious institutions in general.[12] On a very personal level, most Chicana/o and Puerto Rican activists had either grown up in religious families or lived in barrios where it was hard to escape the ubiquity of faith. As Michael Olivas's chapter in this collection describes the early experiences that led him to become an "accidental historian," for these activists the seeds of engagement with faith and politics were planted early in their youth. Visits to church, the prayers of their parents, and the faith evident in their communities shaped their early understandings of a merciful and just God. Even as their rhetoric later condemned the church, their actions presented a narrative of political engagement that championed church reform as a means to better serve Chicana/o and Puerto Rican communities.

Situated within the tense political times of the Black and Brown Power era, the religious movements of Latinas/os reinforce the notion that ethnic nationalist movements are indeed complex and often made up of "an array of Movement agendas and political and cultural positions."[13] Ethnic nationalism and religious devotion, in other words, are not mutually exclusive. Positioning the church takeovers as important moments in Chicana/o and Puerto Rican activism magnifies the multiple and sometimes hidden manifestations of ethnic nationalism during the late 1960s and early 1970s.[14] In this chapter we see activism engage with faith and, in turn, shape faith toward new activist expressions.

The Politics of Chicano and Latino Religious History

Focusing on Chicano and Puerto Rican civil rights provides an important contribution to the field of American religious studies. Aside from the obvious references to César Chávez and the religious overtones of the farmworker movement, most studies continue to frame debates around race, resistance, and social movements within a black/white racial binary. Consider Michael Emerson and Christian Smith's now classic book *Divided by Faith: Evangelical Religion and the Problem of Race in America*. In recent memory no book has captured the imagination of race and religious studies scholars in such a significant way. Entire conferences, edited books, and journal articles have been organized around this one book and its fascinating look into the historic links between race and evangelicalism. In the midst of obtaining its "classic" status, the book has also spawned a litany of critiques from scholars who believe its narrow focus on black/white race relations ignored the demographic shifts of the late twentieth century stemming from increased Asian and Latin American immigration.[15] The critiques leveled on *Divided by Faith* confirm the need to move beyond a black/white binary when writing about race and religion in the United States. Since the publication of *Divided by Faith*, however, religious scholars have generated a flurry of studies on multiethnic/multiracial congregations and on the racialized histories of single ethnic churches. These recent studies provide fresh insights into how religious institutions function as multiethnic spaces and reveal how even in single ethnic group churches the politics of race, class, gender, and sexuality remain omnipresent.[16]

While religion remains a marginal topic in Chicana/o history, the last fifteen years has seen a rise in studies that deal with the relationship between religion, activism, and culture.[17] There are several reasons behind this heightened interest, many of which can be attributed to the demographic boom and growing religious pluralism of the Latino community. Even as a majority of Latinos in the United States are Catholic (nearly 55 percent), 22 percent adhere to an eclectic mix of mainline Protestantism and Pentecostalism while the remaining 18 percent are religiously unaffiliated, a number that has grown rapidly in the last few years. These percentages are nothing new when you consider that Latinos/as have danced to the "rhythms of religious affiliation and disaffiliation" for over a century in the United States.[18] But this religious diversity does offer new clues into the ways Latinos/as have forged transnational networks, participated in electoral politics and immigrant rights movements, and transformed public space via storefront churches or sidewalk shrines. Moving beyond religion as simply an additive category carries with it the possibility of revealing these transnational cultures, migrant streams, activist politics, and diverse forms of "spiritual *mestizaje*" that make up the new visibilities and expressions of Latino religious life.[19]

This recent trajectory of Chicana/o and Latina/o religious history, however, is only one part of a longer evolution that began with institutional church histories in the nineteenth century. Sponsored by specific Christian denominations and intended for Christian audiences, these studies were soon replaced by the important works of Samuel Ortegón and Carlos Castañeda during the middle part of the twentieth century.[20] Ortegón and Castañeda's scholarship provided important insights about Mexican Catholics and Protestants even as it presented a romanticized view of Christianity that uncritically linked religion and social uplift. That approach shifted significantly again in the 1960s and 1970s. Motivated to a great extent by the political tenor of the times, the rearticulation of religious history symbolized a political act that stressed racial identity as well as resistance to church hierarchy. The writings of liberation theologians in Latin America, especially the Peruvian theologian Gustavo Gutierrez, as well as the Chicana/o and Puerto Rican civil rights movements inspired an entire generation of Latina/o theologians and religious scholars in the United States in the 1970s.[21]

Theologians like Justo González, Orlando Costas, Virgilio Elizondo, and Ada María Isasí-Diaz each offered rich theological reflections that both contextualized the Latina/o experience and challenged Eurocentric assumptions about faith and God.[22] These scholars noted the dialectics of religion as encompassing the power to simultaneously sustain and support the status quo even as it created oppositional cultures that have historically resisted religious imperatives like colonialism. The theologian Carmen Nanko-Fernandez asserts that from the beginning, Latina/o theology as a movement and an academic discipline has "intentionally embraced the cultural dimensions of lived faith."[23]

The academic study of Latina/o religion, then, emerged most powerfully within theological studies in the 1970s. Unfortunately, this rich field of study remained outside the purview of Latina/o historians. The two fields maintained a safe distance even as they both grappled with the workings of colonialism, race, and economic injustice in the Latina/o community. In retrospect, the separate roads taken by Latina/o religious scholars and historians make sense. When the fields of Chicana/o and Puerto Rican studies emerged in the 1960s and 1970s, religion as a topic of investigation remained marginal for reasons that were both appropriate and justified. For Chicana/o and Puerto Rican activists and scholars, the church was seen as the "enemy of the people."[24] These concerns, of course, were rooted in a five-hundred-year history of colonial expansion fueled by a religious ideology of white supremacy. Some Chicano scholars focused on "how the church had failed the Chicano sociologically," or on the obsessive push of Americanization by Protestant churches.[25] And, of course, the one book that is always at the center of the Chicano movement nationalist critique, Rodolfo Acuña's *Occupied America* (1972), made it a point to highlight the tight and historic relationship between the Catholic Church, colonialism, and anti-Mexican racism in the US-Mexico borderlands.[26]

And yet even as Catholic and Protestant institutions stood as markers of oppression in the making of the American West, religious devotions and annual festivals in places like Santa Barbara and San Antonio brought people together and forged vibrant ethnic Mexican communities. This is the point that religious historians such as Robert Wright believe Chicano historians of the 1970s deliberately overlooked. In his essay on Mexican Catholicism in the Southwest, for example, Wright argues that much of the literature that emerged in the late 1970s as part of the "social history turn" ignored religion and was full of "poorly substantiated Chicano assumptions." But although Wright's critiques merit consideration, his assertion that Chicano historians monopolized the field and even went as far as to pressure at least one religious scholar to write "a mostly negative account of California Catholicism" is farfetched. Placing blame on "California Chicano negativity," as Wright does, simplifies a scholarly oversight and historiographical position that deserves much deeper reflection.[27] Whether in the form of annual Catholic celebrations or in the love that ethnic Mexicans had for their church at La Placita in Los Angeles, there is little doubt that religious devotion mattered especially in the face of an expanding empire and a Catholic hierarchy that remained distant and cold.[28] But Wright is correct when he argues that many of the classic texts in Chicano history that emerged in the late 1970s missed a valuable opportunity when they neglected the importance of Catholicism in the daily lives of ethnic Mexicans.[29]

If scholarship on the late nineteenth and early twentieth century has raised important questions and critiques about the place of religion in the making of ethnic Mexican communities, scholarship on Latino civil rights has emerged as yet another contested arena for religious studies scholars. Again, the historiographic stance is centered on what Chicana/o and Latina/o historians have overlooked rather than how religious studies can revamp our understanding of Chicana/o and Latina/o civil rights history. Take for example the important book, *Latino Religions and Civic Activism in the United States*, edited by Gastón Espinosa, Virgilio Elizondo, and Jesse Miranda. As one of the first collections of essays devoted entirely to religion in the Chicana/o and Puerto Rican civil rights struggles, this was a pathbreaking study that shaped much of my own thinking on the relationship between religion and Latino social movements. And yet the editors follow a familiar historiographical argument in positioning their work as a counter to the 1970s cultural nationalism that characterized the church as an apolitical and oppressive space. In one chapter, the religious historian Gastón Espinosa explained that religion's absence in Chicano movement literature

is the result of "Marxist and socialist teachings during the countercul-
tural movement of the 1960s and 1970s [that] prompted many Latino
scholars" to essentially ignore religion and its connection to civil rights
activism.[30]

While Espinosa is correct when he asserts that ideological commitments kept some Chicana/o scholars from taking religion seriously, the
reality on the ground revealed a much deeper engagement between
Chicana/o and Puerto Rican scholars, activists, and Catholic and Protestant churches. In other words, the radicalism and nationalist politics
of some Latina/o scholars and activists reinforced the need to reform
the church rather than ignore it as an irrelevant institution.[31] The religious politics of Chicana/o and Puerto Rican activists deserve a fresh
look. Perhaps the activists on the ground recognized something that
Chicana/o historians overlooked: that everyday forms of religious devotion have historically provided an "orientation," a way to make sense
of the world and a catalyst to the forms of resistance and adaptation that
have defined the Latino experience in the United States.[32]

Driving Out the Money Changers

In order to examine the interactive relationship between Chicana/o and
Puerto Rican activists and religious institutions, I begin at the place
that most religious scholars point to as the problem: the politics of cultural nationalism. The fundamental belief that undergirded the church
takeovers, vigils, and demonstrations occurring across the country in
1969 was that the church had a social responsibility that extended beyond spiritual matters. Latina/o activists viewed the apathy of religious
leaders as part of the long and tight relationship between the institutional church, colonialism, and genocide in the Americas. That history
structured much of the criticism that both black and Latina/o activists
directed toward the church in the 1960s and 1970s. It is not entirely
clear why 1969 was the year that churches were singled out in such a direct way. One possibility is the work of the former Student Nonviolent
Coordinating Committee activist James Forman. As a member of the
League of Revolutionary Black Workers, Forman presented a "Black
Manifesto" at the National Black Economic Development conference
in Detroit in May 1969 that demanded white Christian churches and
Jewish synagogues pay reparations for the historic role of religious institutions in the enslavement of black people. The Black Manifesto de-

clared: "We are therefore demanding of the white Christian churches and Jewish synagogues which are part and parcel of the system of capitalism, that they begin to pay reparations to black people in this country. We are demanding $500,000,000 from the Christian white churches and Jewish synagogues."[33] By the end of the month, Forman had confronted the United Church of Christ, the United Presbyterian Church, USA, the Lutheran Church in America, the American Baptist Convention, the Roman Archbishop of New York, and church leadership in both the Methodist and Episcopal churches. The interactions between Forman and white church leaders were often "rude and sometimes violent confrontations, and extraordinary, theatrical public displays of great passion and emotion."[34] And in each instance these disruptions worked. By the summer of 1969 mainline Protestant churches across the country were on high alert, fearing their local institutions might be taken over or disrupted by black and brown activists.

While Chicana/o and Puerto Rican activists were likely aware of Forman's "Black Manifesto," it is also clear that they already had plans in motion to engage white religious leaders in Chicago, New York City, Houston, and Los Angeles. In each of these areas, Chicana/o and Puerto Rican activists made a concerted effort to request use of church space to host breakfast programs for children, provide culture classes, push back on urban renewal projects, and offer a variety of other social services. In the case of Católicos in Los Angeles, the group drafted a nine-point plan that included calls for the Catholic Church to build low-cost housing, practice shared governance, grant freedom of speech for all priests and nuns, and make a commitment to the Chicano movement.[35] In each case, however, they were either denied use of church space or ignored completely by church leadership.

When that approach did not work, activists launched a series of political moves that started in Chicago in May 1969 when the Puerto Rican Young Lords took over the newly constructed Stone building on the campus of McCormick Theological Seminary and a month later moved into the Armitage Methodist Church, both of which were located in the middle of Lincoln Park's Puerto Rican community. That move was followed in November by young Mexican American Catholics who took over Camp Oliver in Descanso, California, and renamed it "Centro Cultural de la Raza." They called on the Catholic Church to place Chicanas/os in church leadership positions, demanded that it fund social programs in the Chicano community, and insisted the Church "align itself economically and spiritually to the Chicano movement."[36] In the midst of the takeover of Camp Oliver, participants came together as "Católicos Por La Raza (CPLR)—in their commitment to the Chicano movement and in their determination to make the Catholic Church accountable to Chicanos."[37] These early disruptions signaled a broader and more vigorous move by Chicana/o and Puerto Rican activists that came to a head in the final weeks of December 1969.

As Chicana/o youth took over Camp Oliver, a similar but distinct movement of Católicos Por La Raza coalesced in Los Angeles. Frustrated by the $3 million price tag for the newly constructed St. Basil's Catholic Church, Católicos prepared to disrupt the Christmas Eve Mass in 1969. One of the better-known activists, Oscar Acosta, described St. Basil's Church as a "monstrosity" with a "fantastic organ [that] pumps out a spooky religious hymn to this Christ Child of Golden Locks and Blue Eyes overlooking the richest drag in town."[38] In Los Angeles, Católicos came together under the leadership of Richard Cruz and culled a cadre of leaders (some religious and some not) from Loyola Law School, *La Raza* newspaper, and the United Mexican American Students (UMAS) group at Los Angeles City College.[39]

After several failed attempts to engage Cardinal McIntyre with a list of their demands, Católicos picketed his residence at St. Basil's Church and held candlelight vigils beginning on Thanksgiving Day, 1969. The picketing and vigils lasted throughout the month of December and gained the recognition and support of religious clergy nationwide as well as Chicano Movement activists. The month-long demonstrations came to a head on Christmas Eve as Católicos, frustrated by the lack of concern shown by the Catholic Church leadership, planned to disrupt midnight mass. As demonstrators assembled and marched toward the church, it was clear that the Catholic hierarchy was prepared to respond with force and with the full arm of the law, as police officers disguised as church ushers were embedded at the service. As mass commenced and the front doors to the church closed, activists entered the church through a side entrance that led to a basement sanctuary. Once they were inside, they were ambushed by undercover police officers "wielding their sticks and spraying mace."[40] Five activists were arrested that night and eventually twenty-one people, known as the "St. Basil twenty-one," served jail time for disrupting a religious service. Even though the demonstration turned violent and alienated some Mexican American Catholics, in the end the Catholic Church did take notice. As the pickets and vigils continued, the Church appointed the first Mex-

ican American bishop, Patricio Flores, in 1970 and began more intentional efforts to incorporate Latinos into Church leadership.

Even as Católicos believed that the Church was a racist institution,
they remained on the front lines working from within to reform it and
help it become more responsive to one of its largest constituent groups
in California and across the Southwest—Mexican Americans. In other
words, they understood the importance of the Church. These politics
were stamped on the very name of the group that, according to the historian Mario T. García, was chosen as a way to emphasize that they were
not anti-Catholic. The belief that the Church was an important institution—like other public spaces—was the guiding philosophy that Católicos carried. They proclaimed: "the church belongs to the people." In
doing so, Católicos made it clear they were not "attacking the Church's
theological concepts . . . but asserting that the Church has failed in its
worldly responsibility."[41]

Three days after the demonstration outside St. Basil's Catholic
Church, the Young Lords Party took over the First Spanish Methodist
Church (FSMC) in New York City on a cold Sunday morning. Almost
three months in the making, plans for the occupation followed repeated
failed attempts to meet with church leadership. The Young Lords tried
numerous times to talk with church leaders about the possibility of using church space to offer breakfast programs and other social services
during the week. After months of being ignored by church leaders and
members, the Young Lords took direct action and occupied the church,
refusing to leave until its leaders agreed to let them use the building
for community programs during the week. The occupation on that cold
December morning was as peaceful as it was dramatic. As soon as the
preacher finished his sermon and after the eighty or so parishioners ex-
ited, members of the Young Lords nailed the doors shut with six-inch
railroad spikes and occupied the church.[42]

For members of the Young Lords whose "revolutionary nationalist"
politics were modeled after the Black Panther Party and other revolutionary groups, the takeover of the church was an obvious move.[43] Not
only was it located "right smack dead in the center of the barrio," but it
was used only a few hours a week. The rest of the time it remained "one
big brick that sits on the corner of 111th and Lexington." The political
indifference of the FSMC was even more pronounced when compared
to the work of Catholic churches in the neighborhood that operated various antipoverty programs.[44]

During the eleven-day occupation of the church, the Young Lords organized "free clothing drives, breakfast programs, liberation schools, political education classes, a day care center, free health care programs, and nightly entertainment." Inside the church, the group hung a white sheet with a painted message that read, *Bienvenidos a la Iglesia del Pueblo* (Welcome to the Church of the People). What became known as "the People's Church Offensive" attracted large crowds and helped increase the group's membership. They received letters of support from antipoverty activists such as Reverend David Kirk of Emmaus House, who proudly claimed, "if Christ was alive today, he would have been a Young Lord."[45] The solidarity strengthened the movement and, as Darrel Enck-Wanzer argued, reinforced the larger goal of holding accountable those "institutions they perceived to be advancing dominant interests and failing to serve their community."[46]

But while the move to occupy the church was seen as an important moment for the Young Lords, the reactions that came from those Latinos who attended the church were not positive. "They did not ask, they demanded," Pastor Humberto Carranza told the *New York Times*. He went on to note that the group had no intention of joining the church: "the way they dress, their insignia, it is obvious that they are not bona fide worshippers."[47] On the morning of the occupation, church members did not fight back or ask for police help; instead they lined up on one side of the church and sang hymns in Spanish.[48]

During the occupation of the FSMC, other Puerto Rican churches in the neighborhood were on high alert. At a nearby Pentecostal church, Neftali Torres remembered how "the pastor organized all the men and tried to coordinate this effort so that at the moment that strangers came in to take over the men would stand and take charge."[49] The concerns of area churches were not without merit. Only a few days after ending the takeover of the FSMC, small groups of Young Lords visited half a dozen churches in the area with the hope of garnering support for their breakfast program.

In most cases the groups left without major incident, but at the FSMC an interesting discussion broke out over the goals of the Young Lords Party and the role of the church in the Puerto Rican community. In the aftermath, it was clear that the Young Lords had captured the attention of religious communities across New York. Supporters of the group, including many white progressives, organized press conferences that stressed how these actions served "to challenge the racist Methodist hierarchy."[50]

The takeover in East Harlem was followed up by another church takeover in Houston, Texas. On February 15, 1970, members of the Mexican American Youth Organization (MAYO) took over the Juan Marcos Presbyterian Church located in Houston's Northside neighborhood. Made up of student groups and barrio youth, MAYO was on the forefront of educational and political activism in Texas during the late 1960s and early 1970s. They led school walkouts in south Texas, organized mass demonstrations against the war in Vietnam, and helped give rise to the Raza Unida Party, a Mexican American political party in Texas.[51] With a pragmatic approach to social change and a somewhat uneven commitment to cultural nationalism and internationalism, MAYO's takeover epitomized their eagerness to fight the community's most "sacred cow": the church.[52] Prior to the takeover, the church had been empty for six months as it transitioned from a mostly white congregation to a Mexican American congregation, a reflection of the neighborhood's changing demographics by the early 1970s. MAYO activists had been in talks with the Brazos Presbytery, though they came to the realization early on in that process that "the Anglo congregation had no real desire to work with the Mexican American community." Despite this pessimism, they held out hope that MAYO would be granted permission to use the building.[53] But for reasons that are not yet altogether clear, talks broke down and MAYO's activists were denied access. At that point the activists, who articulated a moral justification for their cause, broke a window and occupied the church.

One of the leaders of the takeover, Yolanda Garza Birdwell, stated, "Our community has spiritual needs, but its social problems are more urgent."[54] MAYO also found support from a familiar ally in the Rev. Antonio Gonzales, the national chaplain for Spanish-speaking affairs in Washington, DC, who visited the church and reminded the young people that they were "not there to fight for property rights, but because they have dignity."[55] MAYO activists occupied the church for three weeks and in that time started a free breakfast program and cultural education classes, and also presented workshops on social services that were available in the area. After the third week, Brazos Presbytery leadership stepped in, cutting the gas and electricity in the building and filing a district court injunction to evict MAYO from the church.[56] MAYO leaders soon evacuated the building, having made their point. But not before José Angel Gutiérrez, state leader of MAYO, used the media to put churches across Texas on notice. He promised that "MAYO would continue to use occupation as a tactic to achieve social change."[57] The demonstrations against Presbyterian churches across Houston continued into April 1970.

Toward a New Chicana/o and Latina/o Religious History

This chapter began as a way to make sense of the interactive relationship between Latinos and the institutional church and, in particular, to argue that the study of religion can open new pathways for understanding the multiple expressions of cultural nationalism in the Brown Power Movements of the late 1960s and early 1970s.[58] Not content with the arguments of religious studies scholars that have blamed cultural nationalism for religion's absence as a topic of study in Chicano and Latino history, this chapter sets out a different path forward grounded in archival research into these diverse local incidents. The first step is to reassess the politics and motivations of radical activist groups such as Católicos, MAYO, and the Young Lords. Rather than languid critiques that blame the nationalist commitments of Latina/o activists and scholars for ignoring religion, we are better served by investigating how the church and other religious institutions were critical and contested spaces for Latina/o activists in neighborhoods across the country that were then on the cusp of being destroyed by urban renewal programs.

Even as Chicana/o and Puerto Rican social movements were for the most part governed by secular ideologies, their actions reflected a grassroots pragmatism that viewed the church as an underutilized space that, in addition to religious worship, could be transformed into a training ground for social change and community renewal. In this way, the activism of Católicos, MAYO, and the Young Lords served as an urgent call for the church to wake from its slumber and become an active presence in people's lives on days other than Sundays or religious holidays. For religious and nonreligious Latina/o activists alike, the church embodied a history of white supremacy, patriarchy, and economic power even as it paradoxically provided hope and liberation. Delicately balancing seemingly paradoxical ideological perspectives about religion and the church, Latina/o activists fiercely challenged religious institutions in the late 1960s and early 1970s. This dynamic and paradoxical relationship generated important resistance movements that for the most part have remained outside the purview of Chicana/o and Latina/o historians.[59]

This should not come as a surprise. Religious reform movements were only one part of the larger and more visible struggles to end the war in Vietnam, to advocate for educational equity, labor rights, political representation, and the fight for a homeland. Even so, the scant coverage that religious activism has received from Chicana/o and Latina/o historians is nonetheless remarkable. The fact that we know very little about the role of the church during the Chicano and Puerto Rican freedom struggles should motivate us as scholars to work to fill in these historiographical gaps. But there is more at stake here than simply telling a new story about Latino civil rights. Activist engagements with religion and the church offer historians new vantage points to the places and spaces of Latina/o civil rights activism in the United States and across the Americas.

In this chapter, the takeovers and clashes in Protestant and Catholic churches revealed the strained, sometimes contradictory position of the church in relation to the civil rights struggle and to community activism, even as they showcased how activists regarded the space of the church. While the response by the churches and their members was mixed at best, the takeovers and clashes thrust churches across the country into a larger conversation about the relationship between activism, faith, and civil rights.

It is also important to note that the clamoring that came from outside groups like the Young Lords and MAYO represented only one part of the sustained religious movements that emerged in Latino communities and churches across the country. This was the subject of my first book, *Latino Mennonites*, where I traced Latina/o religious activism in the Mennonite Church and its relationship to Chicana/o and Puerto Rican movement politics.[60] Latina/o religious activism in the Mennonite Church was one part of a larger religious movement that included PADRES (the Chicano priest movement) and Las Hermanas (a movement led by religious women) in the Catholic Church and La Raza Churchmen in the Presbyterian Church, among other groups. In each case, these groups worked within their own religious traditions to challenge racist and sexist church hierarchies.

In other cases religious activism extended outward from the church into the broader community. In New York City, for example, the Damascus Christian Church ran a church-sponsored drug rehabilitation program in the Bronx through the leadership of the Rev. Leoncia Rosado Rosseau (known to many as "Mama Léo").[61] Sustained almost entirely by church donations, the program was one of the first to help rehabilitate drug abusers, and its success led the program to expand in other New York boroughs in the 1970s. During this time an interethnic mix of *alleluia*-shouting Pentecostals helped nearly three hundred young people, most of them Puerto Rican, who struggled with alcohol or drug addiction. According to the historian Virginia Sánchez Korrol, the programs started by Mama Léo increased the visibility of Pentecostals on the streets and provided a positive example for young Puerto Ricans who wanted to be leaders in the church while also serving their communities outside it.[62]

Halfway across the country, in Davenport, Iowa, the Catholic Interracial Council brought together progressive Anglos, African Americans, and Mexican Americans who together organized programs that addressed issues around housing, education, labor, and police brutality. Here in the heart of the American Midwest, the Catholic Interracial Council stood to "blot out the sin and heresy of racism." For Mexican Americans who were new to the Midwest, the Catholic Interracial Council helped forge an activist impulse that led to the development of several councils of the League of United Latin American Citizens (LULAC) and the American GI Forum across the state of Iowa in the 1950s and 1960s.[63]

When all these cases of religious activism are examined together, what emerges are contested narratives that promise to broaden our understanding of the Chicana/o and Puerto Rican freedom struggles and move us "beyond Aztlán," as Lilia Fernández puts it in her chapter in this collection. New topics and perspectives that, when linked together, provide a narrative thread to weave a relational Latina/o civil rights history—one that takes into account the specific and complex spatial politics of Latino neighborhoods and places them in the broad network of black and brown religious activism that redefined the church's stance on civil rights. If we are to welcome such an approach, then it is imperative that we look anew at the relationship between cultural nationalism and religion. In part this requires complicating the notion that activists simply saw the church—and religion more broadly—as an enemy of radical social change. This approach stresses the relational in Latina/o history, not any singular cultural experience or understanding projected onto a diverse people. These cases highlight the role of churches in community politics and illuminate the varieties of Chicana/o and Puerto Rican cultural nationalisms and internationalisms during the civil rights era. They also offer uncommon possibilities for piecing together Latina/o civil rights narratives that are rooted in the unique politics and movements of multiple metropolitan centers from New York City to Houston to Los Angeles.

In the years that followed the church takeovers and clashes, Latino religious leadership assembled an agenda that moved the church into a closer relationship with civil rights activism. Today the church's political involvement in the immigrant rights movement across the "Nuevo South" and Midwest is a continuation, not a break, from the political tradition of resistance to church hierarchy that was born in the years after World War II. From the Chicano and Puerto Rican movements in the 1960s and 1970s to the Sanctuary movement in the 1980s and now the contemporary immigrant rights movement, the church's involvement has been both cautious and prophetic. What should be clear is how the Chicano and Puerto Rican civil rights movements shaped and (re)formed how the church thought about social justice, resistance, and political involvement. Telling these stories reinforces once again that the power of the Chicano and Puerto Rican civil rights movements resided in neighborhood struggles that were guided and inspired by national and transnational movements for social and political liberation. But they also introduce us to new characters and new themes, both of which promise to reorient our long-held assumptions about the place of religion in these movements. These are important possibilities as we collectively imagine and craft new narratives of those pivotal moments when Chicana/os and Puerto Ricans took over churches and serendipitously transformed the future of Latino churches in the United States.

Notes

1. The Azusa Street revival took place in Los Angeles from 1906 to 1912 and is credited with being an important catalyst for the Pentecostal movement in the Americas and around the globe. See Arlene M. Sánchez Walsh, *Latino Pentecostal Identity: Evangelical Faith, Self, and Society* (New York: Columbia University Press, 2003).

2. I identify the Young Lords in Chicago (and New York) as a "predominantly" Puerto Rican group because they often had Mexican Americans and other Latinos within their membership. See also Lilia Fernández's chapter in this collection.

3. The cases I present in this chapter are part of a larger book project that I am currently working on titled "Apostles of Change: Race, Resistance, and the Latino Religious Fight to End Poverty." A few studies that address church occupations include: Karen Secrist, "*Construyendo Nuestro Pedacito de Patria*: Space and Dis(place)ment in Puerto Rican Chicago" (PhD diss., Duke University, 2009); Elias Ortega-Aponte, "Raised Fist in the Church! Afro-Latino/a Practice among the Young Lords Party: A Humanistic Spirituality Model for Radical Latino/a Religious Ethics" (PhD diss., Princeton Theological Seminary, 2011); Darrel Enck-Wanzer, "Decolonizing Imaginaries: Rethinking 'the

People' in the Young Lords' Church Offensive," *Quarterly Journal of Speech* 98 (2012), 1-23; Mario T. García, *Católicos: Resistance and Affirmation in Chicano Catholic History* (Austin: University of Texas Press, 2010); Brian Behnken, *Fighting Their Own Battles: Mexican Americans, African Americans, and the Struggle for Civil Rights in Texas* (Chapel Hill: University of North Carolina Press, 2011); Lilia Fernández, *Brown in the Windy City: Mexicans and Puerto Ricans in Postwar Chicago* (Chicago: University of Chicago Press, 2012).

4. John T. McGreevy, *Parish Boundaries: The Catholic Encounter with Race in the Twentieth Century Urban North* (Chicago: University of Chicago Press, 1996). For the changes that came with Mexican immigration to the urban North, see Deborah Kanter, "Making Mexican Parishes: Ethnic Succession in Chicago Churches, 1947–1977," *US Catholic Historian* 30, no. 1 (Winter 2012), 35–58. For immigration and religion in the West, see Daniel Ramírez, "Borderlands Praxis: The Immigrant Experience in Latino Pentecostal Churches," *Journal of the American Academy of Religion* (1999), 573–596.

5. Roberto Treviño, *The Church in the Barrio: Mexican American Ethno-Catholicism in Houston* (Chapel Hill: University of North Carolina Press, 2006), 5; see also Alberto Pulido, "Are You an Emissary of Jesus Christ? Justice, the Catholic Church, and the Chicano Movement," *Explorations in Ethnic Studies* 4 (1991): 30; David F. Gomez, *Somos Chicanos: Strangers in Our Own Land* (Boston: Beacon Press, 1973), 156–170.

6. Stephen Lloyd-Moffett, "The Mysticism and Social Action of César Chávez," in *Latino Religions and Civic Activism in the United States*, ed. Gastón Espinosa, Virgilio Elizondo, and Jesse Miranda (New York: Oxford University Press, 2005), 35. The religious historian Gastón Espinosa has argued that "Rodolfo Acuña and others like him have helped shape a generation of Chicano and Latino scholarship on Latino religions and politics." Ibid., 3.

7. Vicki Ruiz, "Dead Ends or Gold Mines? Using Missionary Records in Mexican American Women's History," *Frontiers: A Journal of Women Studies* 22, no. 1 (1991): 51; see also David Gutierrez, "The New Turn in Chicano/Mexicano History: Integrating Religious Belief and Practice," in *Catholics in the American Century: Recasting Narratives of US History*, ed. R. Scott Appleby and Kathleen Sprows Cummings (Ithaca, NY: Cornell University Press, 2012), 112.

8. For more on religion and social change, see García, *Católicos*; Treviño, *The Church in the Barrio*; Richard Martinez, *PADRES: The National Chicano Priest Movement* (Austin: University of Texas Press, 2005); Lara Medina, *Las Hermanas: Chicana/Latina Religious-Political Activism in the US Catholic Church* (Philadelphia: Temple University Press, 2005); Vincent Harding, "Out of the Cauldron of Struggle: Black Religion and the Search for a New America," in *Religion: North American Style*, ed. Patrick H. McNamara (Belmont, CA: Wadsworth, 1984), 256–264; Dwight B. Billings, "Religion as Opposition: A Gramscian Analysis," *American Journal of Sociology* 96, no. 1 (July 1990): 27; Sara M. Evans and Harry C. Boyte, *Free Spaces: The Sources of Democratic Change in America* (New York: Harper & Row, 1986), 183.

9. Gastón Espinosa, "History and Theory in the Study of Mexican American Religions," in *Rethinking Latino(a) Religion and Identity*, ed. Gastón Espinosa and Miguel De La Torre (Cleveland: Pilgrim Press, 2006).

10. Alex Saragoza, "Recent Chicano Historiography: An Interpretive Essay," *Aztlán* 19 (1990): 10–13.

11. Rodolfo Acuña, *Occupied America: The Chicano's Struggle toward Liberation* (San Francisco: Canfield Press, 1972). While Acuña is most often cited when scholars make their point about religion's absence, this critique is really an indictment on much of the Chicana/o historical scholarship produced in the 1970s. I should add that while many of these critiques are on point, they nevertheless fail to offer insights into why religion was left out of most studies, even as many in the Chicana/o and Puerto Rican movements were engaged in questions about the place and role of religion in barrios across the country.

12. For more on this point, see García, *Católicos*, 132. My use of "the church" is meant to be general and representative of both Catholic and Protestant traditions and the buildings where they worship. When Chicana/o and Puerto Rican activists proclaimed that "the church" belongs to the people in takeovers in New York and Houston, they did not mean one particular church but rather all places where Christians gather to worship.

13. George Mariscal, *Brown-Eyed Children of the Sun: Lessons from the Chicano Movement, 1965–1975* (Albuquerque: University of New Mexico Press, 2005), 16. How historians define "ethnic nationalism" remains a heavy debate, but as the historian Jeffrey Ogbar contends, there are fundamental qualities that center on "self-determination, unity . . . people must view themselves as an organic unit, bound together with common experiences, historical myths and culture." Both Ogbar and Mariscal argue that Black and Latino Power Movements practiced complex political forms that went beyond "narrow nationalisms." While Ogbar calls it "polysemic nationalism," Mariscal identifies it as "polycentric nationalism," but both are making similar arguments about the complex narratives of Black and Brown Power in the late 1960s and the need to expand our understandings of cultural nationalism. See Jeffrey Ogbar, "Puerto Rico en mi corazón," *Centro Journal* (Fall 2006): 150; Maylei Blackwell, *¡Chicana Power! Contested Histories of Feminism in the Chicano Movement* (Austin: University of Texas Press, 2011).

14. The work of Ernesto Chávez is important in this regard. Chávez's conceptualization of Chicano nationalism "as a truly American phenomenon that at times encompasses the tenets of American liberalism" is an important framework for understanding the church takeovers. This is a significant point in thinking about the many representations and expressions of Chicana/o and Latina/o politics during the civil rights era. See Ernesto Chávez, *"¡Mi Raza Primero!" Nationalism, Identity, and Insurgency in the Chicano Movement in Los Angeles, 1966–1978* (Berkeley: University of California Press, 2002), 5.

15. Michael O. Emerson and Christian Smith, *Divided by Faith: Evangelical Religion and the Problem of Race in America* (New York: Oxford University Press, 2001). In 2010 Indiana Wesleyan University organized a conference around the book with the theme "Divided by Faith: A Decade Retrospective."

16. See, for example: Sharon Kim, *A Faith of Their Own: Second-Generation Spirituality in Korean American Churches* (New Brunswick, NJ: Rutgers University Press, 2010); J. Russell Hawkins and Phillip Sinitiere, eds., *Christians and the Color Line: Race and Religion after Divided by Faith* (Oxford, UK: Oxford Uni-

versity Press, 2013); Edward J. Blum and Paul Harvey, *The Color of Christ: The Son of God and the Saga of Race in America* (Chapel Hill: University of North Carolina Press, 2014); Gerardo Marti, "Affinity, Identity, and Transcendence: The Experience of Religious Racial Integration in Diverse Congregations," *Journal for the Scientific Study of Religion* 48, no. 1 (2009): 53–68; Antony W. Alumkal, "American Evangelicalism in the Post-Civil Rights Era: A Racial Formation Theory Analysis," *Sociology of Religion* 65, no. 3 (Autumn 2004): 195–213.

17. Mario T. García, "Religion and the Chicano Movement," in *Mexican American Religions: Spirituality, Activism, and Culture*, ed. Gastón Espinosa and Mario T. García (Durham, NC: Duke University Press, 2008), 125. In recent years García has been the most important Chicano historian to include religion in his treatment of Chicana/o history.

18. "The Shifting Religious Identity of Latinos in the United States," Pew Research Center, May 7, 2014, http://www.pewforum.org/2014/05/07/the-shifting-religious-identity-of-latinos-in-the-united-states/; Arlene M. Sánchez Walsh, "Nothing New under the (Pew) Sun," May 9, 2014, http://www.patheos.com/blogs/amsanchezwalsh/2014/05/nothing-new-under-the-pew-sun/.

19. Recent scholarship is pointing us in this direction. See, for example, the work of Sánchez Walsh, *Latino Pentecostal Identity*; Treviño, *The Church in the Barrio*; García, *Católicos*; Medina, *Las Hermanas*; Theresa Delgadillo, *Spiritual Mestizaje: Religion, Gender, Race, and Nation in Contemporary Chicana Narrative* (Durham, NC: Duke University Press, 2011); Elaine A. Peña, *Performing Piety: Making Space Sacred with the Virgin of Guadalupe* (Berkeley: University of California Press, 2011); Timothy Matovina, *Latino Catholicism: Transformation in America's Largest Church* (Princeton, NJ: Princeton University Press, 2011); Gastón Espinosa, *Latino Pentecostals in America: Faith and Politics in Action* (Cambridge, MA: Harvard University Press, 2014); Anne Martínez, *Catholic Borderlands: Mapping Catholicism onto American Empire, 1905–1935* (Lincoln: University of Nebraska Press, 2014); Felipe Hinojosa, *Latino Mennonites: Civil Rights, Faith, and Evangelical Culture* (Baltimore, MD: Johns Hopkins University Press, 2014).

20. Jean Baptiste Salpointe, *Soldiers of the Cross: Notes on the Ecclesiastical History of New Mexico, Arizona, and Colorado* (1898); Thomas Harwood, *History of Spanish and English Missions of the New Mexico Methodist Episcopal Church from 1850–1910*, 2 vols. (1908, 1910); Jay S. Stowell, *A Study of Mexicans and Spanish Americans in the United States* (1920); Theodore Abel, *Protestant Home Missions to Catholic Immigrants* (1933); Samuel M. Ortegón, "The Religious Thought and Practice among Mexican Baptists of the United States, 1900–1947" (1950); Juan Lugo, *Pentecostes en Puerto Rico: La Vida de un Misionero* (Puerto Rico Gospel Press, 1951); Carlos Castañeda, *Our Catholic Heritage in Texas, 1519–1950*, 7 vols. (1936–1958). These works stressed an adaptation approach to the study of Mexicans and Puerto Ricans. For a thorough review of all of these works and the trajectory of Mexican American religious history, see Espinosa, "History and Theory in the Study of Mexican American Religions."

21. Gustavo Gutierrez, *A Theology of Liberation: History, Politics, and Salvation* (Maryknoll, NY: Orbis Books, 1973); Gilbert R. Cadena, "Chicano Clergy and the Emergence of Liberation Theology," *Hispanic Journal of Behavioral Sciences* 11 (May 1989): 107–121.

22. Some of the most important early works include Justo González, *The Development of Christianity in Latin America* (Grand Rapids, MI: Eerdmans, 1969); Orlando Costas, *The Church and Its Mission: A Shattering Critique from the Third World* (Wheaton, IL: Tyndale, 1974); Virgilio Elizondo, *Christianity and Culture: An Introduction to Pastoral Theology and Ministry for the Bicultural Community* (Huntington, IN: Our Sunday Visitor, 1975); Ada María Isasi-Díaz, "The People of God on the Move—Chronicle of a History," in *Prophets Denied Honor: An Anthology on the Hispano Church of the United States*, ed. Anthony M. Stevens-Arroyo (Maryknoll, NY: Orbis Books, 1980).

23. Carmen Nanko-Fernandez, "Latin@ Theology and the Preferential Option for Culture," http://americamagazine.org/issue/latin-theology-and-preferential-option-culture. For another good review of the historical development of Latino/a theologies, see Eduardo C. Fernández, *La Cosecha: Harvesting Contemporary United States Hispanic Theology, 1972–1998* (Collegeville, MN: Liturgical Press, 2000); Anthony B. Pinn and Benjamin Valentin, eds., *The Ties that Bind: African American and Hispanic American/Latino/a Theologies in Dialogue* (New York: Continuum, 2001), 38–57.

24. MAYO Resolutions, October 14, 1971, p. 2, box 1, folder 1, Gregorio Salazar Collection, Houston Metropolitan Research Center (HMRC), Houston, Texas.

25. Alberto Carrillo, "The Sociological Failure of the Catholic Church towards the Chicano," *Journal of Mexican American Studies* (Winter 1971): 75–83.

26. Acuña, *Occupied America*.

27. Richard E. Wright, "Mexican-Descent Catholics and the U.S. Church, 1880–1920: Moving beyond Chicano Assumptions," *US Catholic Historian* (Fall 2010): 73–97. Wright makes this claim in footnote 10 (p. 75) when he discusses Jeffrey M. Burns's work. In another essay, Stephen Lloyd-Moffett makes a similar claim about the intentional efforts to silence religious approaches in Chicano history when he asserts that "the liberal intelligentsia and Chicano activists—embarked on a conscious, consistent, and comprehensive agenda to secularize [César] Chávez." Lloyd-Moffett, "The Mysticism and Social Action of César Chávez," in Espinosa et al., *Latino Religions and Civic Activism in the United States*, 35.

28. The writings of Tomás Almaguer and Rodolfo Acuña, both of whom initially employed the "internal colonial" model for understanding the Chicano experience in the 1970s, are rightfully critiqued for their assumptions about the homogeneity of the Mexican-origin population and the limits of cultural nationalism. But these works were only a small part of the larger body of work that, when examined, can shed new light on the ideologies, dynamics, and power struggles of the 1960s and 1970s. The religious writings of Jorge Lara-Braud, Bishop Patricio Flores, César Chávez, and the ubiquitous coverage of religion in Chicano and Puerto Rican activist newspapers suggest that the discourses and politics of cultural nationalism manifested themselves in multiple forms and from a variety of perspectives. See Tomás Almaguer, "Toward the Study of Chicano Colonialism," *Aztlán* 2 (Spring 1971): 7–21; "Historical Notes on Chicano Oppression: The Dialectics of Racial and Class Domination in North America," *Aztlán* 5 (Spring, Fall 1974): 27–56; Acuña, *Occupied America*.

29. In particular, Wright is critical of the works of Leonard Pitt, *The Decline*

of the Californios: A Social History of the Spanish-Speaking Californians, 1846–1890 (Berkeley: University of California Press, 1966); Albert Camarillo, *Chicanos in a Changing Society: From Mexican Pueblos to American Barrios in Santa Barbara and Southern California, 1848–1930* (Cambridge, MA: Harvard University Press, 1979); Richard Griswold del Castillo, *The Los Angeles Barrio, 1850–1890: A Social History* (Berkeley: University of California Press, 1982); Ricardo Romo, *East Los Angeles: History of a Barrio* (Austin: University of Texas Press, 1983).

30. Espinosa et al., *Latino Religions and Civic Activism in the United States*, 3.

31. See, for example, Patrick H. McNamara, "Social Action Priests in the Mexican American Community," *Sociology of Religion* 29 (1968): 177–185; Ralph Guzman, Leo Grebler, and Joan Moore, *The Mexican American People: The Nation's Second Largest Minority* (New York: Free Press, 1970); César Chávez, "The Mexican-American and The Church," *El Grito* 4 (1968): 215–218.

32. Thomas Tweed argues that religions function as "watch and compass" that help in locating "devotees in a religious-nationalist historical narrative and situating them in social space and the natural landscape." From there, religious devotees "map, construct, and inhabit ever-widening spaces: the body, the home, the homeland, and the cosmos." Thomas Tweed, *Crossing and Dwelling: A Theory of Religion* (Cambridge, MA: Harvard University Press, 2008), 81–84. The notion of religion as "orientation" can be seen in Tomás Summers-Sandoval Jr.'s work on the role of Guadalupe Church in San Francisco during the late nineteenth and much of the twentieth century. Summers-Sandoval, *Latinos at the Golden Gate: Creating Community and Identity in San Francisco* (Chapel Hill: University of North Carolina Press, 2013).

33. James Forman, "Black Manifesto," presentation given and adopted by the National Black Economic Development Conference, Detroit, April 26, 1969, box 3, file 71, GC Voluntary Service, Series 11, Gulfport VS Unit, VII.R, Mennonite Library and Archives, North Newton, Kansas; James F. Findlay Jr., *Church People in the Struggle: The National Council of Churches and the Black Freedom Movement, 1950–1970* (New York: Oxford University Press, 1997), 199–225.

34. Findlay, *Church People*, 203.

35. García, *Católicos*, 147–148.

36. Pulido, "Are You an Emissary of Jesus Christ?" 26–29.

37. Ibid., 25.

38. Oscar Zeta Acosta, *The Revolt of the Cockroach People* (New York: Vintage Books, 1989), 11–12.

39. Ibid., 134–138.

40. Ibid., 158.

41. Ibid., 137; Pulido, "Are You an Emissary of Jesus Christ?" 26.

42. Michael T. Kaufman, "Puerto Rican Group Seizes Church in East Harlem in Demand for Space," *New York Times*, December 29, 1969.

43. Enck-Wanzer, "Decolonizing Imaginaries," 2. For many young Latinas/os, the Young Lords Party was one of the most visible examples of the rising ethnic nationalism of the late 1960s.

44. National Council of Churches, "Young Lords Organization: What We Want," 27.

45. Darrel Enck-Wanzer, *The Young Lords: A Reader* (New York: New York University Press, 2010), 206.

46. Enck-Wanzer, "Decolonizing Imaginaries," 7.

47. Michael T. Kaufman, "8 Hurt, 14 Seized in a Church Clash," *New York Times*, December 8, 1969.

48. Kaufman, "Puerto Rican Group Seizes Church." Church members asked that the police not intercede on their behalf and instead filed an injunction to bar the group from further disruptions of its services.

49. Hinojosa, *Latino Mennonites*, 106.

50. "Young Lords Mar Services, Including East Harlem's," *New York Times*, January 12, 1970.

51. Armando Navarro, *Mexican American Youth Organization: Avant-Garde of the Chicano Movement in Texas* (Austin: University of Texas Press, 1995), 118–148, 176–182.

52. Ibid., 75.

53. "MAYO Out, but Fighting," *Houston Post*, n.d., box 1, folder 1, Gregorio Salazar Collection, HMRC.

54. "MAYO Group Seizes Control of Church," box 1, folder 1, *Houston Post*, February 16, 1970, Salazar Collection, HMRC.

55. Jim Bishop, "Church Seeks Court Help in MAYO Case," *Houston Post*, March 1970, box 1, folder 1, Salazar Collection, HMRC.

56. "Church Suit Asks Eviction of MAYO," *Houston Post*, March 5, 1970, box 1, folder 1, Salazar Collection, HMRC.

57. J. D. Arnold, "Chicanos Eye More Church Takeovers," *Houston Chronicle*, March 1970, box 1, folder 1, Salazar Collection, HMRC.

58. I second Carlos Blanton's contention in this collection that studying this formative period gets at the heart of the meaning of Chicana/o and Latina/o history today.

59. Works that cover these important movements include Leo D. Nieto, "The Chicano Movement and the Gospel," in *Hidden Stories*, ed. David Cortes-Fuentes and Daniel R. Rodriguez-Diaz (AETH, 1994); Paul Barton, "*Ya Basta!*" in Espinosa et al., *Latino Religions and Civic Activism in the United States*; Martinez, *PADRES*; Medina, *Las Hermanas*.

60. Hinojosa, *Latino Mennonites*.

61. Ibid.; Espinosa, "Your Daughters Shall Prophesy: A History of Women in Ministry in the Latino Pentecostal Movement in the United States," in *Women and Twentieth-Century Protestantism*, ed. Margaret Lamberts Bendroth and Virginia Lieson Brereton (Urbana: University of Illinois Press, 2001), 37–38.

62. Virginia Sánchez Korrol, "In Search of Unconventional Women: Histories of Puerto Rican Women in Religious Vocations before Midcentury," in *Unequal Sisters: An Inclusive Reader in US Women's History*, 4th ed., ed. Vicki L. Ruiz with Ellen Carol Dubois (New York: Routledge, 2008), 148–49.

63. Letter from M. A. Mottet, Chaplain, to Archbishop Carboni, November 20, 1962, box 3, file 4, John L. Schneiders Topical Files, CIC Administration 1962–1969, Putnam Museum, John L. Schneiders Collection, Davenport, Iowa.

CHAPTER SIX

Chicanas in the US-Mexican Borderlands: Transborder Conversations of Feminism and Anarchism, 1905–1938

SONIA HERNÁNDEZ

A comment made by my dissertation adviser during a conference at Veracruz, Mexico, over a decade ago has resonated with me throughout these past years. "You can get the girl out of the *norteño* but you can't get the *norteño* out of the girl," he chuckled when I insisted I wanted *fajitas de res* during a group dinner after the panel. I did not care for the various local seafood dishes that constituted the typical *Veracruzano* cuisine. I recently thought about this exchange when considering the links, tensions, debates, and missed opportunities concerning Chicana/o and borderlands history.[1] The historical trajectory of Chicanas/os along the US-Mexican borderlands has made me consider the following variation on my adviser's quip: you can get the borderlands out of the Chicana/o but you can't get the Chicana/o out of the borderlands. That is, one can study communities of Chicanas/os in the Midwest and now in the US South, as do my colleagues Perla M. Guerrero and Lilia Fernández in this collection. These are regions distant from the border (although, conceptually speaking, one can obviously study "borders" within these communities/regions). Yet to study the borderlands without the Chicana/o does not make much sense historically, historiographically, or methodologically.

Along the US-Mexican borderlands, communities of Chicanas/os with a long historical trajectory tied to the rich history of indigenous populations are so integral to our understanding of the creation and the everyday process of the geopolitical border that any US-Mexican borderlands study, even if the focus is on a distinct and particular ethnic and/or racial group in a precise time period, must take the historical position of Chicanas/os into account. It is within this context of linkages, tensions, and perhaps missed methodological and historiographical opportunities between Chicana/o and borderlands history that I explore the relationship between Chicanas, *Mexicanas*, and women from Latin America. With a geographical anchor in the greater south Texas region—an *encrucijada*[2] in its own right—I investigate the way in which Chicanas engaged in transborder conversations of feminism, anarchism, and other radical thought with *norteñas* from Tamaulipas and Nuevo León and women from Mexico City and from across Latin America. I chart these conversations over the course of the pivotal early twentieth century and through the immediate post–Mexican Revolution period ending with the Lázaro Cárdenas and Franklin D. Roosevelt administrations. The periodization employed here serves as guideposts for this study and attempts to fill a gap in Chicana historiography that covers the years prior to the Chicana/o Movement.[3]

In a 2004 synthesis of the state of Chicana/o history, particularly as it relates to race, ethnicity, and labor, Vicki Ruiz aptly explained its trajectory. She summarized this historiography as guided by the theme of a "fervent sense of *Mexicanidad*." Historians wrote about "workers as community builders and proletariats politicized by material circumstances and, at times, Mexican revolutionary ideals; this approach served as the common interpretive thread running throughout *Chicana/o* labor studies."[4] Research has also addressed the formation of collective or individual labor identities and consciousness. As Sarah Deutsch pointed out almost two decades ago in a review of Chicana/o labor and gender history that specifically examined the genre of autobiographies in the field, "identity and consciousness are constructed and emerge through contest and struggle."[5] Yet with few exceptions, Chicana/o scholars, while acknowledging certain external and global influences, leave the characters and history that happened beyond Chicana/o communities outside of the narrative despite their crucial role in such communities. While our understanding of the Mexican American experience has been broadened by the scholarship on Chicanas/os or Mexican American claims to citizenship, whiteness, and activism during the 1920s through the 1940s, particularly in organizations such as League of United Latin American Citizens (LULAC) and the American GI Forum, it presents little in the way of women's participation in leftist politics, particularly in Texas, and its transnational implications and connections.[6]

The historian Maylei Blackwell recognizes this gap, and in her recent book, *¡Chicana Power! Contested Histories of Feminism in the Chicano Movement*, she urges scholars to further historicize and examine *Mexicana* and Chicanas' role in radical politics.[7] Similarly, in addressing the labor activism and political strategies of Latina and other female garment factory workers in the Tex-Son Garment Factory in San Antonio, Lori A. Flores recognizes the gap in Chicana labor history in the post-1950s. In her 2009 article, Flores observes, "The existing literature on *Tejanas*' labor activism is almost exclusively limited to discussing the San Antonio pecan shellers' strike of 1938 and the Farah Clothing strike of 1972, with little else in-between."[8]

To this end, I take Blackwell's and Flores's leads and build upon the works of historians who have examined the ideology and the practice of the 1910 Mexican Revolution within a transnational framework, mainly Emma Pérez, Clara Lomas, James Sandos, and Devra Weber.[9] Pérez and Lomas examine the activism of women in the revolution as writers, activists, combatants, and pioneers in promoting what were the modern origins of a Mexican feminist consciousness. In *Rebellion in the Borderlands*, Sandos places the Plan de San Diego in a binational context and traces the anarchist influence on this failed rebellion. He argues that the plan was anarchist in origin, and while scholars have recently debated its beginnings, what concerns my research is the extent to which women from south Texas were attracted to radical ideologies and how they made sense of their struggles by using ideas and creating networks of support with women from different parts of the globe.[10] More recently, Devra Weber examines the role of indigenous labor radicals and their connections to the PLM (Partido Liberal Mexicano) and International Workers of the World (IWW). Her work fills an important gap in the literature in that she focuses on indigenous transborder individuals attracted to the ideology espoused by such organizations.[11]

The *Encrucijada* of Historical Imagination on Chicanas and *Mexicanas*

In a rarely cited anarcho-syndicalist organization's archive in Tampico, I discovered correspondence between women from south Texas, Tampico, Mexico City, and Latin America. Using these and other archival records from various repositories, I further expand on the "role that Mexicanas in the United Sates played in left politics," as Blackwell emphasizes, and place it within the larger global, transborder, transnational context.[12] Such an approach will enrich our understanding of Chicanas and present them as active agents who were not isolated, provincial, or disconnected, but kept abreast of local as well as global developments, particularly as they related to other women.

Thinking about and approaching Chicana/o history in this way also opens the possibility of investigating the field's multiple connections to other disciplines and historiographies. Charting such connections via multinational archival research helps to investigate Chicanas' and *Mexicanas'* transnational reach and repositions women more centrally along the border. It also helps us understand the flow of ideas in the making of borders and transnational networks. With a long historical presence given Chicanas' indigenous and mestizo origins, any study on the greater US-Mexican borderlands must account for their role, particularly vis-à-vis other racial and/or ethnic groups, in creating, adapting, exporting, promoting, and negotiating capital, ideologies, or cultural practices in the process of border-making. Chicanas are indispensable to the study of this bordered space and to the myriad racial and ethnic populations that inhabit it. Not only do Chicanas illuminate our understanding of borders, but studying them reveals their influence, connections, and deeper relevance on a transnational and global scale.[13] As Luis Alvarez argues in this collection, Chicanas/os' identity drew from distinct cultures and political ideologies and simultaneously shaped the identity of those with whom they interacted and mingled.

What do such theoretical notions mean? In my work, the women engaged in these global conversations, and localized struggles and issues framed themselves in language that was understood beyond any specific region or site. Through these conversations via correspondence and radical literature, women from south Texas and beyond shaped one another's identities. While not excluding ethnicity or race, these identities were mostly informed by the particular ideological discourses that they were involved in creating. In this way, the research conducted in archival repositories in Texas, New York, Mexico, and other places reveals that Chicanas were not *gente cerrada* (narrow-minded); they influenced other women just as much as they were influenced. This research and perspective of connecting historiographies and charting transnational conversations is indeed part of "the promise of *Chicana* and *Chicano* history" that thematically and historiographically guides this anthology. It is also part of the new preoccupation with borderlands and transnationalism in the field that Carlos Blanton discusses in his chapter of this book. Such ways of thinking about history break down disciplinary and nationalistic mind-sets for more expansive perspectives that reconsider this bordered space.

Tracing the conversations that took place between *Mexicanas* who lived and worked in the Gulf of Mexico region, Chicanas and *Tejanas* from the Texas-Mexico borderlands (and other parts of the state), and women from across the Atlantic evidenced in various media, particularly literature, correspondence, and propaganda, reveals how a global language of activism and survival was promoted and appropriated by women to make sense of their local conditions. In this way, women took part in "monumental change," helping to advance one of the most radical ideologies of the twentieth century.[14]

The transnational research employed here points to how women used radical ideology—particularly anarcho-syndicalist thought—to advance women's rights at the turn of the twentieth century and up through the 1920s. In the early twentieth century, ethnic Mexican women used anarcho-syndicalist ideas and other radical forms of thought prevalent in PLM branches to advocate for women's rights. This advocacy included higher wages, better working conditions, and the promise of dignity for all families. The transborder conversations that took place among women reveal the way in which localized struggles and local and regional ideas of women's rights, citizenship, and community were framed in a global context. Chicanas or *Tejanas* appropriated language and strategies used by their female counterparts from across geopolitical borders and international lines to address a variety of issues in their communities.[15]

A decline in the global anarchist movement came in 1920, despite women's central role in advocating and spreading such radical thought.[16] By the late 1920s and into the 1930s, the transborder conversations had become increasingly marked by a gendered rhetoric whereby women were promoted as partners, supporters, and *compañeras*, but not as individuals capable of independent action. It was a kind of modern domestic language to define the new postrevolutionary modern Mexican woman from both sides of the border. Gender inequity remained, but was framed in a new modern context. As the historian Nichole Sanders has argued, for middle-class, professional women, their new role in society became one tied to reforms that eventually led to the establishment of a modern nation-state. Furthermore, new state welfare policies, while promoting science and "modern" lifestyle methods that encouraged good hygiene, "were not designed to enable women to live or work on their own," and thus "state paternalism was strengthened."[17] The "modernization" of the state also involved the co-optation of more radical labor groups. Radical labor-based groups became marginalized, and by the mid-1930s labor-based organizations, including those with large numbers of women, became co-opted by the state during the Cárdenas period to promote the idea of a united Mexican family. This idea extended to ethnic Mexican women across the border as well, and examining it within the context of changing Mexican gender politics provides a more nuanced understanding of shifting gender ideologies and practices along the border. In this way, examining the intersections and links of various historiographies from the perspective of an *encrucijada* also illuminates how gender could operate sometimes in different ways and other times in similar ways.[18]

Students of women's history have examined the various ways in which women addressed issues affecting their families, work, and general socioeconomic and political conditions, and have also studied the origins or development of a feminist agenda. Early organizing efforts were based on social issues and ran along ethnic or class lines, as well as by gender and/or trade. Activism by ethnic Mexican women along the US-Mexican borderlands at the turn of the twentieth century consisted mostly of mutual-aid groups and labor-based organizations with female auxiliaries. Women addressed issues individually or collectively, and did not function in isolation.[19] That is, their gendered, racial and ethnic, and class-based forms of activism were informed by their relationship to other women from different locales and their interactions with men. As Deutsch reminds us, "women's labor organizations grew out of a particular framework of a family economy and a sexual division of labor."[20]

What was always present in discussions of labor and women's work was the question of their role in society or what was referred to as "the Woman Question." Nineteenth-century ideas of domesticity and femininity guided much of the discussion about women's place in Mexican society, particularly in labor matters. Such ideologies about the proper role of women and men reflected deeply entrenched social values.[21] In 1912, for example, one Mexican writer explained women's "natural" school was in fact the "family" and that the best "teacher was the mother."[22] As the Mexican Revolution unfolded, the general sentiment regarding women's place in society was that of domesticity, including the promotion of home economics in schools in Mexico, the United States, and Latin America.[23] Knowing the home and caring for the home and the family "elevate[d] the woman socially and ennoble[d] her very function . . . and ultimately ma[de] her a key factor in economic development," the editorial continued.[24] While historians have demonstrated how even in the most radical and egalitarian of movements, entrenched gender ideologies of expected behavior have informed women's position, on a global scale such movements provided a space for women to voice concerns.

Furthermore, the topic of feminist thought or the development of a feminist agenda and the use of the term itself (or not) has been a contentious issue among scholars of women's history in all fields of study. Historians have debated the meaning of feminism, its origins, and its successes and limitations.[25] I am concerned less about whether Chicanas or *Mexicanas* embraced the term "feminism" than about how women used the language of radical thought such as anarchism and anarcho-syndicalism to advance ideas that are commonly thought to be part of a feminist agenda. Of further significance is how ideas crossed borders and how women adapted, modified, and embraced such ideas to make sense of their own conditions.

The relational aspect of such sharing of struggles and collaborations can be understood as a "remapping" or rethinking of how we have approached the study of populations in this country by "border thinking," as borderlands literary scholar José Saldívar notes. The region between Texas and Mexico and its links to the Gulf of Mexico ports, as well as to the Atlantic world more broadly, can be approached and examined as "sites of thinking from dichotomous concepts rather than ordering the world in dichotomies."[26] The point here is to chart connections while acknowledging differences and disjunctions within this conceptual framework, neither neglecting the role of the nation-state nor assigning it privilege as the sole history-making entity.[27] In such trans-border conversations, women also underscored their position as workers or as being interested and concerned about their sons, brothers, or husbands' role as workers. Their ties through gender, race, and ethnicity cut across such conversations of solidarity.[28] These conversations were in great part facilitated by the collective, more egalitarian idea of socialist and anarchist thought. If seen from an *encrucijada* lens, these otherwise disconnected women cross one another in multiple ways, not only bringing history and historiography together but also revealing how they produced knowledge about one another while advancing their particular localized agendas.

Transnational Radicalism

Socialism and anarchism made headway in North America during the nineteenth century. They spread through the formation of reading clubs, secret societies, and mutual-aid groups that sought to change their local communities by applying such ideologies. Thinkers such as France's Pierre-Joseph Proudhon and Russia's Mikhail Bakunin disseminated anarchist thought (in its varied forms). While there are variations in the way anarchism has been defined and continues to be defined, Emma Goldman's 1910 essay "Anarchism: What It Really Stands For" captured the essence of the particular kinds of gendered anarchist thought in the correspondence I examine here between Latinas throughout the Americas. The Russian-born Goldman argued, "[A]narchism was the philosophy of a new social order based on liberty unrestricted by man-made law, the theory that all forms of government rest on violence, and are therefore wrong and harmful, as well as unnecessary."[29] Goldman attracted not only women sympathetic to anarchism but also men and women drawn to socialism and those interested in building alliances or organizations based on class and labor solidarity, such as Ricardo Flores Magón, the well-known anarcho-syndicalist from Mexico.[30] Certainly divergent strands of anarchism and socialist thought circulated and in many cases aligned nicely with varieties of Communist thought (in the Marxist tradition). Most of the conversations that took place between women via letters, newspapers, and pamphlets had an anarcho-syndicalist inclination. As the historians John Mason Hart and Ward Albro have documented, anarcho-syndicalism fused collectivist ideas of worker autonomy with ideas of self-governance.[31] It is also important to note that there were few women (and men) who self-identified as anarchists or socialists, but many were certainly labeled as such, as their behavior or rhetoric was perceived to be in line with radical ideology.

In the late 1870s, Bakunin wrote to advocate the abolition of hereditary property, redistribution of land, and equality for women. Mexican intellectuals and foreigners living in Mexico during the post–French Intervention such as the philosopher Plotino Rhodakanaty advocated similar ideals. Rhodakanaty helped to establish *La Social* in Mexico emphasizing "liberty, equality, and fraternity" through a pan-nationalist movement. Rhodakanaty also espoused women's rights. In fact, he was among the most progressive of his European anarchist contemporaries when it came to women's equality. He recruited women to serve in his organization and some, including Soledad Sosa, later served as delegates to the Mexican National Labor Congress.[32] Such anarchist thought came to be an attractive ideology for women, particularly women workers, who found its language useful in articulating their global subordinate position.

Besides Goldman, the Michigan-born French-American Voltairine de Cleyre was among the early anarcho-feminists and "freethought" writers. She condemned the institution of marriage, the nation-state, and the overwhelming control held by religion over women's bodies and lives. By the mid- to late nineteenth century, French anarchist Louise Michel had also articulated a feminist agenda couched in the language of anarchism. Her "Why I am an anarchist," written in 1895, was reprinted in the port of Tampico (Tamaulipas) newspaper *Sagitario* in 1926. In the manifesto, Michel argued that anarchism was the ideology "closest to freedom."[33] Such women's writings on the topic of anarchism and women's autonomy and general rights written by prominent female writers, as well as by lesser-known women, formed a critical part of a knowledge base that circulated among radical women and men.

Throughout the 1910 Mexican Revolution and in the immediate postrevolutionary years, Goldman remained in communication with Ricardo Flores Magón. Ricardo, Enrique, and Jesús, better known as the Flores Magón brothers, represented what historians have called the "precursor phase" of the revolution and were among the most radical of thinkers and political and social activists of the late nineteenth/ early twentieth century. Yet as more recent interpretations of Ricardo Flores Magón reveal, his actions were in fact revolutionary and not prerevolutionary.[34] Ricardo died in 1922 but left a legacy of social reform grounded on ideas of worker autonomy. *Mexicanas* and Chicanas found the writings of the Flores Magón brothers appealing, discovering in the PLM a space in which they could express their localized agendas and act upon them. What exactly were these localized agendas, what were the issues that women were concerned with, and why were the politics and language of anarchism and socialism appealing to them? If, as the political philosopher Martha Ackelsberg noted in her book on the Mujeres Libres of 1930s Spain, "domination in all its forms—whether exercised by governments, religious institutions, or through economic relations—is for anarchists the source of all social evil," then anarchism went beyond a Marxist Socialist perspective in that it "develop[ed] an independent critique of the state, of hierarchy, and of authority relations in general."[35] It extended beyond "the division of labor in the economy," Ackelsberg added. Furthermore, she noted that anarchist language appealed to women because it acknowledged that domination and marginalization also involved factors besides those of an economic nature.[36]

Unquestionably, one of the major turning points in the twentieth century was the 1910 Mexican Revolution. The first of a series of major revolutions, the Mexican Revolution was driven in great part—at least early on—by anarcho-syndicalist ideology. As early as the 1880s in mining centers across the Mexican northern borderlands mainly in Chihuahua, Coahuila, Nuevo León, and Tamaulipas, radical literature circulated among miners who felt alienated by privileges afforded to foreign interests.[37] Residents and transients alike who knew the borderland terrain and had contacts or relatives on the south bank of the *Río Grande* plotted a series of revolts from the north bank of the river. Women would come to support revolutionary efforts on both sides of the international line.[38]

In the midst of the revolution in 1913, just a year before the radical newsletter of the Flores Magón brothers, *Regeneración*, was suspended, Luisa Guajardo Soto spoke to a congregation of workers from Buda, Rosebud, and Waco to commemorate the founding of a PLM branch in Gurley, Texas. Teodoro Velásquez read PLM manifestos aloud while Soto detailed "the rights of women." Luisa's sister, Gumersinda Miranda Soto, described as "an intelligent woman" in the pages of *Regeneración*, explained to the crowd—predominantly agricultural and railroad workers—that women's fate would remain uncertain if "the regime [referring to Díaz sympathizers] would remain in power and continue to oppress all humanity." The young sisters from the Miranda Soto family of Lorena, Texas, a small community several miles from Waco, joined the speakers who were scheduled to close the meeting. A newly written "global" manifesto produced by the Grupo Regeneración Humana from Havana, Cuba, was the focal point for the young sisters and a young boy. As the manifesto was read, the sisters sang revolutionary songs while the young Mexican boy recited a poem.[39]

That the young women referenced a manifesto by a Cuban organization sympathetic to the ideals of the PLM suggests that these groups were bound by similar ideals that transcended international borders. Mexico, mainly through its ports such as Tampico, served as a conduit between ethnic Mexicans and residents from Cuba, the Caribbean, and Latin America in general. In 1918, eight years into the revolution, American and other foreign observers visiting Mexico were writing about the "dangers of socialism" and how it "intruded itself upon the horizon of the Mexican peon . . . preached . . . by peripatetic agitators."[40]

Ports were sites of cultural exchange, and Tampico was home to women and men of all backgrounds lured by economic opportunities resulting from the lucrative oil industry. The port city sustained cultural ties with other ports along the Gulf of Mexico, including Brownsville, New Orleans, and Havana. Tampico became a hot spot for labor activism in Mexico.[41] Not surprisingly, 25 percent of Mexico's 1.5 million industrial workers had some affiliation with either a mutual-aid society or cooperatives, or were members of the radical pro-worker Casa del Obrero Mundial (COM), which had a significant base in Tampico.[42] Such ports of entry, however, were closely supervised to safeguard them from suspected radicals, regardless of gender.

Women's *actual* physical mobility could be limited, especially if considered of "ill-repute," for those who "had been corrupted by the ideas of socialism, anarchism." Such women—like their male counterparts—could be barred from entering Mexican ports or crossing into the United States, or at least they had a difficult time doing so.[43] For example, two women aboard the steamship *Monterrey* from the ports of New York and Havana attempted to enter Tampico in 1920. Immigration authorities immediately asked for proper documentation given their port of origin and demanded that they prove their "honest and moral" character. While there was no indication of what kind of documentation women could and should provide, as these measures were used arbitrarily, such proof was nonetheless required for legal admission. Reports circulated in major ports and urban centers urged immigration officers and consuls to keep a close eye on individuals suspected of radical behavior. Officials from the industrial capital of Monterrey reported that "[while] the state of women is like that all over the country . . . in Monterrey they are not protected [from such ideology] as well as in other cities."[44] Immigration officers from Tampico submitted a detailed report on how the port had for some time witnessed a "flood" of *"gente de mal vivir."*[45] Tampico was a bustling cosmopolitan port with "a good many foreigners from all parts of the world," according to US intelligence reports. There were Chinese, Belgians, Italians, Spanish, Syrians, Arabs, Greeks, Hollanders, Americans, British, and of course Mexicans. The report added that residents "have little respect for any government and are good material from which revolutionary leaders can recruit a force of bandit outlaws."[46] Yet according to the same report, these radicals were also a "lazy-set of people who work when they have to and loaf as much as they can."[47]

Mexican immigration officers seemed to echo US officials' reports on Mexicans. Officers of the US Military Intelligence Division compared Mexican "peons from the border" to "the type found in Texas and are vastly inferior as laborers and citizens." With regard to border Mexicans, the officers wrote that "[they] are experienced in running contraband, a good shot as Mexicans go, and altogether considers himself [*sic*] superior to the people farther south."[48] US officials of the Military Intelligence Division grew concerned about such political currents in Monterrey, given its relatively close proximity to the Texas border. A report detailed the way in which "labor is organized in nearly every trade . . . tending to increase the individual's ideas of his personal importance." It concluded, "[T]he Socialistic-Bolshevik movement is at present exerting a strong influence on social conditions."[49]

Women exhibiting "radical behavior," influenced by *"gente de mal vivir"* such as Caritina M. Piña, would come to be categorized as part of the women of "ill-repute." Piña was comparable to the likes of the *Tejana* and self-proclaimed Communist and former LULACer Emma Tenayuca of San Antonio.[50] A Tamaulipas native, Piña became involved in Esteban Méndez Guerra's anarcho-syndicalist group. Méndez had fought for the Villistas in northern Mexico, and after the revolution came to a close he founded a pro-labor, anarcho-syndicalist organization. Compared to suffragists in Mexico or those involved with reforming education who practiced what the historian Gabriela González has called the "politics of benevolence," Piña was considered much more radical. Piña was a member of the small circle of Méndez's group based in Tampico and contributed to *Sagitario*, an anarcho-syndicalist newspaper. She quickly became involved in numerous pro-worker causes while remaining in communication with women from south Texas as well as those from different parts of the globe.[51]

Piña served as the Secretaria de Corespondencia (in charge of correspondence and communication with other organizations) for the Comité Internacional Pro-Presos Sociales, a committee that raised funds to release imprisoned workers from across the world. Most of the organizations in which Piña served in multiple capacities reflected an inclusive membership where women could be found in the upper ranks.[52] Piña's activism included raising monies and securing general support for detainees who were involved in labor activism, regardless of the political ideology to which they subscribed (Socialist, anarchist, Communist, syndicalist, etc.). She kept in touch with individuals such as the Spanish anarchist Jesús Louzara de Andres (through the pseudonym R. Lone of Steubenville, Ohio) during PLM organizer Librado Rivera's imprisonment.[53] Piña received Lone's letter of support for Rivera when he was apprehended in 1927 and asked him if he could contribute an essay to the radical and pro-labor newspaper *La Encuesta*. Lone and others had petitioned Washington, DC, for Rivera's release and kept Piña in the loop.[54] She and her colleagues' involvement extended beyond Ohio; she and other women petitioned on behalf of workers in Baja California, Nuevo León, Texas, San Luis Potosí, New York, Buenos Aires, and Barcelona.[55]

Piña and her colleagues kept themselves up-to-date with the latest happenings in labor issues, conflicts, strikes, and women's organizations and general women's issues. Her office received *Alma Obrera*, a pro-labor newspaper from the north-central Mexican state of Zacatecas, and Piña then forwarded such materials to women in south Texas and beyond. *Alma Obrera* frequently included editorials and stories that extended beyond women's suffrage—which by the late 1920s had made headway as one of several main issues concerning women. *Alma Obrera* printed across its pages, "*No es libre la mujer que depende económicamente de otro individuo*/A Woman who depends economically on another is not free."[56]

Throughout the 1920s and 1930s, south Texas workers maintained close ties with those across the border. As was the case during the decade of the revolution, the state of Texas and the greater south Texas area in particular counted over one hundred PLM branches and several other pro-labor organizations. For residents such as Luz Mendoza, maintaining open communication with fellow *camaradas* from across borders helped them to keep abreast of labor developments. These strong networks of support helped to spread not only ideas but also news coverage on events that shaped the labor movement, such as the Sacco and Vanzetti case. In her communications to Mendoza, Piña frequently asked for "any updates" as well as for additional materials.[57]

Throughout the 1920s, the Harlingen resident Luz Mendoza received radical literature from Piña and her colleagues featured in *Sagitario*. Mendoza and Piña articulated their separate localized struggles and socio-economic conditions in global terms and argued that it was absolutely "necessary for workers around the globe to be familiar with such abuses suffered by the most sincere of supporters."[58] While it is difficult to produce hard numbers for those directly involved in pro-anarchist organizations in the greater south Texas region and in other parts of the state, individuals such as Mendoza were knowledgeable about the world beyond south Texas.[59]

Piña's updates and aid reached south Texas; in the meantime, labor news and related information also was sent to her supporters from the border states of Baja California and Coahuila. She also kept workers from that state informed about the Sacco and Vanzetti case. In the late 1920s, over two hundred agricultural workers associated with the

Unión Agraria "Miguel Hidalgo" petitioned the governor of Massachusetts and none other than the president of the United States, Herbert
Hoover, with support from Piña.[60]

Post-Radical Turn

The politics behind determining women's role in society or the so-called
Woman Question, preoccupied both men and women involved in labor
activism. The "appropriate" role of women remained a contentious issue
up through the late nineteenth century and the long twentieth century.
While women's activism shaped the larger conversation about labor and
labor rights, their presence and direct involvement in the revolution did
not overturn the system of gender inequality. Women's role in remuner-
ated labor and society in general was still circumscribed by an ideology
of domesticity and femininity—which lingered from Gilded Age/*Porfi-
riato* understandings of society. However, the postrevolutionary period
ushered in a new era of Mexican nationalism for Chicanas and *Mexicanas* on both sides of the border, promoted by the state and its representatives. In this way, gender politics in Mexico were guided by the
idea of Mexican unity and nationalism where the nation and its citizens
were defined as the great Mexican family. Mexicans abroad also were included.[61] The idea of the new Mexican woman was articulated in *compa-
ñerismo* language as "*compañera* and not a slave." The new *Mexicana* was
described as valuable to the nation because she was the key to reproduc-
ing community and the mother of hard-working *Mexicanos* and *Mexicanas* on both sides of the US-Mexican borderlands.[62] Women were cast in
this new light across Mexico and Latin America.

   The rhetoric of "*cooperación de los sexos*" spread throughout the Mexican northern borderlands during the late 1920s and 1930s and resembled
the discourse on the modern woman in places such as Argentina. Chicanas as well as *Mexicanas* from Tampico and Monterrey were aware of the
situation of Argentinean women, and they learned about "women's conditions" in that country and the way in which women were viewed. Florinda Mondini, from Tindal, near the Argentinean coast, wrote that "as
a mother, sister, and *compañera*, I extend to you my emaciated but honest hand, so together we can fight for our sisters who live in an unconscious state." Mondini continued, "[W]e need to make them haughty
women."[63] She concluded by stating, "[T]he man fights an earnest battle
yet he cannot advance as he wishes to, he needs the woman next to him

so that he can reach a total emancipation. Oh Woman! Let's go to them! I send you a fraternal hug and let us fight for humanity's redemption!"[64]

Working-class *Mexicana* conditions resembled those in Argentina. In Buenos Aires, for example, protests over the exploitation of women and girls occurred in 1903 as the first factories there opened: "In some places one's attention is grabbed easily when one sees *pequeñas obreritas*; in one factory focused on the production of bags, girls of six to seven years of age are employed . . . working up to fourteen hours a day." By the end of 1903 there were 11,723 women and 10,922 children under sixteen years of age, and 1,197 children younger than fourteen years of age, working in the city's factories.[65] Women's exposure to substandard factory conditions, unequal wages, and other injustices was a familiar story for Mexicans. And Mondini's message reprinted in the newspaper *Sagitario* reached Piña and women of south Texas.

The Great Depression, the gradual state consolidation of labor unions in Mexico under the huge Confederación de Trabajadores de México (CTM), and the challenges and risks involved in labor organizing in conservative Texas ushered in a new era of activism for both women and men. The Unión de Mujeres Americanas (UMA), composed of a majority of the ethnic Mexican women in the small northeastern Texas town of New York in present-day Henderson County, reflected a shift in the activist approach of women. The internationally recognized UMA was founded by Margarita Robles de Mendoza in 1933.[66] Robles de Mendoza came to symbolize a type of transnational cultural-labor broker, and by the late 1930s she led a suffragist movement in Mexico City. UMA was a transnational organization headquartered in New York City. UMA branches became widespread, existing even in remote places. Yet tiny as it may have been, the UMA in New York, Texas, was quite active and spread its message across borders, most likely with the help of UMA members elsewhere. One editorial that highlighted UMA's efforts commented on how the organization had been able to garner the support of "a great number of Hispanic nations" and were now advocating "women's rights." Neither anarchist nor Communist in its ideological orientation, UMA promoted a discourse that sounded quite similar to that of other anarcho-syndicalist organizations and radical newspapers such as *Sagitario*: "We need to promote and safeguard the friendship of women from all of the Americas. . . . we need to reform the laws . . . those that still maintain women's inequality . . . and maintain solidarity ties with other organizations . . . those that identify with the ideals of suffrage, regardless of creed, color, race, or nationality."[67]

What UMA proposed to do was quite radical in that it posited that all of the Americas could be united "via its ladies (*damas*)." UMA placed Pura Roma Silva as its New York, Texas, branch president. New York (Texas) members included Estrella de Díaz, Hermelinda de Briones, Clotilde B. Jaeger, and Ana Esther Trujillo who were married, while Blanca Calvez, Carolina Rosas, Ofelia Morales, Amafia [*sic*] Kiug, and Evangelina Anlay were single. Citing their involvement in the "modern feminist movement," the women claimed to "aid their men in the persistent progressive agenda of all America."[68] While New York (Texas) seemed so distant from Tampico and even from south Texas, its residents appeared to promote a discourse similar to ones that had circulated in previous decades.

UMA called for cooperation between women from the United States and Latin America. Carolina Munguía, an educator and refugee of the Mexican Revolution from Puebla, believed in the advancement of women via a similar *cooperación de los sexos* strategy and felt that those who were more privileged had a responsibility to those who lacked resources. Munguía moved with her family from Puebla to San Antonio, Texas, in 1926. A contemporary of Emma Tenayuca, Munguía became the first "Mexican" woman on radio. In 1937 Munguía founded the Círculo Social Femenino de México, whose primary goal was to aid Mexican-origin women from the area and whose motto was "all for the *patria* and *hogar* (home)." Members from the Círculo as well as Munguía not only maintained ties with other women from Mexico but also played a key role in carrying ideas across the border. Munguía "propagaría los nobles ideales del club/promoted the organization's noble ideals" in 1938 when she took her message to Linares, Nuevo León, approximately fifty miles south of the capital of Monterrey.[69] Yet the "organizations comprised of our sisters" preached a benevolent stance, stating, "our sisters *de raza* who are less fortunate than us . . . live in a state of economic, intellectual and moral decline."[70] It appeared that while Munguía and her colleagues from the Círculo Social and their *Mexicana* counterparts were united by the fact that "they were *raza* sisters," social class cut sharply and created differences. Similar class divisions were evident across the border. Already by the late 1930s, the kind of discourse promoted by Munguía and her colleagues that dealt with the general "Woman Question" was articulated in a more socially conservative context.

While the Unión de Mujeres Americanas and Munguía were no anarchists, their discourse was in line with the shift to an agenda that by the 1930s was becoming more conservative even among radical outlets such as *Sagitario*. In her research on Chilean anarchist organizations and women's involvement, the historian Elizabeth Quay Hutchison noted the change in discourse regarding women's position in revolutionary politics among Chilean anarchists. Certainly by the 1920s, Chilean anarchists, much like those from across the globe, had moved away from "their former enthusiasm for women's participation in revolutionary politics" to take a "more conservative" position regarding sexual politics, which affected women's participation in such organizations and was reflected in the writings of female and male anarchists. As Hutchison rightly points out, "international anarchism" took on a more conservative approach on the "woman question."[71] That was certainly the case for the organizations that had sustained links across the Texas-Mexican borderlands. Yet for this particular borderlands, state-led efforts to create a new postrevolutionary government included women as part of the greater Mexican family. Women continued to debate issues and connect with one another over reform and the betterment of their lives and the lives of others. As indicated in Felipe Hinojosa's chapter in this collection, the absence of radicalism is not an absence of activism.

In the early twentieth century, women from south Texas, Tampico, and other parts of Mexico and Latin America sustained conversations based on ideas of worker independence and women's rights that continued during the Mexican Revolution and its aftermath. Such conversations, couched in a global, anarcho-syndicalist framework, gave women a much-needed space in which to share their local struggles and make sense of them. While women in pro-anarchist organizations or who were sympathetic to the ideology were described in terms of their individuality, their economic power, and their role as revolutionaries, by the late 1920s and well into the 1930s a combination of state-led efforts to create a sense of nationalism guided by the idea of *cooperación de los sexos* defined *Mexicanas* as new and improved or modernized women, and by extension defined ethnic Mexican women across the border in a similar way. More so than the rise of labor movements that were sympathetic to communism and more mainstream labor unions, the consolidation of labor unions under the state-led CTM by 1938 led to the marginalization of women's issues.

For *Tejanas* and Chicanas, the 1930s, despite some gains in labor and the persistence of labor leaders such as Emma Tenayuca and others, was a decade of massive deportations and continued segregation. Already by the late 1920s, "hordes of Mexicans" were encouraged to cross "back" into Mexico," as several south Texas newspapers put it. Ethnic Mexicans from Brownsville, Hidalgo, and a long list of other south Texas cities witnessed the deportation or repatriation of "thousands of . . . families."[72] For a segment of the *Tejana* population, organizations such as LULAC provided some space, though a far less radical one, in which to continue voicing their concerns.[73]

A generation later in the late 1960s and 1970s, Chicanas revisited *magonista* literature to reenergize their base; their *compañeras* on the opposite side did the same. Late nineteenth-century anarchist writings and revolutionary-era proclamations were reprinted. As the Los Angeles–based Prensa Sembradora put it in a 1974 foreword to a translation of Flores Magón's "¡A la Mujer!" to commemorate International Women's Day, "if we are to examine seriously and critically our historic revolutionary tradition, it is obligatory that we deal with Magón's essay. . . . There is a rekindled revolutionary attitude among Chicanas today which will not be appeased by tokenism and patronage."[74] Such "rekindled revolutionary attitude" formed the basis of a new era of political and socioeconomic activism in which Chicanas reasserted their role as leaders of and participants in revolutionary politics to address decades of gender, political, social, and economic inequities. During the civil rights movement, Chicanas renewed ties with women from across borders and international lines.

In this greater transnational network of women who spoke each other's language stood Chicanas along the border. They formed a critical component of the production and circulation of knowledge in the form of radical ideas. Transnational approaches, as Kelly Lytle Hernández noted in a recent article on transnationalizing borderland history, can recover "topics that have been pushed to the periphery of US national history but sit loudly in Mexican, Canadian, and Caribbean archives." Examining Chicana history within the context of borderlands history and through a transnational archival and methodological approach provides a more nuanced interpretation of Chicanas' role in sustaining and promoting radical thought. Chicanas helped to sustain and were a crucial component of global networks.[75] As indicated in Carlos Blanton's chapter in this collection, breaking down not just physical borders, but borders of the mind, helps to identify the intricate links between Chicana and borderlands history. This opens up a wider historical imagination. Examining global history through the prism of Chicana/o or Latina/o history is not just possible, but a revelation. The repositioning of Chicanas as central historical actors in the borderlands, or refusing to "get the *Chicana* out of the borderlands," re-presents Chicanas and *Mexicanas* on both sides of the border as key players in the global circulation of ideas and the global women's movement, and places their activism and experiences at the heart of global processes. This *is* part of the "promise" of Chicana/o history.

Notes

I would like to thank Carlos Blanton, Felipe Hinojosa, Lisa Ramos, and audience members of the *Breaking Free, Breaking Down: The New Chicana/o History in the Twenty-First Century* symposium (Texas A&M University, Fall 2013) for their insightful comments. Parts of this research were also presented at the Illustrating Anarchy and Revolution: Mexican Legacies of Global Change Conference (Center for Mexican American Studies, University of Texas at Austin, Spring 2014), and I thank the audience members for their questions and comments. Special thanks to Carlos Blanton for his editorial precision; thanks also to the anonymous reviewers.

1. While I acknowledge the time-specificity when using "Chicana/o" as a politicized term during the height of the civil rights movement, in this chapter I use it to identify people of Mexican/mestizo origin (regardless of citizenship) who do or did reside in the United States regardless of periodization. I use Mexican American, ethnic Mexican, and Chicana/o interchangeably. Antonia Castañeda provides an excellent discussion on the need to extend beyond national categories and to expand our understanding of regional history. While not focusing exclusively on why historians can and should employ the term "Chicana" or "Chicana/o history" in examining the pre-1848 period, she makes a case for it, revealing the limits of the nation/region/traditional historiography. See Antonia Castañeda, "'Que se Pudieran Defender (So You Could Defend Yourselves)': Chicanas, Regional History, and National Discourses," *Frontiers: A Journal of Women Studies* 22, no. 3 (2001): 116–142, in particular 118–119.

2. As the Chicana scholar and theorist Gloria Anzaldúa puts it, the US-Mexican border is a "crossroads" in its own right, its own "*encrucijada*." Gloria Anzaldúa, *Borderlands/La Frontera: The New Mestiza* (San Francisco: Aunt Lute Books, 1987).

3. This chapter draws from a larger book project, *Conversations across Borders: Chicanas, Mexicanas, Españolas y 'las de Argentina' in Anarchist-Feminist Organizations, 1900–1960*. In this project I examine the connections between anarchism, feminism, and socialism (in its varied forms) in women's transnational and global networks of support, particularly those groups or individuals involved in demanding labor rights. I examine women from Texas, Tampico, Monterrey, Mexico City, New York, and their connections to women in similar labor organizations in Buenos Aires and Barcelona. For this chapter I only include a discussion of Chicanas and *Mexicanas*, and some information on women from Latin America. See also the numerous newspaper clippings and correspondence between Mendez's organization and other pro-labor, Socialist, an-

archist, and Communist groups from Europe, Latin America, and the United States, in Archivo Histórico de Esteban Mendez, hereafter cited as AHEM, IIH-UAT.

4. Vicki Ruiz, "Morena/o, blanca/o y café con leche: Racial Constructions in Chicana/o Historiography," *Mexican Studies/Estudios Mexicanos* 20, no. 2 (Summer 2004): 343–360, quotation on p. 348.

5. Sarah Deutsch, "Gender, Labor History, and Chicano/a Ethnic Identity," *Frontiers: A Journal of Women Studies* 14 (1994): 2.

6. There are some exceptions. See Cynthia Orozco, *No Mexicans, Women, or Dogs Allowed: The Rise of the Mexican American Civil Rights Movement* (Austin: University of Texas at Austin Press, 2009). On labor and activism, see Emilio Zamora, *The World of the Mexican Worker in Texas* (College Station: Texas A&M University Press, 1993), and *Claiming Rights and Righting Wrongs in Texas: Mexican Workers and Job Politics during World War II* (College Station: Texas A&M University Press, 2009). See also Benjamin Johnson, "The Cosmic Race in Texas: Racial Fusion, White Supremacy, and Civil Rights Politics," *Journal of American History* 98, no. 2 (September 2011): 404–419.

7. Maylei Blackwell, *¡Chicana Power! Contested Histories of Feminism in the Chicano Movement* (Austin: University of Texas Press, 2011), 49.

8. Lori A. Flores, "An Unladylike Strike Fashionably Clothed: Mexicana and Anglo Women Garment Workers against Tex-Son, 1959–1963," *Pacific Historical Review* 78, no. 3 (August 2009): 370.

9. For an interdisciplinary and global perspective on the meaning of transnationalism, see Hastings Donnan and Thomas M. Wilson, *Borders: Frontiers of Identity, Nation, and State* (Oxford, UK: Berg, 2001); Devra Weber, "Keeping Community, Challenging Boundaries: Indigenous Migrants, Internationalist Workers, and Mexican Revolutionaries, 1900–1920," in *Mexico and Mexicans in the Making of the United States*, ed. John Tutino (Austin: University of Texas Press, 2012).

10. James Sandos, *Rebellion in the Borderlands: Anarchism and the Plan of San Diego, 1904–1923* (Norman: University of Oklahoma Press, 1992).

11. Emma Pérez, *The Decolonial Imaginary: Writing Chicanas into History* (Bloomington: Indiana University Press, 1999); Ruiz, "Morena/o"; Blackwell, *¡Chicana Power!* Sandos dedicated the entirety of his monograph to the Plan de San Diego, breaking new ground in that little research had been done on this radical manifesto by either American or Mexican historians. While he includes a discussion of women involved in PLM activities, his focus was not entirely on women or the role of gender ideologies in the creation of the PSD and anarchist sympathies in south Texas; see *Rebellion in the Borderlands*, especially chap. 4. See also Shirlene Soto, *Emergence of the Modern Mexican Woman: Her Participation in Revolution and Struggle for Equality, 1910–1940* (Denver: Arden Press, 1990). For anarchism and feminism as well as general issues of gender and sexuality, see Dora Barrancos, *Anarquismo, educación y costumbres en la Argentina de principios de siglo* (Buenos Aires: Ed. Contrapunto, 1990); Maxine Mlyneux, "'No God, No Boss, No Husband': Anarchist Feminism in Nineteenth-Century Argentina," *Latin American Perspectives* 13 (1986): 119–145; see also Sonia Saldívar-Hull, *Feminism on the Border: Chicana Gender Politics and Litera-*

ture (Berkeley: University of California Press, 2000) and the foundational work by Juan Gómez-Quiñones, *Sembradores: Ricardo Flores Magón y el Partido Liberal Mexicano: A Eulogy and Critique* (Los Angeles: Aztlán Publications, 1973).

12. Blackwell, *¡Chicana Power!* 49.

13. Literature on Chicanas' transnational role, particularly through the lenses of literary works, educational policy, and feminist frameworks, also informs my historical approach in this chapter. See C. Alejandra Elenes, "Reclaiming the Borderlands: Chicana/o Identity, Difference, and Critical Pedagogy," *Educational Theory* 47, no. 3 (Summer 1997): 359–375; Michelle Joffroy, "El Espacio Relacional/Las Relaciones Espaciales: La Práctica del Feminismo Chicano en la Literatura Fronteriza Contemporánea," *Revista Iberoamericana* 71, no. 212 (July–September 2004): 801–814; Chandra Talpade Mohanty, "Transnational Feminist Crossings: On Neoliberalism and Radical Critique," *Signs* 8, no. 4 (Summer 2013): 967–991; Mohanty, "Under Western Eyes: Feminist Scholarship and Colonial Discourses," *Feminist Review* 30 (Autumn 1988): 61–88; and Mohanty, "'Under Western Eyes' Revisited: Feminist Solidarity through Anticapitalist Struggles," *Signs* 28, no. 2 (Winter 2003): 499–535. See also Aída Hurtado, "Sitios y Lenguas: Chicanas Theorize Feminisms," *Hypatia* 13, no. 2 (Spring 1998): 134–161.

14. I borrow from Deena J. Gonzalez, who demonstrates in *Refusing the Favor: The Spanish-Mexican Women of Santa Fe, 1820–1880* (New York: Oxford University Press, 1999) that women also took part in monumental change.

15. While there is a specific historical activism tied to the identity label of "Chicana," I use "Chicana" and *"Tejana"* interchangeably to refer more generally to ethnic Mexican women residing or working in Texas and the United States. *"Mexicana"* is used to identify women living or working in Mexico.

16. Latin Americanists, including those who were interested in Latina and Chicana concerns, also began to employ a gendered analysis as early as the 1970s, albeit most were in the social sciences and were not historians. See Sueann Caulfield, "The History of Gender in the Historiography of Latin America," *Hispanic American Historical Review* 81, nos. 3–4 (2001): 449–490.

17. Nichole Sanders, *Gender and Welfare in Mexico: The Consolidation of a Postrevolutionary State* (University Park: Pennsylvania State University Press, 2011), 3, 7. See also Jocelyn Olcott, *Revolutionary Women in Postrevolutionary Mexico* (Durham, NC: Duke University Press, 2005).

18. For a discussion of the shifting gender politics concerning the "new, modern" woman in Brazil, Chile, and Mexico, see Susan K. Besse, *Restructuring Patriarchy: The Modernization of Gender Inequality in Brazil, 1914–1940* (Chapel Hill: University of North Carolina Press, 1996); Elizabeth Quay Hutchison, Labors Appropriate to Their Sex: *Gender, Labor, and Politics in Urban Chile, 1900–1930* (Durham, NC: Duke University Press, 2001); Jocelyn Olcott, Mary Kay Vaughan, and Gabriela Cano, eds., *Sex in Revolution: Gender, Politics, and Power in Modern Mexico* (Durham, NC: Duke University Press, 2006).

19. For newer work on the legacy of *mutualistas* led by Mexican and Mexican Americans in the United States, see Julie Leninger Pycior, *Democratic Renewal and the Mutual Aid Legacy of US Mexicans* (College Station: Texas A&M University Press, 2014).

20. Deutsch, "Gender, Labor History, and Chicano/a Ethnic Identity," 3.

21. María Teresa, Fernández Aceves, Carmen Ramos Escandón, and Susie Porter, coord., *Orden Social eidentidad de género: México, siglos XIX y XX* (Guadalajara: Universidad de Guadalajara, 2006).

22. "La Economía Doméstica en la Escuela Primaria," Segunda Parte, *El Cauterio* (Victoria, Tamps.), June 30, 1912, in Hemeroteca, del Instituto de Investigaciones Históricas de la Universidad Autónoma de Tamaulipas, IIH-UAT, hereafter cited as Hemeroteca, IIH-UAT. For a more comprehensive treatment of the woman question and the ideology and practice of feminism, see Esperanza Tuñón Pablos, *Mujeres que se organizan: El Frente Único pro Derechos de la Mujer, 1935–1938* (Mexico City: Universidad Nacional Autónoma de México, 1992); Stephanie Mitchell and Patience A. Schell, eds., *The Women's Revolution in Mexico, 1910–1953* (Lanham, MD: Rowman and Littlefield, 2007); Olcott, Vaughan, and Cano, *Sex in Revolution*. See also Vicki Ruiz, *Cannery Women, Cannery Lives: Mexican Women, Unionization, and the California Food Processing Industry, 1930–1950* (Albuquerque: University of New Mexico Press, 1987); Ruiz, *From Out of the Shadows: Mexican Women in Twentieth-Century America* (New York: Oxford University Press, 2008).

23. "La Economía Doméstica en la Escuela Primaria," *El Cauterio*, June 23, 1912, in Hemeroteca, IIH-UAT.

24. "La Economía Doméstica en la Escuela Primaria," Segunda Parte, *El Cauterio*, June 30, 1912, in Hemeroteca, IIH-UAT. The original Spanish text is: "socialmente eleva y ennoblece la función de la mujer . . . haciendo de ella un poderoso factor de bienestar económico."

25. Joan Scott, *Gender and the Politics of History*, rev. ed. (New York: Columbia University Press, 1999); Pérez, *The Decolonial Imaginary*; Judith Butler, *Gender Trouble: Feminism and the Subversion of Identity* (New York: Routledge, 2006).

26. José D. Saldívar, *Border Matters: Remapping American Cultural Studies* (Berkeley: University of California Press, 1997).

27. See also Vicki L. Ruiz and Leisa D. Meyer, "Ongoing Missionary Labor": Building, Maintaining, and Expanding Chicana Studies/History, an Interview with Vicki L. Ruiz," *Feminist Studies* 34, nos. 1–2 (Spring–Summer 2008): 33.

28. For the potential of such methodological approaches on the contemporary feminist movement, see Beatriz M. Pesquera and Denise A. Segura, "With Quill and Torch: A Chicana Perspective on the American Women's Movement and Feminist Theories," in *Chicanas/Chicanos at the Crossroads: Social, Economic, and Political Change*, ed. David R. Maciel and Isidro D. Ortiz (Tucson: University of Arizona, 1996), 246. In their 1996 analysis on the American women's movement and Chicana concerns, they wrote, "The future potential of feminism to forge a progressive praxis depends on the manner in which activist and intellectual currents take into account the intersection of race/ethnicity, culture, and class, as well as gender."

29. Emma Goldman, "Anarchism: What Does It Really Stand For?" in the Paul Avrich Collection, Robert Wagner Labor Archives, Tamiment Library, New York University, hereafter cited as PAC-RWL.

30. Emma Goldman was born in 1869 and died in 1940. See the correspon-

dence between Ricardo Flores Magón (during his imprisonment in St. Louis) and Emma Goldman in the Rare Books Room, US Library of Congress.

31. Ward Albro, *Always a Rebel: Ricardo Flores Magón and the Mexican Revolution* (Fort Worth: Texas Christian University Press, 2003); John Mason Hart, *Anarchism and the Mexican Working Class, 1860–1931* (Austin: University of Texas Press, 1978).

32. John Mason Hart, "The Evolution of the Mexican and Mexican-American Working Classes," in Hart, ed., *Border Crossings: Mexican and Mexican-American Workers* (Wilmington, DE: Scholarly Resources, 1998), 24.

33. Louise Michel, "Por Que Soy Anarquista," 1895; repr., *Sagitario*, June 1926, AHEM, IIH-UAT.

34. Claudio Lomnitz, "Ideological Incoherence and Ideological Purity in the Mexican Revolution," keynote address at the Illustrating Anarchy and Revolution: Mexican Legacies of Global Change Conference, Center for Mexican American Studies, University of Texas at Austin, February 5–7, 2014; Lomnitz, *The Return of Comrade Ricardo Flores Magón* (New York: Zone Books, 2014); in addition to the classic work *Sembradores* by Juan Gomez-Quiñones, see James D. Cockcroft, *Intellectual Precursors of the Mexican Revolution, 1900–1913* (Austin: University of Texas Press, 1968).

35. Martha Ackelsberg, *Free Women of Spain: Anarchism and the Struggle for the Emancipation of Women* (Bloomington: Indiana University Press, 1991), 16–17.

36. Ibid, 17.

37. Hart, *Anarchism and the Mexican Working Class*, 18. See also Friedrich Katz, *The Secret War in Mexico: Europe, the United States, and the Mexican Revolution* (Chicago: University of Chicago Press, 1984).

38. For works that deal with socioeconomic and race relations in the greater south Texas region, see David Montejano, *Anglos and Mexicans in the Making of Texas* (Austin: University of Texas Press, 1986); Omar Valerio-Jiménez, *River of Hope: Forging Identity and Nation in the Rio Grande Borderlands* (Durham, NC: Duke University Press, 2012); Benjamin Johnson, *Revolution in Texas: How a Forgotten Rebellion and Its Bloody Suppression Turned Mexicans into Americans* (New Haven, CT: Yale University Press, 2003); Rodolfo Rocha, "The Influence of the Mexican Revolution on the Texas-Mexico Border" (PhD diss., Texas Tech University, 1981). In addition, see the film documentary *Border Bandits* by Kirby Warnock (2005).

39. "Mitin en Gurley," *Regeneración*, November 8, 1913, http://www.archivomagon.net/ Periódico/Regeneración/ CuartaEpoca/PDF/e4n164.pdf; list of donors and donations as printed in the January 13, 1912, issue of *Regeneración*, http://www.archivomagon.net/Periódico/Regeneración/; for an examination of *fronteriza* women such as Jovita Idar who also wrote and fought in support of the Mexican Revolution, see Sonia Hernández, "Women's Labor and Activism in the Greater Mexican Borderlands," in *War along the Border: The Mexican Revolution and Tejano Communities*, ed. Arnoldo De León (College Station: Texas A&M University, 2012); see also José E. Limón's examination of El Primer Congreso Mexicanista in which Jovita Idar and the Idar family participated, "El Primer Congreso Mexicanista de 1911," *Aztlán* 5 (Spring, Fall 1974).

40. Lewis Spence, *Mexico for the Mexicans*, May 31, 1918, 34, in Edward Doheny Research Foundation, Occidental College, box 1, 1309-Labor folder 1674–1685, "Effects of Revolution on Labor Conditions," hereafter cited as EDRF.

41. "Mexican Laborer a Real Autocrat," *Washington Star*, February 3, 1918, box 1, 1309-Labor folder 1674–1685, "Effects of Revolution on Labor Conditions," EDRF.

42. Hart, *Border Crossings*, 18.

43. "Se impidió desembarcar a dos mujeres extranjeras," *La Opinión: Diario Independiente de la Tarde* (Tampico), April 12, 1924, Hemeroteca, IIH-UAT.

44. *Mexico Handbook on Approaches to San Luis Potosí and Tampico from the North and East through Zone E*, prepared by the Military Intelligence Division General Staff, US War Department, 1920, copy no. 196 (Washington, DC: Government Printing Office), 74.

45. "Invasión de gentes de mal vivir, que ha unos años de esta parte ha inundado la ciudad," *La Opinión: Diario Independiente de la Tarde* (Tampico), April 12, 1924, Hemeroteca, IIH-UAT.

46. *Mexico Handbook on Approaches to San Luis Potosí and Tampico.*

47. Ibid.

48. Ibid., 36; for a discussion of the linkages between cultural views of Mexicans held by Americans and Mexican elites, see Gilbert G. González, *Culture of Empire: American Writers, Mexico, and Mexican Immigrants, 1880–1930* (Austin: University of Texas Press, 2004).

49. *Mexico Handbook on Approaches to San Luis Potosí and Tampico.*

50. As the historian Cynthia Orozco has pointed out, Emma Tenayuca was a member of LULAC before she joined the Texas Communist Party; see *No Mexicans, Women, or Dogs Allowed*. Tenayuca and other Texas-based female labor activists had been influenced by labor activists in Mexico and their radical ideas. Roberto R. Calderón and Emilio Zamora, "Manuela Solis Sager and Emma Tenayuca," in Teresa Córdova, Norma Cantú et al., *Chicana Voices: Intersections of Class, Race, and Gender* (National Association for Chicano Studies, 1990), originally published by the Center for Mexican American Studies, UT-Austin, 1986.

51. For example, see Carolina Munguía and the role of the *Círculo Social Femenino de México*, "Junta reglamentaria del CSFM," Carolina M. Munguía, October 2, 1938, Rómulo Munguía Collection, Nettie Lee Benson Library, hereafter cited as RMC-NLB. See Gabriela González, "Carolina Munguía and Emma Tenayuca: The Politics of Benevolence and Radical Reform," *Frontiers: A Journal of Women Studies* 24, nos.2–3 (2003): 200–229; for an in-depth examination of Caritina M. Piña, Esther Mendoza, Domitila Jiménez, and their Tampico-based labor network, see Sonia Hernández, "Revisiting *Mexican(a)* Labor History through *Feminismo Transfronterista*: From Tampico to Texas, and Beyond, 1910–1940," *Frontiers: A Journal of Women's Studies*, special issue on Transnational Feminisms, forthcoming.

52. "A todas las organizaciones obreras de parte del Sindicato Defensor de Poseedores del Obrero Organizado" (Tampico, Tamps.), July 6, 1930, AHEM, IIH-UAT.

53. Paul Avrich, *Anarchist Voices: An Oral History of Anarchism in America* (Princeton, NJ: Princeton University Press, 1995).

54. R. Lone (Steubenville, Ohio) to Librado Rivera (Tampico, Tamps.), May 13, 1927, AHEM, IIH-UAT.

55. See newspaper clippings and correspondence between Mendez's organization and other pro-labor, Socialist, anarchist, and Communist groups from Europe, Latin America, and the United States, AHEM, IIH-UAT.

56. See cover page of *Alma Obrera: Quincenal de propaganda sindicalista, Órgano del grupo sindicalista "Alma Obrera" de Zacatecas*, March 15, 1925, in Hemeroteca, IIH-UAT.

57. Luz Mendoza (Harlingen, Texas) to Juan J. Montemayor (Villa Cecilia, Tamps.), November 11, 1929, AHEM, IIH-UAT; The citation on the number of PLM branches comes from Sandos, 77.

58. Caritina Piña (Comité Internacional Pro-Presos Sociales, Villa Cecilia y Tampico) to Grupo Libertario 'Sacco y Vanzettí," June 7, 1929, AHEM, IIH-UAT.

59. Luz Mendoza (Harlingen, Texas) to Juan J. Montemayor (Villa Cecilia, Tamps.), November 11, 1929, AHEM, IIH-UAT; Caritina Piña (Comité Internacional Pro-Presos Sociales, Villa Cecilia y Tampico) to Grupo Libertario "Sacco y Vanzettí," June 7, 1929, AHEM, IIH-UAT.

60. Newsletter, *Grupo Sagitario*, n.d., 1927, AHEM, IIH-UAT; IWW members also showed solidarity and supported the workers from Massachusetts.

61. Johnson, "The Cosmic Race in Texas," 404–419.

62. Sonia Hernández, "'¡Cooperación de los Sexos para el bien de la Nación!' Relaciones de Género en el Tamaulipas PosRevolucionario, 1920–1930," *Revista Internacional de Ciencias Sociales y Humanidades* 20, no. 1 (January–June 2010): 85–105.

63. De Florinda Monidini, *Sagitario*, February 27, 1927, AHEM, IIH-UAT.

64. Ibid.

65. "V: Ley 5291, Reglamentaria del Trabajo de Mujeres y Menores," in José Panettiri, *Las Primeras Leyes Obreras* (Argentina: Centro Edirot de America Latina Biblioteca Política, 1984), 39.

66. Unión de Mujeres Americanas, *Artes y Letras* (New York, TX), October 1, 1934, Hispanic Recovery Project Online database, hereafter cited as HRP. It is possible that Amafia (probably Amalia) was in fact Amalia King and not Amalia Kiug, given the role of the King family (Richard King 1824–1885, born in New York City, patriarch of the King Ranch) from Texas.

67. Ibid.

68. Ibid. See also Olcott's examination of Robles de Mendoza in *Revolutionary Women in Postrevolutionary Mexico*, chap. 5.

69. "Junta reglamentaria del CSFM," Carolina M. Munguía, October 2, 1938, RMC-NLB.

70. Ibid.

71. Elizabeth Quay Hutchison, "From 'La Mujer Esclava' to 'La Mujer Limón': Anarchism and the Politics of Sexuality in Early-Twentieth Century Chile," *Hispanic American Historical Review* 81, nos. 3–4 (2001): 519–554, 522.

72. "Mexicans in Texas Leave for Old Home," *Harlingen Star*, 19 (24?), CNI,

NLB; "Varias Familias de Mexicanos se Repatrian," *El Fronterizo*, 19(?), CNI, NLB.

73. For the struggle that led to women's participation in LULAC, see Orozco, *No Mexicans, Women, or Dogs Allowed*.

74. Ricardo Flores Magón, *A La Mujer*, trans. La Prensa Sembradora (Oakland, CA: La Prensa Sembradora, 1974), 2.

75. It also helps to address what Vicki Ruiz noted in her published interview, "Ongoing Missionary Labor," as a movement away from a "Chicano/a Nationalist project." Ruiz and Meyer, "Ongoing Missionary Labor"; Kelly Lytle-Hernández, "Borderlands and the Future of the American West," *Western Historical Quarterly* 42, no. 3 (Autumn 2011): 17.

CHAPTER SEVEN

Eastside Imaginaries: Toward a Relational and Transnational Chicana/o Cultural History

LUIS ALVAREZ

In 2013 the band Quetzal from East Los Angeles won the Grammy for "Latin rock, urban or alternative" for their album *Imaginaries*. Released by Smithsonian Folkways Recordings, the album brilliantly fuses the group's activism and energy for issues ranging from immigrant rights to Chicana feminism with their unique sonic blend. The *Los Angeles Times* remarked that *Imaginaries* was "a characteristically ambitious foray into cumbia, neo-'80s style R&B, Cuban *charanga* and Brazilian *pandeiro*, charged with the band's collectivist political passion."[1] Singer Martha Gonzalez underscored the album's remarkable scope when she noted that the title track was inspired by Emma Pérez's Chicana feminist intellectual project *The Decolonial Imaginary*.[2] The term "imaginaries," Gonzalez explained, is

> useful in explicating the ways in which our music and art community has been functioning. When we become critical of the discourses that teach an outlook of community assessment through a lens of deficit and instead look to our communities from an asset-based perspective, we stand to create something much more sustainable. In this sense, we imagine. We visualize. We gather our resources. We design and construct. Taking part in communities that have exercised decolonializing methods such as these, as well as dialoguing and learning from communities that survived by adopting the same strategies and principles, inspired this song.[3]

Imaginaries calls our attention to the musical, social, and political possibilities of art-based community making, as opposed to community-based art making.[4] Inspired by anticolonial struggles from Chiapas to

Palestine and by issues from environmentalism to spatial politics in the neoliberal city, the cuts on *Imaginaries* draw their aesthetic groove from musical traditions associated with the Afro-Mexican son jarocho, Peruvian cajón, Cuban charango, African American soul, and US West Coast Latin jazz. *Imaginaries* sketches a musical and political cartography that cements Quetzal's Eastside Chicana/o origins in a multiracial and global map of sound and communities in struggle. Through their music and politics, Quetzal articulates a Chicana/o identity that is relational and transnational, one where relationships with non-Chicana/o people and places matter deeply. Describing the band's efforts to push the boundaries of Chicana/o music, founding member Quetzal Flores said, "The most important thing is how does 'Chicano' relate to the rest of the world? We don't exist in a vacuum."[5]

This chapter examines the longer history of relational and transnational impulses in Chicana/o culture recalled by Quetzal's *Imaginaries*. Far from a detailed chronological narrative, this is more a series of riffs on what seemingly disparate figures and moments might teach us about postwar Chicana/o cultural history. Drawing on examples from Los Angeles's Eastside, I argue there was a postwar stream of Chicana/o cultural politics determined less by racial or territorial logic than by multiracial and hemispheric, even global, social and political currents. With its diverse and iconic history, East LA may seem an obvious place to make such a case. Perhaps less obviously, I focus on the production of Chicana/o culture by those who were not Mexican American. Some might not consider them to be Chicana/o at all! I consider, for instance, the role of a Jew in the 1950s Eastside music scene, a Puerto Rican–Hungarian in *Movimiento*-era TV, and a Japanese entrepreneur integral to the recent globalization of Chicana/o music. More than historical anomalies or oddities, these figures reveal the racial and geographic crossings of Chicanas/os and their cultural politics. They underscore how postwar consumerism and commercialized leisure served as incubators for oppositional memory and utopian hopes at the same time that they highlighted political limits and cleavages in Chicana/o pop culture. The deep connections between these seemingly incongruent people, the places they came from, and LA's Eastside ultimately show how Chicana/o cultural history gave rise to a myriad of new social relations and political formations in the decades following World War II.

I am less interested in the notion of Chicana/o cultural history without Chicanas/os, however, than I am in excavating those moments when people drew their Chicana/o identity from their politics instead of drawing their politics from their Chicana/o identity. I agree with Felipe Hinojosa's contention in this collection that political activism informs identities once assumed to be static aspects of culture. Rather than prioritize the racial and spatial transgressions of Mexican Americans, however, I consider what we might learn from thinking about Chicana/o history from the outside-in as much as the inside-out.[6] By viewing the Eastside as part of a relational and transnational cartography, we see how the outer edges of Chicana/o culture reveal its inner workings.[7] More to the point, I consider how those presumed to be on the ethnic, racial, or national margins of Chicana/o culture fueled its ultimate circulation and rendered a reordering of Chicana/o identity and politics. From this disorienting angle, there are few assumptions about who is or is not considered Chicana/o, where Chicana/o history happens, and what constitutes Chicana/o politics. While claims to cultural authenticity were paramount for some, others disavowed any racial, ethnic, or national litmus test for a Chicana/o identity that transcended such boundaries. An outside-in sight line helps us see that Chicana/o cultural history must account for how the Chicana/o experience was *imagined* to be part of a larger matrix of struggle over race, civil rights, and everyday life.[8]

This chapter highlights instances where relational or transnational Chicana/o culture and politics grew from the spaces in between capitalist networks and the commercial and consumer practices they presumed to, but could not totally, control. The people and cultural commodities I scrutinize were deeply embedded in local circuits of the Eastside economy and global capital in the years after the Second World War. Their history, however, is not simply a case of resistance to, or seduction by, neoliberalism's growth. Their stories are instead a complicated and, at times, contradictory mix of the two. As it connected and invigorated social movements between seemingly disparate places and people, the commercialization of Chicana/o culture also risked losing its meaning across time and geography, silencing or excluding voices, and obscuring patterns of violence, sexism, and structural inequity.

The concept of "imaginaries" helps unravel these many strands of Chicana/o culture because it illuminates the possibilities and limits of people's world-making aspirations.[9] Chicana/o cultural imaginaries took various shapes, including in music, television, and stylistic expressions. Depending on how they emerged in popular culture, some imaginaries made stronger links between communities than others, some were more readily translatable into political collaboration, and still others revealed gender or ethnic tensions.[10] Chicana/o cultural imaginaries were never guaranteed to be radical, but they did show how ordinary folk made sense of their present and envisioned a different future. They reveal how people engaged and constructed the world around them, recalling that social change must be imagined before it can be practiced. Such imaginaries were not simply the stuff of dreams, however. They were grounded in real places, relationships, and everyday activities. Their often gendered construction suggested that masculinity was sometimes the shortest way through to multiracial coalition and, as Sonia Hernández finds in her chapter in this collection, that imaginaries could also be women-centered. Chicana/o imaginaries were also mobile, stretching across time and space to connect the people who inhabited them.

These Eastside imaginaries contain important lessons for Chicana/o cultural history. First, the field radiates in at least three directions: the "cross" (as in cross-ethnically and cross-racially), the "intra" (as in intra-ethnic relations of citizenship, gender, class, and sexuality) and the "trans" (as in the transnational reach of the Chicana/o experience).[11] Second, we must think beyond paradigms of *"mestizaje"* and "borderlands" to fully account for the relational and transnational dimensions in Chicana/o cultural history.[12] The folks I write about here demonstrate that there have long been relational and transnational circuits of Chicana/o cultural politics that are not overdetermined by relationships with Mexicans or Mexico. Third, and finally, postwar Chicana/o cultural history is as much about continuity as it is discontinuity. The figures and moments I discuss complicate the conventional periodization of Chicana/o history that emphasizes rupture between the Mexican American, Chicana/o, and post-*Movimiento* generations.

Utopian Rhythms, Cold War Blues

In 1956, Lil' Julian Herrera had one of the biggest rhythm and blues hits of the year in Los Angeles. His soulful, doo-wop ballad, "Lonely Lonely Nights," turned Herrera into an overnight sensation. He was soon known across the city for spectacular live performances that drew comparisons to a young James Brown. He became a teen idol and heartthrob among Mexican American girls on the Eastside. What many of his fans may not have known, however, was that Herrera was neither Mexican American nor from LA. He was an East Hungarian Jew who had run away from his Massachusetts home at age eleven. His given name was Ezekiel, though his probation officer knew him as Ron Gregory. After hitchhiking to Southern California, he was taken in by a Mexican American family in the Boyle Heights neighborhood of East LA, eventually taking their surname as his own.[13]

The legendary Johnny Otis produced "Lonely Lonely Nights." Born the son of Greek immigrants in Vallejo, California, Otis came of musical age as a drummer and bandleader playing in African American jazz and blues joints along LA's Central Avenue. By the mid-1950s when he helped launch Lil' Julian Herrera into local stardom, Otis already was a formidable figure in the LA music scene. He soon became known as the "Godfather of Rhythm and Blues" and produced records, hosted radio and television programs, and organized dances and concerts. He was also regularly harassed by local authorities for making and promoting music whose performers and audiences often crossed racial lines. Otis, in fact, considered himself "black by persuasion." He once remarked, "Genetically, I'm pure Greek. Psychologically, environmentally, culturally, by choice, I'm a member of the black community."[14] Emblematic of the Eastside music scene's diversity in the 1950s, "Lonely Lonely Nights" was a pop hit produced by a Greek American who considered himself African American and performed by a Hungarian Jew who considered himself Mexican American.

In an era marked by red baiting, demands for cultural conformity, and the continuation of Jim Crow and Juan Crow segregation across the Southwest, "Lonely Lonely Nights" mapped a different set of racial possibilities. Amidst escalating fears of domestic subversion and foreign invasion fueled in part by Soviet economic and political advances, expressions of racial, national, and cultural difference were attacked and discouraged. Yet many of those in the Eastside music scene imagined and put into practice alternative ways of living that championed the area's diversity. As George Sánchez noted, even though parts of East LA were becoming increasingly Mexican during the 1950s, the area was home to rich exchanges among its Mexican American, African American, Japanese American, Jewish, and Russian residents.[15]

"Lonely Lonely Nights" was far from an isolated case. There were also the likes of Big Jay McNeely, Joe Houston, and Chuck Higgins, a trio of African American saxophonists with huge followings on the Mexican American Eastside. Higgins's numbers, for instance, included odes to LA's Mexican American community such as "Beanville," "Tortas," and "Pachuko Hop," in honor of the Mexican American *pachu-*

cos and zoot suiters of the World War II years. Across the Eastside and the rest of the city, such cultural interchanges went the other way too. Avant-garde Mexican American jazz players Anthony Ortega and Gil Bernal were touring with the likes of Lionel Hampton's Orchestra by the late '50s, but got their start studying alongside black Angelino artists like Horace Tapscott, Charles Mingus, and Buddy Collette. Bernal recalled that his "real roots were with the black style of playing, the black musicians. I felt there was more soul, more energy in that music. I liked the sound, the attack, that's the way I played."[16] It is important to note that most of these performers were male and that many of their connections with one another were likely made on gendered terrain. And it is not far-fetched to think that many young black and brown performers interpreted insults to their race and class identities in Cold War America as crises of manhood, let the longer history of hyper-sexualizing young Mexican American women in LA go unchallenged, or presumed as male performers to know what women wanted or how they should behave.

Still, the multiracial imaginary evident in the Eastside sound of the 1950s was grounded in the daily life of ordinary people and real places.[17] One such place was Phillips Music Company on Brooklyn Avenue in Boyle Heights. William Phillips was a Jew from Rochester, New York, who ran away from home and joined the Navy before he turned eighteen. He eventually settled in East LA, where he married, started a family, and opened a music store in the 1930s. While Phillips never assumed a Mexican American identity like Lil' Julian Herrera, his two sons remember "he felt more comfortable with Mexican Americans."[18] Despite eventually moving his family to Beverly Hills, Phillips kept his business in Boyle Heights, where by the 1950s the store had become a kind of "community melting pot."[19] It was a local hangout where youth of all racial stripes from across the Eastside could buy or just listen to the Latin jazz, rock, cumbia, and Yiddish swing records that helped make up the multinational audio thicket of the Eastside scene. Years later, Boyle Heights native Lola Fernandez recalled that

> The Phillips Music store was like stepping into a world of its own. . . . It was the first encounter with how music was made and I think as a young Mexican American person, that, especially for kids that didn't have that opportunity, it was a great place to go and be acquainted with the actual instruments that we heard the music being made from. . . . It was a marvelous experience to go into the store and it was the kind of place where

you could go into and they didn't shoo you away. . . . I remember that as a young person they didn't make you leave because they knew you weren't gonna buy anything. They were happy that you were there.[20]

Phillips, who learned to play the drums in the Navy and had performed across LA, permitted local kids with an interest in music to jam in the store after hours. He also had an eye for talent and introduced young Mexican American musicians to his industry contacts in Hollywood and the music joints along Central Avenue.[21] A recent retrospective on Boyle Heights noted that Phillips's customers, including Mexican Americans who became members in bands like Thee Midniters, Los Lobos, and Ollin, "provided a soundtrack to the social and cultural transformations that defined the Eastside."[22] In a gesture reflective of the kind of place the store was and the kind of person Phillips was, shortly after the war he gave a corner of his store to Kenji Taniguchi upon his return to Boyle Heights from the internment camps. Taniguchi sold sporting goods equipment, soon opened his own store down the street, and became the biggest provider of sporting goods on the Eastside.

Herrera, Phillips, and others like them eliminate any doubt that Mexican American identity was constructed in relation to others, and that culture reflected and refracted the political possibilities of the time. As George Lipsitz argues, it is important to understand music as more than "a way of posing imaginary solutions to real problems." It is also a form of politics and an arena of social experimentation that is integrally linked to a much wider world of political action.[23] The Eastside sound emerged when the city was structured by a white spatial imaginary in the decade after World War II. From Brooklyn's perennially underachieving baseball team taking possession of a stadium erected upon the foundations of one of the city's oldest Mexican American neighborhoods at Chavez Ravine to freeway construction that allowed increasingly suburbanized white populations to pass between points of interest with less direct interpersonal contact with nonwhite people than before, LA was resegregated instead of desegregated.[24] Against and amidst this resegregation of the city, figures like Herrera, Phillips, and those they crossed paths with charted an alternative racial cartography in their music and in the places where they performed and conducted business.

Political organizing across communities of color in Los Angeles during the 1950s mirrored the Eastside music scene. Activists organized their own interracial political performance. As the historian

Shana Bernstein shows, the political landscape of 1950s LA was deeply shaped by interracial coalitions. Organizations like the Mexican American Community Service Organization (CSO) and League of United Latin American Citizens (LULAC) collaborated with the National Association for the Advancement of Colored People (NAACP), the Japanese American Citizens League (JACL), and the Jewish Community Relations Committee (CRC). The conservative Cold War political climate forced these groups to strike a delicate, difficult balance between their collective push for civil rights and the rigid anticommunism of the era.[25] Despite the volatile political terrain, it should not come as a surprise, for example, that more than two thousand people attended a four-day celebration of ethnic culture at the Soto-Michigan Jewish Community Center in East LA in 1952. The event was cosponsored by the NAACP, JACL, and Jewish Centers Association and was indicative of the growing bonds between such groups.[26] Nor should it be surprising that Bill Phillips sat on the Soto-Michigan board of directors or that he campaigned for Ed Roybal, the popular Mexican American city council member from 1949 to 1963 (and later US congressional representative for the district). Like the music sold in his store, Cold War ideologies never fully contained the interracial and cross-cultural character of his politics.

Movimiento Imaginaries

From 1974 to 1978 *Chico and the Man* aired on NBC. Starring Freddie Prinze and Jack Albertson, the situation comedy was set in the East LA barrio. Its storyline centered on the relationship between Chico, an enterprising young Chicano Vietnam War veteran from the neighborhood played by Prinze, and Ed Brown, a curmudgeonly, racist, Archie Bunker type played by Albertson. Brown owned a run-down mechanic's garage, from where he watched his neighborhood and clientele become increasingly Mexican. Based on Ed's racist sense of humor and Chico's witty and endearing jokes in return, the series tracked the two men's cultural and generational conflict, respect and affection for one another, and business partnership. The show was the first in prime time to feature a Chicana/o character and made Chico's ethnic identity and politics known from the beginning. In the pilot episode, for instance, Chico encounters two white police officers who interrogate him in the garage. They suspect him of a robbery, call him "Pancho" and "beaner," and ask if he has papers to prove he was born in the United States. Chico responds by saying: "Why? You got papers to prove where you were born? I'm a Chicano, man! I was born in this country! And, what's more, we had it first. You people are the outsiders! I *habla* your English. Why can't you *habla* a little of my Español?" As did other 1970s sitcoms for the African American ghetto experience, *Chico and the Man* introduced the Chicana/o Movement and life in the barrio to a mainstream audience that averaged forty million viewers a week. However, many LA-area Chicana/o activists protested the show as soon as the pilot aired. Their main complaint was that Freddie Prinze was not Chicano. He just played one on TV. Prinze was actually half Puerto Rican and half Hungarian, and referred to himself as a "Hungarican" from New York.

The ensuing controversy over Prinze and the show revealed the range of political views held by Chicanas/os in the early 1970s. The spectrum ranged from hardcore ethnic nationalism to the strident internationalism of what has since been called the US third world left. The debate over *Chico and the Man* also underscored that Chicana/o cultural imaginaries were contested, never guaranteed to be progressive, and readily susceptible to being hijacked by commercial interests. This was especially the case in the immediate post–civil rights movement years when the future of racial politics was so unsettled.

Despite its early ratings success and novelty in starring a Chicano character, *Chico and the Man* drew considerable ire from Chicana/o media activists in LA. Following a long history of Latina/o groups protesting Hollywood's casting of non-Chicanas/os to play Chicana/o or Mexican parts, including by the League of United Latin American Citizens, Mexican American Legal Defense and Educational Fund, and the National Council of La Raza, complaints poured in from viewers and groups like El Teatro Nacional de Aztlán (a Chicana/o theater group known as TENAZ) and Justice for Chicanos in the Motion Picture and Television Industry (Justicia). In this instance, Chicana/o viewers complained that Prinze's Spanish sounded Puerto Rican and that "even his gestures and body movements are not convincingly Chicano."[27] Prinze and the "distinctly Caribbean flavor" of Puerto Rican singer José Feliciano's theme song for the show came under attack as an inauthentic portrayal of life in East LA.[28] For his part, Prinze rebutted, "I wish I knew what they wanted. . . . They say Chicanos talk a certain way, walk a certain way. I know lots of Chicanos. All different. They don't want an actor. They want a stereotype: a wind up Chicano."[29]

Critics, however, further lambasted the show's humor as racist and degrading. In a letter to NBC's president, Robert Howard, the Los Angeles Hispanic Urban Center argued that *Chico and the Man* "is a sad continuation of the racist history of the media that has made us almost invisible." The center's founder and director, Vahac Mardirosian, and nine of its faculty accused the program and NBC of presenting Chico in a "demeaning, 'serf-master' relation to 'The Man,'" ridiculing his "language, speech, habits, and overall presence" and reinforcing overused stereotypes of "simplistic" and dishonest Mexicans that were a "great disservice to the Mexican-American population."[30] Another viewer summarized much of the outcry when he said that the "show portrays a Chicano in a subservient role; demeans the Chicano character and gives Chico little opportunity to demonstrate pride in himself and his ethnic origin. The humor utilized is dangerously close the Step 'n Fetchit portrayals."[31]

Much of this criticism took on a thinly veiled gender bent. Mirroring the well-documented masculinist ethos of the *Movimiento*, some argued that the show denied Chico (meaning "boy" in Spanish) his manhood when he was juxtaposed to Ed Brown as the "Man." Brown's paternalism toward Chico (in one episode Chico even chose Ed over his own Mexican immigrant father) led Chon Noriega to claim it advanced "an oedipalized masculinity."[32] Ray Andrade, an associate producer of the show and former president of the group Justicia upon whom creator James Komack partially based the Chico character, argued many of these problems stemmed from the lack of Chicanas/os involved in production of the show, especially as writers.[33] The uproar over *Chico* quieted soon after its debut in 1974 and its subsequent success, but not before there were threats of advertiser boycotts and a picket of KNBC's Burbank studios where the series was taped.[34]

The controversy over *Chico and the Man* was more than a protest against the misrepresentation of Chicanas/os or their exclusion from the TV industry. It was a debate about who and what was considered Chicana/o. The longer story behind Vahac Mardirosian and the Hispanic Urban Center's protest against *Chico* illustrated the point as much as Prinze. Mardirosian was born in Syria after his parents escaped the Armenian genocide by the Turkish government, migrated with them to Mexico City at age two in 1926, came of age in Tijuana, and eventually settled in LA after becoming a minister. When East LA high school students walked out of classes in 1968 to protest inferior education and dropout rates higher than 50 percent, Mardirosian organized with Lincoln High teacher Sal Castro, picketed with the students at Roosevelt, and negotiated on behalf of the Eastside community with the school board and city authorities. When parents, teachers, and clergy met following the walkouts, they formed the Educational Issues Coordinating Committee (EICC) and elected Mardirosian its president. The EICC soon took on other issues, including educational resources, poverty, and police harassment. Mardirosian soon founded the Hispanic Urban Center to continue this work that, in 1974 at least, included lambasting NBC over *Chico and the Man*.[35]

Chico and the Man also instructs us that the pop cultural form of Chicana/o imaginaries mattered deeply. Television and film informed viewer's commonsense understanding of the world, were extremely profitable, and, as indicated by Michael Olivas in his chapter in this volume, even spurred scholars to investigate the past. The TV industry created new programming in the 1970s that dealt with African American life (*Good Times, Sanford and Son, What's Happening*), multiracialism (*Barney Miller, Welcome Back, Kotter, The White Shadow*), and racial reconciliation (*All in the Family, The Jeffersons, Chico and the Man*). Like *Chico and the Man*, the rest of these shows sought to increase profit and tap younger demographics by addressing racial issues of the day. In so doing, however, they often presented black and Latino characters as nonthreatening, immature, and, in most (but not all) cases, divorced from the radical politics of the previous decade's social movements. Also, the content of these shows curtailed the racial possibilities of the moment by emphasizing gender and class as a shortcut to multiracial coalition and racial conciliation. In Komack's *Chico and the Man*, for instance, Chico and Ed were ultimately able to navigate their racial and generational differences largely because they identified with one another through their shared masculinity and working-class ethos in the gendered space of the garage.[36]

However legitimate the claims *Chico and the Man* was racist and inauthentic, its creators and critics alike obscured the multiracial and internationalist political and cultural currents in which the show existed. Mardirosian's Armenian-Mexican-Chicanoness and Prinze's multiracialism and Chico's Puerto Ricanness (in an episode of season one it is revealed, perhaps in response to the outcry, that Chico is half Puerto Rican) mirrored the relational and transnational milieu of both East LA and the Chicana/o Movement. Alternative readings of *Chico and the Man* might have cast it as part of a larger matrix of that era's pan-Latina/o politics, perhaps in conversation with Chicana artist Linda Lucero's *Lolita Lebrón*, a poster honoring the Puerto Rican nationalist who led the

1954 armed attack on the US House of Representatives in the name of Puerto Rican independence.[37] That such pan-Latina/o constructions did indeed exist during the Chicana/o Movement is, as evidenced by Lilia Fernández's chapter in this collection, apparent in the ways today's historians analyze the era.

Others may have found in *Chico and the Man* some faint echoes of the multiracial brown-eyed soul music of the 1960s and 1970s that could be heard in the streets of East LA, the place that the show was intended to portray. In the tradition of the '50s scene, bands like El Chicano, Tierra, War, and Mark Guerrero increasingly politicized the *Movimiento*-era Eastside sound. Seeing *Chico and the Man* as part of this cultural milieu reminds us of the *Movimiento*'s reach and complexity. On the one hand, the response to *Chico and the Man* was derivative of the fragmentation of the civil rights movement into strands of black, brown, yellow, red, gay, and women's power that helps explain the deeply seeded cultural nationalism and often divisive gender and sexual relations that bifurcated interracial and intra-ethnic relationships. On the other hand, even though responses to the show reflected the hardening of racial and ethnic divisions, *Chico and the Man* was part of a larger cultural conversation that rested on Chicana/o connections with other people, places, and struggles.

Making sense of *Chico and the Man* demands that we not neglect the relational and transnational dimensions of the *Movimiento*. This assertion gets at the heart of Chicana/o history and is further explored in the chapters by Felipe Hinojosa and Carlos Blanton of this collection. Like some blacks, Native Americans, and Asian Americans, Chicanas/os claimed a Third World identity in an effort to connect to streams of anti-imperialist politics. Laura Pulido analyzed how El Centro de Accion Social y Autonomo (CASA) shared political space and principles with LA chapters of the Black Panthers and the predominantly Japanese American organization East Wind.[38] Lorena Oropeza and Ernesto Chávez detailed how the biggest protest of the Chicana/o Movement in Los Angeles was when tens of thousands showed up to protest the Vietnam War as part of the Chicano Moratorium in May 1970.[39] Like the historian Dan Berger in his anthology *The Hidden 1970s: Histories of Radicalism*, Cynthia Young pushed the periodization of the 1960s to include revolutionary filmmaking by Chicana/o, Latina/o, black, Middle Eastern, and Asian American students at UCLA in the '70s.[40] Furthermore, many of these studies and the politics they chronicle acknowledged the ways in which Chicana feminist critiques pushed the *Movimiento* to face up to its multiracial and internationalist past and present.[41] While this landscape of Chicana/o politics may have been lost on most of *Chico and the Man*'s viewers, the controversy over Prinze's Puerto Ricanness and the show's representation of Chicana/o life pointed to a contested *Movimiento*-era cultural politics that was chock full of relational and transnational veins.

Globalization and the Far Eastside Scene

In 1999 Hector Gonzalez saw a peculiar-looking Japanese man standing outside of his home in East LA wearing a Pendleton-type shirt and dark shades and sporting a goatee. Gonzalez recalled, "He looked like a homeboy from the Eastside barrios."[42] Gonzalez was head of Rampart Records, an iconic record label that helped originate the Eastside sound in the mid-1960s when it released music by bands like Cannibal and the Headhunters, the Premiers, and the Blendells. Ramparts founder Eddie Davis, an Anglo who grew up in the Flats area of East LA and worked closely with Billy Cardenas to produce and manage Eastside bands from the 1950s onward, envisioned Rampart as the Chicana/o Motown. The Japanese guy was Shin Miyata. He wanted to release Rampart Records songs in Japan, where there was a growing fascination with Chicana/o lowrider culture. By 2002, Miyata had re-released the first Rampart Records album by the Village Callers in Japan on his Barrio Gold label, a subsidiary of his new venture Music Camp, Inc. In the years since then, Miyata has released dozens of Chicana/o "oldies" in Japan from Rampart and other LA-based labels, incorporated Chicana/o rap and new Eastside bands like Quetzal into his repertoire, and helped grow a niche market for Chicana/o culture and music in Tokyo. For its part, Rampart Records has since re-released its songs in as many as fifty other countries and inked a deal with a Sony Music–affiliated global digital distributor. The Eastside imaginary is now as globally consumed as it was globally constructed.[43]

The story of how Shin Miyata came to pioneer what might be playfully called the Far Eastside Chicana/o scene in Japan is instructive for charting the globalization of Chicana/o music and culture. The intensification of neoliberal economics and the global markets it relies upon has, for better or worse, stretched Chicana/o cultural imaginaries. Neoliberalism fuels cultural exchange in ways that can spark new politics across time and space. Yet it also runs the risk of voiding Chicana/o culture of its political substance in foreign contexts. This can exacerbate hyper-masculinity as a central linkage between faraway people and places, or make acts of transcoding cultural texts and politics virtually impossible. In raising these issues, Miyata's experience sheds light on the political possibilities and limits of Chicana/o cultural imaginaries in the late twentieth and early twenty-first century.

Miyata first encountered Chicana/o culture and lowriders when he watched 1970s American TV shows. The drama *CHiPs*, starring Eric Estrada as a Mexican American motorcycle highway patrolman named "Ponch," and *Chico and the Man* were among his early influences. Miyata was especially enthralled by the episodes of *CHiPs* that featured East LA barrio life and soon found ways to absorb as much Chicana/o music, TV, and film as he could. He also decided to study Spanish when he went to university in Japan, and instead of going to Spain or Latin America to study abroad as did many of his fellow Japanese Spanish language students, Miyata took a year off from school to live in East LA. In 1984 when he was twenty-one years old, Miyata landed in Boyle Heights, the same barrio where Bill Phillips had his music store. Miyata immersed himself in Chicana/o life and culture. He took classes in Chicana/o Studies at East Los Angeles College, cruised with lowriders along Whittier Boulevard, and heard as much live music by East LA bands like Los Lobos as he possibly could. When he returned to Japan, he began writing about Chicana/o music and culture for Japanese media outlets, including *Lowrider Japan* with its more than seventy thousand readers. After working in the music industry for BMG in Tokyo, Miyata broke out on his own to start Music Camp, Inc. and Barrio Gold. His enterprise has grown over the years, releasing more records, interviewing dozens of musicians, and bringing East LA bands and artists to perform in Japan, including a 2006 tour that paired Quetzal with the Chicano author Luis J. Rodriguez.[44]

Miyata's lifelong encounter with Chicana/o music and culture underscores how its circulation and consumption resulted in variant meanings. Having made the trip to East LA at least fifty times since his first visit in 1984, Miyata recalls James Clifford's contention that travel enables "reflections on conditions for human connection, alliances cutting across class, race, gender, and national locations."[45] And Miyata's experience represents an interpretive break from the relentless triumphalism with regard to globalization that appears in many intellectual discourses, as also indicated by Perla M. Guerrero in her chapter for this collection. In a time when people everywhere face "a brand of economic fundamentalism favoring free markets," Miyata's links to Chicana/o culture reveal a kind of globalization from below.[46] He connects the Eastside with Tokyo and Chicanas/os with Japanese through informal networks, hard work, and circuits of pop culture. My point here is not that Miyata and Eastside Chicanas/os, let alone his Japanese customers, share a single interpretation of Chicana/o culture, identity, or politics. Nor is it that Miyata's Barrio Gold label stripped Chicana/o culture of its meaning by capitalizing on its exotic appeal to those that bought his re-released Chicano oldies. Rather, to borrow from Walter Benjamin, it is that Miyata's and Japan's fascination with Chicana/o culture is not simply with its content, but also with the historical conditions in which it was produced.[47]

Miyata himself links this cultural consumption with the historical and political contexts of the Eastside. He notes, for example, that Japanese youth are drawn to Chicana/o music precisely because it "is a kind of a mix" and its longer history of multiracialism and transregional connections encouraged links across place, race, and time. Beyond sharing "skin tones," he argues, many Japanese youth relate to "things against the mainstream," and that the anti-authoritarian political currents in *Movimiento*-era Chicana/o music and culture resonate in a society "so structured and controlling" like Japan's.[48] As did Clifford, Miyata seems to intuitively understand that his movement creates new contacts with Chicana/o culture while sustaining ideas of home, dwelling, and discrete regions. These "roots" with a double "o" and "routes" with an "ou" that Clifford describes are very much alive in Miyata's engagement with Eastside music and Chicana/o culture.

With such extensive travel and encounter as Miyata's, Clifford reminds us, comes the need for cultural translation. It is vital if people are to make sense of connections with new places and those different from themselves.[49] In Miyata's case, there is often the need for literal translation. For instance, in a 2013 interview on the Boyle Heights Internet-based community radio station Radio Sombra, Miyata served as his own translator. After answering questions in English, mixed in with a bit of Spanglish, he repeated his answers in Japanese for anyone listening via the web from his home country. If the literal and figurative translation of Chicana/o culture by Miyata and his customers risks distorting its meaning, it also fuels its circulation and cultivates identification with the longer history of racial struggle on the Eastside.

Miyata and the Far Eastside scene invoke a Chicana/o diaspora that is less defined by shared connections to place or ethnicity than by people's cultural exchange and shared experiences of alienation in a globalized, neoliberal world. Miyata's links to Chicana/o culture suggest a diaspora that is as much forward-looking to possible political and cultural connections as it is backward-looking to any shared home, ancestral land, or appeal to common kinship or race.[50] Much as Vivek Bald describes overlapping ethnic diasporas in the early twentieth-century United States, Miyata shows that Chicana/o cultural imaginaries include "movements and relations between multiple locations," move "away from an overdetermining focus on 'homeland,'" and depart from "a singular emphasis on particular racial, ethnic or national groups."[51] For Bald and Miyata, diaspora operates more as "a process of encounter, intermixture, and the negotiation of difference across all these lines."[52] These connections are at once historically rooted in place, whether Boyle Heights or Tokyo, and are dependent on exchanges across such sites.

There is no clear recipe for how Miyata's brand of Chicana/o cultural politics leads to other kinds of political or social movements. If it does—and that is no sure thing—then there is no certainty that such movements will be progressive. Like *Chico and the Man*, for instance, Miyata's story raises important questions about the possibilities and limits of a Chicana/o cultural diaspora when its links are often, though not always, male and masculine. Yet the power of Chicana/o cultural imaginaries to touch seemingly disparate people and places far away or close to home is not in doubt. Shin Miyata reminds us, as did Bill Phillips and Freddie Prinze, that culture and politics in this Chicana/o diaspora flow in multiple directions. The host of the show *Discos Inmigrantes* on Radio Sombra made this point when he remarked during his interview with Shin Miyata that it was Miyata's friendship and passion for Chicana/o music that helped him understand his own Chicana/o identity. He recalled that when he first met Miyata in the late 1990s, he considered himself to be an "angry Xicano" (with an "X"). When he saw Miyata's enthusiasm for Chicana/o music, he half-jokingly acknowledged that it helped him rediscover his "Chicano" identity with a "C-h" and reconnect with the history of struggle embedded in Chicana/o culture.

Beyond Aztlán?

The night before they won the Latin Grammy, Quetzal played a gig at the Breed Street Shul, a synagogue in Boyle Heights that was around when Bill Phillips first arrived in LA. The show reflected the neighborhood's deep Jewish roots, multiethnic history, and complex Chicana/o culture. One attendee observed that

> the place was packed, the sound was muddy but there was a vibe in the air. Something was up. A culturally mixed crowd of academics (our homies George Lipsitz, Josh Kun and Victor Viesca spoke brilliantly between sets), activists, musicians, artists, and those that have been following Quetzal from the start. The fact that it was a pre-Grammy show took a back seat. It was a true gathering of community—in the fullest sense of the word—of coming together to honor our culture, our history, and our historians. So much history ran through my head: the dramatic poly-cultural social history of Boyle Heights, its legendary musical history, and its volatile political history reverberated off the walls of that 1915 shul along with the cooking rhythms of son jarocho. Quetzal winning the Grammy was cool, but Quetzal had already won—the hearts of a Community.[53]

Like Bill Phillips, Freddie Prinze, and Shin Miyata before them, Quetzal's Breed Street Shul show brought into focus the way Eastside cultural imaginaries transcended boundaries and conventional thinking about what "Chicano" is and ought to be. All of them showed in their own way that Chicana/o culture has long flowed from and through circuits that extend beyond racial and national borders, what José David Saldívar calls the "outernational."[54]

Quetzal and its generation have also brought new forms of Chicana/o cultural politics to the fore. More directly than their predecessors, their music and activism supports George Yudice's contention that some cultural practices and venues have the potential to be turned into resources that might "be mobilized in the pursuit of social justice under certain circumstances."[55] Drawing inspiration from the Ejército Zapatista de Liberación Nacional's struggle against neoliberalism and co-organizing the 2002 "Encuentro Chicano/Jarocho" in Veracruz, for instance, dramatically influenced Quetzal's musical and political work.[56] Further, unlike much previous Eastside cultural expression, Quetzal and others of their ilk deliberately articulate a woman-centered political vision. Martha Gonzalez noted that she and the band's violinist Rocio Marron "have come to realize the scarcity of female musicians" and that they "work really hard to resist and redefine" women as "tokens" or "eye candy" rather than serious artists.[57] Quetzal also challenge the idea that (hyper)masculinity serves as an effective shortcut to multiracial or transnational coalition. Quetzal Flores noted that nowadays "the whole East LA scene is into the mode of making a conscious effort to acknowledge the struggle of women and for us as men to act on that as well."⁵⁸ Despite the injection of new social movements and gender politics into recent Eastside imaginaries, it is still not difficult, as journalist Rubén Martínez reminds us, to connect "the mysterious Lil' Julian Herrera, the Hungarian Jewish-Chicano rock 'n' roller of 1950s Boyle Heights" to "the latest generation of jarana-picking neo-folkies-with-a-pomo-twist."⁵⁹

I begin and end this chapter with Quetzal because they have explicitly sought to reimagine "Chicana/o" through their music and activism. Though they did so differently from the outside-in, Herrera, Bill Phillips, Freddie Prinze, and Shin Miyata also reimagined "Chicana/o." Accounting for them in the longer history of Eastside imaginaries remaps Chicana/o identity and politics as relational and transnational. It recognizes the shifting and porous racial and political boundaries of Chicana/o communities. Ultimately, it stretches the contours of how we understand Chicana/o cultural history. Eyeing the field through the experiences of "non-Chicanas/os" underscores that cultural dialogue, exchange, and intersection are operative devices in how we as scholars might reimagine our work in Chicana/o studies.

Such an approach unearths a Chicana/o cultural history that reformulates our understanding of Aztlán. As a historical, political, and scholarly paradigm signifying a physical and spiritual Chicana/o homeland, the idea of Aztlán has often rested on tropes of *mestizaje* and borderlands. With its claims to national and biological ties that originated prior to the founding of the United States, stretched south to pre-Columbian Mexico, and emphasized indigenous history, Aztlán gave legitimacy to Chicana/o claims for civil rights against what many perceived to be a racist and hegemonic order.⁶⁰ While much of Chicana/o history has been generatively filtered through such approaches, however, Aztlán can mask as much as it reveals. The concept of *mestizaje* can elide multiple racial identifications for an idealized Indian identity. Borderlands, while underscoring the migrations of a transnational Mexican labor force and related cross-border circuits of economic, political, and cultural exchange, have not always accounted for Chicana/o linkages that extend toward other hemispheric points, the Pacific Rim, and elsewhere. Thinking beyond *mestizaje* and borderlands means accounting for the multiracial and global Chicana/o experiences that have been fueled by neoliberalism's reach in both recent years and decades past.

Quetzal Flores underscored this argument for the contemporary moment when he said, "The concept of Aztlan has changed a little. It's a spiritual safe haven, the place I travel to in my dreams and find comfort and relax for a minute, you know? It's just a model, the one that we have right now. If other people of color want to take that model and build something bigger and more beautiful that would be great for me—I'd follow it."[61]

The Eastside imaginaries discussed herein also complicate the periodization of Chicana/o cultural history. Much of the literature underscores the discontinuity between the World War II, *Movimiento*, and post-Movement eras. It emphasizes generational and political rupture between earlier efforts for accommodation and assimilation, the militancy and radicalism of the middle period, and a slow spiral of depoliticization or declension into the Hispanic or Latina/o age, the latter of which Carlos Blanton takes issue with elsewhere in this collection as wrong and divisive. Rather than assume Chicana/o cultural history followed this single narrative, we would do better to see the variant relational and transnational impulses, connections, and politics that surfaced throughout the postwar period. Far from suggesting the 1950s generation was as militant as the next or that global *Latinidad* carries the political potency Chicanisma/o did in the heyday of the *Movimiento*, I do think we have too quickly dismissed alternative periodizations in Chicana/o cultural history.

When Shin Miyata was asked about José Feliciano's theme song for *Chico and the Man* in a recent interview, he said, "Well, he is not Chicano and on TV the main actor [Freddie Prinze] was not Chicano. But, anytime I see the YouTube of *Chico and the Man*, the opening scene is so beautiful. Filmed on the Eastside and it shows original Impala low riders cruising, the kids are playing in the park. You know, it's beautiful. I like that song."[62] Feliciano and Prinze were not Chicano, but, at least for Miyata, they encapsulated a quintessential, if romantic, Chicana/o cultural imaginary. Add to this a final observation by Quetzal Flores: "I think that being Chicano now is still valid and still very important in terms of identity and self-determination, but I think more and more people are starting to take this position: how to create an identity as a way to build a foundation so that you can communicate and collaborate with other communities."[63] Miyata and Flores might have said as much to one another when Quetzal toured Japan in 2006 at Miyata's invitation. Perhaps we can imagine either of them stepping into Phillips Music Company in the 1950s or responding to the 1974 controversy over

Chico and the Man. Among the most important lessons we might learn from all of these figures and moments? *Imagine.*

Notes

1. "Quetzal's 'Imaginaries' Wins Latin Alternative Award," *Los Angeles Times,* February 10, 2013.

2. Emma Pérez, *The Decolonial Imaginary* (Bloomington: Indiana University Press, 1999).

3. Russell Rodriguez and Martha Gonzalez, "Track Notes," Quetzal, *Imaginaries,* Smithsonian Folkways Recordings, 2012.

4. George Lipsitz, *American Studies in a Moment of Danger* (Minneapolis: University of Minnesota Press, 2001), 181.

5. Patricia Zavella, *I'm Neither Here nor There: Mexicans' Quotidian Struggles with Migration and Poverty* (Durham, NC: Duke University Press, 2011), 213.

6. For a useful discussion of how Chicanas/os, African Americans, and Asian Americans crossed, passed, and sidestepped the color line in the twentieth-century urban United States, see, for example, Albert Camarillo, "Navigating Segregated Life in America's Racial Borderhoods, 1910s–1950s," *Journal of American History* 100, no. 3 (December 2013): 645–662.

7. For an excellent discussion of conducting Chicana/o history through a relational lens, see Natalia Molina, "Examining Chicana/o History through a Relational Lens," *Pacific Historical Review* 82, no. 4 (November 2013): 520–541.

8. Matthew Pratt Guterl, *Seeing Race in Modern America* (Chapel Hill: University of North Carolina Press, 2013), 10–11.

9. Alicia Schmidt Camacho notes that imaginaries function as a "symbolic field in which people come to understand and describe their social being." Camacho, *Migrant Imaginaries: Latino Cultural Politics in the US-Mexico Borderlands* (New York: NYU Press, 2008), 5.

10. Inderpal Grewal, *Transnational America: Feminisms, Diasporas, Neoliberalisms* (Durham, NC: Duke University Press, 2005), 23. Grewal notes the complex and multiple character of transnational "connectivities" (as opposed to outright "connections") where there are a "variety of connections that exist," "weak and strong connectivities," "some unevenly connected, others strongly connected," "some get translated and transcoded," and "still others incommesurable and untranslatable."

11. Juan Flores, "Reclaiming Left Baggage: Some Early Sources for Minority Studies," *Cultural Critique* 59 (Winter 2005): 187–206.

12. Nicole Guidotti-Hernández, *Unspeakable Violence: Remapping US and Mexican National Imaginaries* (Durham, NC: Duke University Press, 2011), 14.

13. David Reyes and Tom Waldman, *Land of a Thousand Dances: Chicano Rock 'n' Roll from Southern California* (Albuquerque: University of New Mexico Press, 1998), 33.

14. Ihsan Taylor, "Johnny Otis, Godfather of Rhythm and Blues, Dies at 90," *New York Times,* January 19, 2012.

15. George J. Sánchez, "What's Good for Boyle Heights Is Good for the

Jews: Creating Multiracialism on the Eastside during the 1950s," *American Quarterly* 56, no. 3 (September 2004): 633–661; Anthony Macías, "Multicultural Music, Jews, and American Culture: The Life and Times of William Phillips," in *Beyond Alliances: The Jewish Role in Reshaping the Racial Landscape of Southern California*, ed. George J. Sánchez (West Lafayette, IN: Purdue University Press, 2012), 33–70.

16. Reyes and Waldman, *Land of a Thousand Dances*, 27.

17. George Lipsitz, *How Racism Takes Place* (Philadelphia: Temple University Press, 2011).

18. Interview with Allan and Bruce Phillips by Josh Kun, August 18, 2011, accessed September 12, 2013, http://phillipsmusiccompany.tumblr.com.

19. "Celebrating a Piece of Boyle Heights History," *Los Angeles Times*, August 27, 2011; Jessica Perez, "The Democracy of Music in Boyle Heights," *Boyle Heights Beat*, August 4, 2011. Perez's article includes an interview with USC professor Josh Kun, who spearheaded the Phillips Music Company historical project funded by the National Endowment for the Arts and the California Council for the Humanities. The project's website can be viewed at http://phillipsmusiccompany.tumblr.com.

20. Interview with Lola Fernandez by Josh Kun, August 24, 2011, accessed September 12, 2013, http://phillipsmusiccompany.tumblr.com.

21. Sánchez, "What's Good for Boyle Heights," 644–645; Macías, "Multicultural Music, Jews, and American Culture," 33–70.

22. "Celebrating a Piece of Boyle Heights History," *Los Angeles Times*, August 27, 2011.

23. George Lipsitz, *Time Passages: Collective Memory and American Popular Culture* (Minneapolis: University of Minnesota Press, 2006), 152.

24. On race, space, and popular culture in postwar LA, see, for example, Gaye Theresa Johnson, *Spaces of Conflict, Sounds of Solidarity: Music, Race, and Spatial Entitlement in Los Angeles* (Berkeley: University of California Press, 2013); Eric Avila, *Popular Culture in the Age of White Flight: Fear and Fantasy in Suburban Los Angeles* (Berkeley: University of California Press, 2004).

25. Shana Bernstein, *Bridges of Reform: Interracial Civil Rights Activism in Twentieth-Century Los Angeles* (New York: Oxford University Press, 2011).

26. "2009 Persons Attend Cultural Programs at Soto, Michigan," *California Eagle*, November 23, 1952.

27. Alicia Sandoval and Paul Macías, "Chico and the Man: Some Chicanos Are Not Amused," *Los Angeles Times*, October 27, 1974. Sandoval was a USC PhD candidate in education and a local talk show host. Macías was an actor at Universal Studios and a member of El Teatro Nacional de Aztlan (TENAZ), a national network of Chicana/o theater groups.

28. Ibid.

29. *TV Times*, supplement to the *Los Angeles Times*, November 10, 1974. Quoted in Mary C. Beltrán, *Latina/o Stars in US Eyes: The Making and Meanings of Film and TV Stardom* (Urbana: University of Illinois Press, 2009), 102.

30. Letter from Los Angeles Hispanic Urban Center to NBC President Robert Howard, reprinted in "Under Fire: Chico and the Man," *Los Angeles Times*, September 30, 1974.

31. John H. Brinsley, letter to the editor, "Chico and the Man," *Los Angeles Times*, November 18, 1974.

32. Chon Noriega, *Shot in America: Television, the State, and the Rise of Chicano Cinema* (Minneapolis: University of Minnesota Press, 2000), 71.

33. "Chico's Associate Producer Andrade Unhappy over Show's Chicano Image," *Daily Variety*, September 19, 1974; Greg Oguss, "Whose Barrio Is It? *Chico and the Man* and the Integrated Ghetto Shows of the 1970s," *Television & New Media* 6, no. 1 (February 2005): 3–21.

34. Sandoval and Macías, "Chico and the Man: Some Chicanos Are Not Amused."

35. Luis Torres, *Doña Julia's Children: The Life and Legacy of Educational Reformer Vahac Mardirosian* (N.p.: Xlibris, 2013).

36. It is important to note that Freddie Prinze's portrayal of Chico occasionally disrupted the "macho," masculine trope.

37. Lipsitz, *American Studies in a Moment of Danger*, 176.

38. Laura Pulido, *Black, Brown, Yellow, and Left: Radical Activism in Los Angeles* (Berkeley: University of California Press, 2006).

39. Lorena Oropeza, *¡Raza Si! ¡Guerra No! Chicano Protest and Patriotism during the Viet Nam War* (Berkeley: University of California Press, 2005); Ernesto Chávez, *"¡Mi Raza Primero!" Nationalism, Identity, and Insurgency in the Chicano Movement in Los Angeles, 1966–1978* (Berkeley: University of California Press, 2002).

40. Dan Berger, ed., *The Hidden 1970s: Histories of Radicalism* (New Brunswick, NJ: Rutgers University Press, 2010); Cynthia Young, *Soul Power: Culture, Radicalism, and the Making of a US Third World Left* (Durham, NC: Duke University Press, 2006).

41. Maylei Blackwell, *¡Chicana Power! Contested Histories of Feminism in the Chicano Movement* (Austin: University of Texas Press, 2011).

42. Hector Becerra, "Eastside Record Label Still Spinning Out the Music," *Los Angeles Times*, January 8, 2013.

43. Ibid.

44. Mark Guerrero, "Shin Miyata: Chicano Music's Bridge to Japan," based on Guerrero's interview of Miyata on December 9, 2007, accessed September 3, 2013, http://www.markguerrero.com/misc_63.php; interview with Shin Miyata on *Discos Inmigrantes*, April 24, 2012, aired on Radio Sombra, a community-based Internet radio station in Boyle Heights, East Los Angeles.

45. James Clifford, *Routes: Travel and Translation in the Late Twentieth Century* (Cambridge, MA: Harvard University Press, 1997), 18.

46. George Lipsitz, *Footsteps in the Dark: The Hidden Histories of Popular Music* (Minneapolis: University of Minnesota Press, 2007), 70.

47. Walter Benjamin, "The Author as Producer," in *Reflections: Essays, Aphorisms, Autobiographical Writing*, ed. Peter Demetz (New York: Schocken Books, 1986), 220–238.

48. Guerrero, "Shin Miyata: Chicano Music's Bridge to Japan."

49. Clifford, *Routes*, 18.

50. Ibid.; Paul Gilroy, *The Black Atlantic: Modernity and Double Consciousness* (Cambridge, MA: Harvard University Press, 1993).

51. Vivek Bald, "Overlapping Diasporas, Multiracial Lives: South Asian Muslims in US Communities of Color, 1880–1950," *Souls: A Critical Journal of Black Politics, Culture, and Society* 8, no. 4 (2006): 7.

52. Ibid.

53. Comment by Ruben Guevara in response to Rubén Martínez, "Eastside Grammy Story," accessed August 31, 2013, http://rubenmartinez.la/blog/eastside-grammy-story/.

54. José David Saldívar, *Trans-Americanity: Subaltern Modernities, Global Coloniality, and the Cultures of Greater Mexico* (Durham, NC: Duke University Press, 2012).

55. George Yudice, "Afro Reggae: Parlaying Culture into Social Justice," *Social Text* 19, no. 4 (2001): 53.

56. Interview with Quetzal Flores by Chris Gonzalez Clarke, *In Motion Magazine*, March 27, 1999, accessed September 10, 2013, http://www.inmotionmagazine.com/quetz.html; Victor Viesca, "The Battle of Los Angeles: The Cultural Politics of Chicana/o Music in the Greater Eastside," *American Quarterly* 56, no. 3 (September 2004): 719–739; Zavella, *I'm Neither Here nor There*, 211; Russell Rodriguez, "Introduction" to liner notes, Quetzal, *Imaginaries*, Smithsonian Folkways Recordings, 2012.

57. Zavella, *I'm Neither Here nor There*, 208–209.

58. Viesca, "The Battle of Los Angeles," 729.

59. Martinez, "Eastside Grammy Story."

60. Josefina Saldaña Portillo, "Who's the Indian in Aztlán? Re-writing Mestizaje, Indianism, and Chicanismo from the Lacandón," in *The Latin American Subaltern Studies Reader*, ed. Ileana Rodríguez (Durham, NC: Duke University Press, 2001), 402–423.

61. Interview with Quetzal Flores by Chris Gonzalez Clarke.

62. Interview with Shin Miyata on *Discos Inmigrantes*, April 24, 2012.

63. Viesca, "The Battle of Los Angeles," 730.

Select Bibliography of Recent Publications in Chicana/o History

Acuña, Rodolfo. *The Making of Chicana/o Studies: In the Trenches of Academe*. New Brunswick, NJ: Rutgers University Press, 2011.

Alamillo, José M. *Making Lemonade out of Lemons: Mexican American Labor and Leisure in a California Town, 1880–1960*. Urbana: University of Illinois Press, 2006.

Almaráz, Félix D., Jr. *Knight without Armor: Carlos Eduardo Castañeda, 1896–1958*. College Station: Texas A&M University Press, 1999.

Alonzo, Armando C. *Tejano Legacy: Rancheros and Settlers in South Texas, 1734–1900*. Albuquerque: University of New Mexico Press, 1998.

Alvarez, Luis. "From Zoot Suits to Hip Hop: Towards a Relational Chicana/o Studies." *Latino Studies* 5, no. 1 (Spring 2007): 53–75.

———. *The Power of the Zoot: Youth Culture and Resistance during World War II*. Berkeley: University of California Press, 2008.

Alvarez, Luis, and Daniel Widener. "A History of Black and Brown: Chicana/o–African-American Cultural and Political Relations." *Aztlán* 33, no. 1 (Spring 2008): 143–154.

Arredondo, Gabriela F. *Mexican Chicago: Race, Identity, and Nation, 1916–1939*. Urbana: University of Illinois Press, 2008.

Arreola, Daniel D., ed. *Hispanic Spaces, Latino Places: Community and Cultural Diversity in Contemporary America*. Austin: University of Texas Press, 2004.

———. *Tejano South Texas: A Mexican American Cultural Province*. Austin: University of Texas Press, 2002.

Badillo, David A. *Latinos and the New Immigrant Church*. Baltimore, MD: Johns Hopkins University Press, 2006.

Barajas, Frank P. *Curious Unions: Mexican American Workers and Resistance in Oxnard, California, 1898–1961*. Lincoln: University of Nebraska Press, 2012.

Barr, Juliana. *Peace Came in the Form of a Woman: Indians and Spaniards in the Texas Borderlands*. Chapel Hill: University of North Carolina Press, 2007.

Barton, Paul. *Hispanic Methodists, Presbyterians, and Baptists in Texas*. Austin: University of Texas Press, 2006.

Bebout, Lee. *Mythohistorical Interventions: The Chicano Movement and Its Legacies*. Minneapolis: University of Minnesota Press, 2011.

Behnken, Brian D. *Fighting Their Own Battles: Mexican Americans, African Americans, and the Struggle for Civil Rights in Texas.* Chapel Hill: University of North Carolina Press, 2011.

Bernstein, Shana. *Bridges of Reform: Interracial Civil Rights Activism in Twentieth-Century Los Angeles.* New York: Oxford University Press, 2011.

Blackwell, Maylei. *¡Chicana Power! Contested Histories of Feminism in the Chicano Movement.* Austin: University of Texas Press, 2011.

Blanton, Carlos Kevin. "The Citizenship Sacrifice: Mexican Americans, the Saunders-Leonard Report, and the Politics of Immigration, 1951–1952." *Western Historical Quarterly* 40, no. 3 (Autumn 2009): 299–320.

———. "From Intellectual Deficiency to Cultural Deficiency: Mexican Americans, Testing, and Public School Policy in the American Southwest, 1920–1940." *Pacific Historical Review* 72, no. 1 (February 2003): 39–62.

———. "George I. Sánchez, Ideology, and Whiteness in the Making of the Mexican American Civil Rights Movement, 1930–1960." *Journal of Southern History* 72, no. 3 (August 2006): 569–604.

———. *George I. Sánchez: The Long Fight for Mexican American Integration.* New Haven, CT: Yale University Press, 2014.

———. *The Strange Career of Bilingual Education in Texas, 1836–1981.* College Station: Texas A&M University Press, 2004.

Burgos, Adrian, Jr. *Playing America's Game: Baseball, Latinos, and the Color Line.* Berkeley: University of California Press, 2007.

Cadava, Geraldo L. "Borderlands of Modernity and Abandonment: The Lines within Ambos Nogales and the Tohono O'odham Nation." *Journal of American History* 98, no. 2 (September 2011): 362–383.

———. *Standing on Common Ground: The Making of a Sunbelt Borderland.* Cambridge, MA: Harvard University Press, 2013.

Camarillo, Albert M. "Looking Back on Chicano History: A Generational Perspective." *Pacific Historical Review* 82, no. 4 (November 2013): 496–504.

———. "Navigating Segregated Life in America's Racial Borderhoods, 1910s–1950s." *Journal of American History* 100, no. 3 (December 2013): 645–662.

Carrigan, William D., and Clive Webb. "The Lynching of Persons of Mexican Origin or Descent in the United States, 1848–1928. *Journal of Social History* 37, no. 2 (Winter 2003): 411–438.

Carroll, Patrick J. *Felix Longoria's Wake: Bereavement, Racism, and the Rise of Mexican American Activism.* Austin: University of Texas Press, 2003.

Casas, María Raquél. *Married to a Daughter of the Land: Spanish-Mexican Women and Interethnic Marriage in California, 1820–1880.* Reno: University of Nevada Press, 2007.

Castañeda, Antonia. "Que Se Pudieran Defender (So You Could Defend Yourselves)": Chicanas, Regional History, and National Discourses." *Frontiers* 22, no. 3 (2001): 116–142.

Chávez, Ernesto. "Chicano/a History: Its Origins, Purpose, and Future." *Pacific Historical Review* 82, no. 4 (November 2013): 505–519.

———. *"¡Mi Raza Primero!" (My People First!) Nationalism, Identity, and Insurgency in the Chicano Movement in Los Angeles, 1966–1978.* Berkeley: University of California Press, 2002.

. "'Ramón Is Not One of These': Race and Sexuality in the Construction of Silent Actor Ramón Novarro's Star Image." *Journal of the History of Sexuality* 20 (2011): 520–544.

Chávez-García, Miroslava. "Intelligence Testing at Whittier School, 1890–1920." *Pacific Historical Review* 76, no. 2 (May 2007): 193–228.

. "The Interdisciplinary Project of Chicana History: Looking Back, Moving Forward." *Pacific Historical Review* 82, no. 4 (November 2013): 542–565.

. *Negotiating Conquest: Gender and Power in California, 1770s to 1880s.* Tucson: University of Arizona Press, 2004.

. *States of Delinquency: Race and Science in the Making of California's Juvenile Justice System.* Berkeley: University of California Press, 2012.

Cohen, Deborah. *Braceros: Migrant Citizens and Transnational Subjects in the Postwar United States and Mexico.* Chapel Hill: University of North Carolina Press, 2011.

Contreras, Eduardo. "Voice and Property: Latinos, White Conservatives, and Urban Renewal in 1960s San Francisco." *Western Historical Quarterly* 45, no. 3 (Autumn 2014): 253–276.

Crimm, A. Carolina Castillo. *De León: A Tejano Family History.* Austin: University of Texas Press, 2003.

De Genova, Nicholas, ed. *Racial Transformations: Latinos and Asians Remaking the United States.* Durham, NC: Duke University Press, 2006.

De Genova, Nicholas, and Ana Y. Ramos-Zayas. *Latino Crossings: Mexicans, Puerto Ricans, and the Politics of Race and Citizenship.* New York: Routledge, 2003.

De la Teja, Jesús F. *San Antonio de Béxar: A Community on New Spain's Northern Frontier.* Albuquerque: University of New Mexico Press, 1996.

. "Why Urbano and María Trinidad Can't Get Married: Social Relations in Late Colonial San Antonio." *Southwestern Historical Quarterly* 112, no. 2 (October 2008): 121–146.

De León, Arnoldo. *Racial Frontiers: Africans, Chinese, and Mexicans in Western America, 1848–1890.* Albuquerque: University of New Mexico Press, 2002.

, ed. *War along the Border: The Mexican Revolution and Tejano Communities.* College Station: Texas A&M University, 2012.

Delgado, Grace Peña. *Making the Chinese Mexican: Global Migration, Localism, and Exclusion in the US-Mexico Borderlands.* Stanford, CA: Stanford University Press, 2012.

Díaz, George T. *Border Contraband: A History of Smuggling across the Rio Grande.* Austin: University of Texas Press, 2015.

Echeverría, Darius V. *Aztlán Arizona: Mexican American Educational Empowerment, 1968–1978.* Tucson: University of Arizona Press, 2014.

Escobar, Edward J. "Bloody Christmas and the Irony of Police Professionalism: The Los Angeles Police Department, Mexican Americans, and Police Reform in the 1950s." *Pacific Historical Review* 72, no. 2 (May 2003): 171–199.

. *Race, Police, and the Making of a Political Identity: Mexican Americans and the Los Angeles Police Department, 1900–1945.* Berkeley: University of California Press, 1999.

Escobedo, Elizabeth R. *From Coveralls to Zoot Suits: The Lives of Mexican Amer-*

ican Women on the World War II Home Front. Chapel Hill: University of North Carolina Press, 2013.

———. "The Pachuca Panic: Sexual and Cultural Battlegrounds in World War II." *Western Historical Quarterly* 38, no. 2 (Summer 2007): 133–156.

Espinosa, Gastón. "'El Azteca': Francisco Olazábal and Latino Pentecostal Charisma, Power, and Faith Healing in the Borderlands." *Journal of the American Academy of Religion* 67, no. 3 (September 1999): 597–616.

Espinosa, Gastón, and Mario T. García, eds. *Mexican American Religions: Spirituality, Activism, and Culture.* Durham, NC: Duke University Press, 2008.

Espinoza, Dionne. "'Revolutionary Sisters': Women's Solidarity and Collective Identification among Chicana Brown Berets in East Los Angeles, 1967–1970." *Aztlán* 26, no. 1 (Spring 2001): 16–58.

Fernandez, Delia. "Becoming Latino: Mexican and Puerto Rican Community Formation in Grand Rapids, Michigan, 1926–1964." *Michigan Historical Review* 39, no. 1 (Spring 2013): 71–100.

Fernández, Lilia. *Brown in the Windy City: Mexicans and Puerto Ricans in Postwar Chicago.* Chicago: University of Chicago Press, 2012.

———. "Of Migrants and Immigrants: Mexican and Puerto Rican Labor Migration in Comparative Perspective, 1942–1964." *Journal of American Ethnic History* 29, no. 3 (Spring 2010): 6–39.

Fink, Leon. *The Maya of Morganton: Work and Community in the Nuevo New South.* Chapel Hill: University of North Carolina Press, 2003.

Flores, Juan. "Reclaiming Left Baggage: Some Early Sources for Minority Studies." *Cultural Critique* 59 (Winter 2005): 187–206.

Flores, Lori A. "An Unladylike Strike Fashionably Clothed: Mexicana and Anglo Women Garment Workers against Tex-Son, 1959–1963." *Pacific Historical Review* 78, no. 3 (August 2009): 367–402.

Flores, Ruben. *Backroads Pragmatists: Mexico's Melting Pot and Civil Rights in the United States.* Philadelphia: University of Pennsylvania Press, 2014.

Foley, Neil. *Quest for Equality: The Failed Promise of Black-Brown Solidarity.* Cambridge, MA: Harvard University Press, 2010.

———. *The White Scourge: Mexicans, Blacks, and Poor Whites in Texas Cotton Culture.* Berkeley: University of California Press, 1997.

García, Ignacio M. *Chicanismo: The Forging of a Militant Ethos among Mexican Americans.* Tucson: University of Arizona Press, 1997.

———. *Hector P. Garcia: In Relentless Pursuit of Justice.* Houston: Arte Público Press, 2003.

———. *Viva Kennedy: Mexican Americans in Search of Camelot.* College Station: Texas A&M University Press, 2000.

———. *White but Not Equal: Mexican Americans, Jury Discrimination, and the Supreme Court.* Tucson: University of Arizona Press, 2009.

García, Juan R. *Mexicans in the Midwest, 1900–1932.* Tucson: University of Arizona Press, 1996.

García, Mario T. *Católicos: Resistance and Affirmation in Chicano Catholic History.* Austin: University of Texas Press, 2008.

———, ed. *The Chicano Movement: Perspectives from the Twenty-First Century.* New York: Routledge, 2014.

García, Mario T., with Sal Castro. *Blowout! Sal Castro and the Chicano Struggle for Educational Justice.* Chapel Hill: University of North Carolina Press, 2011.

García, Matt. *From the Jaws of Victory: The Triumph and Tragedy of Cesar Chavez and the Farm Worker Movement.* Berkeley: University of California Press, 2012.

———. *A World of Its Own: Race, Labor, and Citrus in the Making of Greater Los Angeles, 1900–1970.* Chapel Hill: University of North Carolina Press, 2001.

Garcilazo, Jeffrey M. "McCarthyism, Mexican Americans, and the Los Angeles Committee for Protection of the Foreign-Born, 1950–1954." *Western Historical Quarterly* 32, no. 3 (Fall 2001): 273–295.

Garza-Falcón, Leticia M. *Gente Decente: A Borderlands Response to the Rhetoric of Dominance.* Austin: University of Texas Press, 1998.

Getz, Lynne Marie. *Schools of Their Own: The Education of Hispanos in New Mexico, 1850–1940.* Albuquerque: University of New Mexico Press, 1997.

Gómez, Laura E. *Manifest Destinies: The Making of the Mexican American Race.* New York: New York University Press, 2007.

González, Deena J. *Refusing the Favor: The Spanish-Mexican Women of Santa Fe, 1820–1880.* New York: Oxford University Press, 1999.

González, Gabriela. "Carolina Munguía and Emma Tenayuca: The Politics of Benevolence and Radical Reform." *Frontiers* 24, nos. 2–3 (2003): 200–229.

González, Gilbert G. *Culture of Empire: American Writers, Mexico, and Mexican Immigrants, 1880–1930.* Austin: University of Texas Press, 2004.

———. *Mexican Consuls and Labor Organizing: Imperial Politics in the American Southwest.* Austin: University of Texas Press, 1999.

González, John Morán. *Border Renaissance: The Texas Centennial and the Emergence of Mexican American Literature.* Austin: University of Texas Press, 2009.

Gonzalez, Phillip B. *Forced Sacrifice as Ethnic Protest: The Hispano Cause in New Mexico and the Racial Attitude Confrontation of 1933.* New York: Peter Lang, 2001.

———. "'La Junta de Indignación': Hispano Repertoire of Collective Protest in New Mexico, 1884–1933." *Western Historical Quarterly* 31, no. 2 (Summer 2000): 161–186.

Gordon, Linda. *The Great Arizona Orphan Abduction.* Cambridge, MA: Harvard University Press, 1999.

Guglielmo, Thomas A. "Fighting for Caucasian Rights: Mexicans, Mexican Americans, and the Transnational Struggle for Civil Rights in World War II Texas." *Journal of American History* 92, no. 4 (March 2006): 1212–1237.

Guidotti-Hernández, Nicole M. *Unspeakable Violence: Remapping US and Mexican National Imaginaries.* Durham, NC: Duke University Press, 2011.

Gutiérrez, David G., ed. *The Columbia History of Latinos in the United States since 1960.* New York: Columbia University Press, 2004.

———. "Migration, Emergent Ethnicity, and the 'Third Space': The Shifting Politics of Nationalism in Greater Mexico." *Journal of American History* 86, no. 2 (September 1999): 481–517.

———. *Walls and Mirrors: Mexican Americans, Mexican Immigrants, and the Politics of Ethnicity.* Berkeley: University of California Press, 1995.

Gutiérrez, Ramón A. "Internal Colonialism: An American Theory of Race." *Du Bois Review* 1, no. 2 (2004): 281–295.

Gutiérrez, Ramón A., and Elliott Young. "Transnationalizing Borderlands History." *Western Historical Quarterly* 41, no. 1 (Spring 2010): 26–53.

Haas, Lisbeth. *Conquests and Historical Identities in California, 1769–1936.* Berkeley: University of California Press, 1996.

Hämäläinen, Pekka, and Samuel Truett. "On Borderlands." *Journal of American History* 98, no. 2 (September 2011): 338–361.

Haney-López, Ian F. *Racism on Trial: The Chicano Fight for Justice.* Boston: Belknap, 2004.

Hernández, José Angel. *Mexican American Colonization during the Nineteenth Century: A History of the US-Mexico Borderlands.* New York: Cambridge University Press, 2012.

Hernández, Kelly Lytle. "The Crimes and Consequences of Illegal Immigration: A Cross-Border Examination of Operation Wetback, 1943 to 1954." *Western Historical Quarterly* 37, no. 4 (Winter 2006): 421–444.

———. *Migra! A History of the US Border Patrol.* Berkeley: University of California Press, 2010.

Hernández, Sonia. *Working Women into the Borderlands.* College Station: Texas A&M University Press, 2014.

Hinojosa, Felipe. *Latino Mennonites: Civil Rights, Faith, and Evangelical Culture.* Baltimore, MD: Johns Hopkins University Press, 2014.

———. "¡Medicina Sí Muerte No! Race, Public Health, and the 'Long War on Poverty' in Mathis, Texas, 1948–1971." *Western Historical Quarterly* 44, no. 4 (Winter 2013): 437–458.

Innis-Jiménez, Michael. *Steel Barrio: The Great Mexican Migration to South Chicago, 1915–1940.* New York: New York University Press, 2013.

Johnson, Benjamin H. "The Cosmic Race in Texas: Racial Fusion, White Supremacy, and Civil Rights Politics." *Journal of American History* 98, no. 2 (September 2011): 404–419.

———. *Revolution in Texas: How a Forgotten Rebellion and Its Bloody Suppression Turned Mexicans into Americans.* New Haven, CT: Yale University Press, 2003.

Kaplowitz, Craig A. *LULAC: Mexican Americans and National Policy.* College Station: Texas A&M University Press, 2005.

Katzew, Ilona, and Susan Deans-Smith, eds. *Race and Classification: The Case of Mexican America.* Stanford, CA: Stanford University Press, 2009.

Kreneck, Thomas H. *Mexican American Odyssey: Felix Tijerina, Entrepreneur and Civic Leader, 1905–1965.* College Station: Texas A&M University Press, 2001.

Levario, Miguel Antonio. *Militarizing the Border: When Mexicans Became the Enemy.* College Station: Texas A&M University Press, 2012.

Limón, José E. *Américo Paredes: Culture and Critique.* Austin: University of Texas Press, 2012.

Lopez, Sarah Lynn. *The Remittance Landscape: Spaces of Migration in Rural Mexico and Urban USA.* Chicago: University of Chicago Press, 2014.

Lozano, Rosina A. "Managing the 'Priceless Gift': Debating Spanish Language Instruction in New Mexico, 1930–1950." *Western Historical Quarterly* 44, no. 3 (Autumn 2013): 271–293.

MacDonald, Victoria-María. *Latino Education in the United States: A Narrated History from 1513–2000.* New York: Palgrave Macmillan, 2004.

MacDonald, Victoria-María, and Benjamin Polk Hoffman. "'Compromising La Causa?' The Ford Foundation and Chicano Intellectual Nationalism in the Creation of Chicano History, 1963–1977." *History of Education Quarterly* 52, no. 2 (May 2012): 251–281.

Mantler, Gordon Keith. *Power to the Poor: Black-Brown Coalition and the Fight for Economic Justice, 1960–1974.* Chapel Hill: University of North Carolina Press, 2013.

Mariscal, George. *Brown-Eyed Children of the Sun: Lessons from the Chicano Movement, 1965–1975.* Albuquerque: University of New Mexico Pres, 2005.

——, ed. *Aztlán and Viet Nam: Chicano and Chicana Experiences of the War.* Berkeley: University of California Press, 1999.

Martínez, Anne M. *Catholic Borderlands: Mapping Catholicism onto American Empire, 1905–1935.* Lincoln: University of Nebraska Press, 2014.

Martinez, Richard Edward. *PADRES: The National Chicano Priest Movement.* Austin: University of Texas Press, 2005.

Matovina, Timothy. *Guadalupe and Her Faithful: Latino Catholics in San Antonio, from Colonial Origins to the Present.* Baltimore, MD: Johns Hopkins University Press, 2005.

May, Glenn Anthony. *Sonny Montes and Mexican American Activism in Oregon.* Corvallis: Oregon State University Press, 2011.

McCormick, Jennifer, and Cesar Ayala. "Felícita 'La Prieta' Méndez (1916–1998) and the End of Latino School Segregation in California." *Centro Journal* 19, no. 2 (Fall 2007): 12–35.

McKiernan-González, John. *Fevered Measures: Public Health and Race at the Texas-Mexico Border, 1848–1942.* Durham, NC: Duke University Press, 2012.

Medina, Lara. *Las Hermanas: Chicana/Latina Religious-Political Activism in the US Catholic Church.* Philadelphia: Temple University Press, 2004.

Meeks, Eric V. *Border Citizens: The Making of Indians, Mexicans, and Anglos in Arizona.* Austin: University of Texas Press, 2007.

Menchaca, Martha. *Naturalizing Mexican Immigrants: A Texas History.* Austin: University of Texas Press, 2011.

——. *Recovering History, Constructing Race: The Indian, Black, and White Roots of Mexican Americans.* Austin: University of Texas Press, 2001.

Mendoza, Alexander. "'For Our Own Best Interests': Nineteenth-Century Laredo Tejanos, Military Service, and the Development of American Nationalism." *Southwestern Historical Quarterly* 115, no. 2 (October 2011): 125–152.

Mitchell, Pablo. *Coyote Nation: Sexuality, Race, and Conquest in Modernizing New Mexico, 1880–1920.* Chicago: University of Chicago Press, 2005.

——. *West of Sex: Making Mexican America, 1900–1930.* Chicago: University of Chicago Press, 2012.

Mohl, Raymond. "Latinization in the Heart of Dixie: Hispanics in Late-Twentieth-Century Alabama." *Alabama Review* 87, no. 4 (2002): 243–274.

Molina, Natalia. "Examining Chicana/o History through a Relational Lens." *Pacific Historical Review* 82, no. 4 (November 2013): 520–541.

———. *Fit to Be Citizens? Public Health and Race in Los Angeles, 1879–1939.* Berkeley: University of California Press, 2006.

———. *How Race Is Made in America: Immigration, Citizenship, and the Historical Power of Racial Scripts.* Berkeley: University of California Press, 2013.

———. "The Long Arc of Dispossession: Racial Capitalism and Contested Notions of Citizenship in the US-Mexico Borderlands of the Early Twentieth Century." *Western Historical Quarterly* 45, no. 4 (Winter 2014): 431–447.

———. "The Power of Racial Scripts: What the History of Mexican Immigration to the United States Teaches Us about Relational Notions of Race." *Latino Studies* 8, no. 2 (2010): 156–175.

Montejano, David. *Quixote's Soldiers: A Local History of the Chicano Movement, 1966–1981.* Austin: University of Texas Press, 2010.

Mora, Anthony P. *Border Dilemmas: Racial and National Uncertainties in New Mexico, 1848–1912.* Durham, NC: Duke University Press, 2011.

———. "Resistance and Accommodation in a Border Parish." *Western Historical Quarterly* 36, no. 3 (Autumn 2005): 301–326.

Nieto-Phillips, John M. *The Language of Blood: The Making of Spanish-American Identity in New Mexico, 1880s–1930s.* Albuquerque: University of New Mexico Press, 2004.

Olivas, Michael A., ed. *"Colored Men" and "Hombres Aquí": Hernandez v. Texas and the Emergence of Mexican American Lawyering.* Houston: Arte Público Press, 2006.

———, ed. *In Defense of My People: Alonso S. Perales and the Development of Mexican-American Public Intellectuals.* Houston: Arte Público Press, 2012.

———. *No Undocumented Child Left Behind: Plyler v. Doe and the Education of Undocumented Schoolchildren.* New York: New York University Press, 2012.

———. "Reflections on Academic Merit Badges and Becoming an Eagle Scout." *Houston Law Review* 43 (2006): 81–124.

———. "The 'Trial of the Century' that Never Was: Staff Sgt. Macario Garcia, the Congressional Medal of Honor, and the Oasis Café." *Indiana Law Journal* 83 (2008): 1391–1403.

Ontiveros, Randy J. *In the Spirit of a New People: The Cultural Politics of the Chicano Movement.* New York: New York University Press, 2014.

Orenstein, Dara. "Void for Vagueness: Mexicans and the Collapse of Miscegenation Law in California." *Pacific Historical Review* 74, no. 3 (August 2005): 367–408.

Oropeza, Lorena. "The Heart of Chicano History: Reies López Tijerina as a Memory Entrepreneur." *The Sixties* 1, no. 1 (2008): 49–67.

———. *¡Raza Sí! ¡Guerra No! Chicano Protest and Patriotism during the Viet Nam War Era.* Berkeley: University of California Press, 2005.

Orozco, Cynthia E. *No Mexicans, Women, or Dogs Allowed: The Rise of the Mexican American Civil Rights Movement.* Austin: University of Texas Press, 2009.

———. "Regionalism, Politics, and Gender in Southwest History: The League of United Latin American Citizens' Expansion into New Mexico from Texas, 1929–1945." *Western Historical Quarterly* 29, no. 4 (Winter 1998): 459–483.

Overmyer-Velázquez, Mark. "Good Neighbors and White Mexicans: Constructing Race and Nation on the Mexico-US Border." *Journal of American Ethnic History* 33, no. 1 (Fall 2013): 5–34.

Pagán, Eduardo Obregón. *Murder at the Sleepy Lagoon: Zoot Suits, Race, and Riot in Wartime L.A.* Chapel Hill: University of North Carolina Press, 2003.

Perales, Monica. "Fighting to Stay in Smeltertown: Lead Contamination and Environmental Justice in a Mexican American Community." *Western Historical Quarterly* 39, no. 1 (2008): 41–63.

———. *Smeltertown: Making and Remembering a Southwest Border Community.* Chapel Hill: University of North Carolina Press, 2010.

Pérez, Emma. *The Decolonial Imaginary: Writing Chicanas into History.* Bloomington: Indiana University Press, 1999.

———. "Queering the Borderlands: The Challenges of Excavating the Invisible and Unheard." *Frontiers* 24, no. 2–3 (2003): 122–131.

Pitti, Stephen J. *The Devil in Silicon Valley: Northern California, Race, and Mexican Americans.* Princeton, NJ: Princeton University Press, 2003.

Pulido, Alberto López, Barbara Driscoll de Alvarado, and Carmen Samora, eds. *Moving Beyond Borders: Julian Samora and the Establishment of Latino Studies.* Urbana: University of Illinois Press, 2009.

Pulido, Laura. *Black, Brown, Yellow, and Left: Radical Activism in Los Angeles.* Berkeley: University of California Press, 2006.

Pycior, Julie Leininger. *Democratic Renewal and the Mutual Aid Legacy of US Mexicans.* College Station: Texas A&M University Press, 2014.

———. *LBJ and Mexican Americans: The Paradox of Power.* Austin: University of Texas Press, 1997.

Quiroz, Anthony. *Claiming Citizenship: Mexican Americans in Victoria, Texas.* College Station: Texas A&M University Press, 2005.

Ramírez, Catherine S. *The Women in the Zoot Suit: Gender, Nationalism, and the Cultural Politics of Memory.* Durham, NC: Duke University Press, 2009.

Ramírez, José A. *To the Line of Fire! Mexican Texans and World War I.* College Station: Texas A&M University Press, 2009.

Ramos, Henry A. J. *The American G.I. Forum: In Pursuit of the Dream, 1948–1983.* Houston: Arte Público Press, 1998.

Ramos, Raúl A. *Beyond the Alamo: Forging Mexican Ethnicity in San Antonio, 1821–1861.* Chapel Hill: University of North Carolina Press, 2008.

———. "Chicano/a Challenges to Nineteenth-Century History." *Pacific Historical Review* 82, no. 4 (November 2013): 566–580.

Reséndez, Andrés. *Changing National Identities at the Frontier: Texas and New Mexico, 1800–1850.* New York: Cambridge University Press, 2005.

Reyes, Bárbara O. *Private Women, Public Lives: Gender and the Missions of the Californias.* Austin: University of Texas Press, 2009.

Rivas-Rodriguez, Maggie, ed. *Mexican Americans and World War II.* Austin: University of Texas Press, 2005.

Rivas-Rodriguez, Maggie, and Emilio Zamora, eds. *Beyond the Latino World*

War II Hero: The Social and Political Legacy of a Generation. Austin: University of Texas Press, 2009.

Rochín, Refugio I., and Dennis N. Valdés, eds. *Voices of a New Chicana/o History.* East Lansing: Michigan State University Press, 2000.

Rodriguez, Marc Simon. "A Movement Made of 'Young Mexican Americans Seeking Change': Critical Citizenship, Migration, and the Chicano Movement in Texas and Wisconsin." *Western Historical Quarterly* 34, no. 3 (Autumn 2003): 274–299.

———. *The Tejano Diaspora: Mexican Americanism and Ethnic Politics in Texas and Wisconsin.* Chapel Hill: University of North Carolina Press, 2011.

Rodríguez, Richard T. *Next of Kin: The Family in Chicano/a Cultural Politics.* Durham, NC: Duke University Press, 2009.

Rosales, F. Arturo. *¡Pobre Raza! Violence, Mobilization, and Justice among México Lindo Immigrants, 1900–1936.* Austin: University of Texas Press, 1999.

Rosales, Steven. "Fighting the Peace at Home: Mexican American Veterans and the 1944 GI Bill of Rights." *Pacific Historical Review* 80, no. 4 (November 2011): 597–627.

Rosas, Ana Elizabeth. *Abrazando el Espíritu: Bracero Families Confront the US-Mexico Border.* Berkeley: University of California Press, 2014.

———. "Breaking the Silence: Mexican Children and Women's Confrontation of Bracero Family Separation, 1942–1964." *Gender and History* 23, no. 2 (August 2011): 382–400.

Ruiz, Vicki L. *From Out of the Shadows: Mexican Women in Twentieth-Century America.* New York: Oxford University Press, 1998.

———. "Morena/o, blanca/o y café con leche: Racial Constructions in Chicana/o Historiography." *Mexican Studies/Estudios Mexicanos* 20, no. 2 (Summer 2004): 343–360.

———. "Neustra America: Latino History as United States History." *Journal of American History* 93, no. 3 (December 2006): 655–673.

———. "Un Mujer Sin Fronteras: Luisa Moreno and Latina Labor Activism." *Pacific Historical Review* 73, no. 1 (February 2004): 1–20.

Ruiz, Vicki L., and Virginia Sánchez Korrol, eds. *Latina Legacies: Identity, Biography, and Community.* New York: Oxford University Press, 2005.

Saldaña-Portillo, María Josefina. "'How Many Mexicans [Is] a Horse Worth?' The League of United Latin American Citizens, Desegregation Cases, and Chicano Historiography." *South Atlantic Quarterly* 107, no. 4 (Fall 2008): 809–831.

Saldívar, Ramón. *The Borderlands of Culture: Américo Paredes and the Transnational Imaginary.* Durham, NC: Duke University Press, 2006.

Sánchez, George J. "What's Good for Boyle Heights Is Good for the Jews: Creating Multiracialism on the Eastside during the 1950s." *American Quarterly* 56, no. 3 (September 2004): 633–661.

Sánchez-Walsh, Arlene. *Latino Pentecostal Identity: Evangelical Faith, Self, and Society.* New York: Columbia University Press, 2003.

Sandos, James A. *Converting California: Indians and Franciscans in the Missions.* New Haven, CT: Yale University Press, 2008.

San Miguel, Guadalupe, Jr. *Brown, Not White: School Integration and the Chicano Movement in Houston.* College Station: Texas A&M University Press, 2001.

———. *Chicana/o Struggles for Education: Activism in the Community.* College Station: Texas A&M University Press, 2013.

———. *Tejano Proud: Tex-Mex Music in the Twentieth Century.* College Station: Texas A&M University Press, 2002.

San Miguel, Guadalupe, Jr., and Richard R. Valencia. "From the Treaty of Guadalupe Hidalgo to *Hopwood*: The Educational Plight and Struggle of Mexican Americans in the Southwest." *Harvard Educational Review* 68 (Fall 1998): 353–412.

Schmidt Camacho, Alicia R. *Migrant Imaginaries: Latino Cultural Politics in the US-Mexico Borderlands.* New York: New York University Press, 2008.

Smith, Heather A., and Owen J. Furuseth. *Latinos in the New South: Transformations of Place.* Burlington, VT: Ashgate, 2006.

Soldatenko, Michael. *Chicano Studies: The Genesis of a Discipline.* Tucson: University of Arizona Press, 2009.

Stern, Alexandra Minna. "On the Road with Chicana/o History: From Aztlán to the Alamo and Back." *Pacific Historical Review* 82, no. 4 (November 2013): 581–587.

Summers-Sandoval, Tomás F. *Latinos at the Golden Gate: Creating Community and Identity in San Francisco.* Chapel Hill: University of North Carolina Press, 2013.

Treviño, Roberto R. *The Church in the Barrio: Mexican American Ethno-Catholicism in Houston.* Chapel Hill: University of North Carolina Press, 2006.

Tutino, John, ed. *Mexico and Mexicans in the Making of the United States.* Austin: University of Texas Press, 2012.

Valencia, Richard R. *Chicano Students and the Courts: The Mexican American Legal Struggle for Educational Equality.* New York: New York University Press, 2008.

———. *Dismantling Contemporary Deficit Thinking: Educational Thought and Practice.* New York: Routledge, 2010.

Valerio-Jiménez, Omar S. "New Avenues for Domestic Dispute and Divorce Lawsuits along the US-Mexico Border, 1834–1893." *Journal of Women's History* 21, no. 1 (March 2009): 10–33.

———. *River of Hope: Forging Identity and Nation in the Rio Grande Borderlands.* Durham, NC: Duke University Press, 2013.

Vargas, Zaragosa. *Labor Rights Are Civil Rights: Mexican American Workers in Twentieth-Century America.* Princeton, NJ: Princeton University Press, 2005.

———. "Tejana Radical: Emma Tenayuca and the San Antonio Labor Movement during the Great Depression." *Pacific Historical Review* 66, no. 4 (November 1997): 553–580.

Webb, Clive, and William D. Carrigan. *Forgotten Dead: Mob Violence against Mexicans in the United States, 1848–1928.* New York: Oxford University Press, 2013.

Weber, Devra. *Dark Sweat, White Gold: California Farm Workers, Cotton, and the New Deal.* Berkeley: University of California Press, 1994.

Weber, John. "Homing Pigeons, Cheap Labor, and Frustrated Nativists: Immigration Reform and the Deportation of Mexicans from South Texas in the 1920s." *Western Historical Quarterly* 44, no. 2 (Summer 2013): 167–186.

Weise, Julie M. *Corazón de Dixie: Mexicanos in the US South since 1910.* Chapel Hill: University of North Carolina Press, 2015.

———. "Mexican Nationalisms, Southern Racisms: Mexicans and Mexican Americans in the US South, 1908–1939." *American Quarterly* 60, no. 3 (September 2008): 749–777.

Wilson, Stephen H. "Brown over 'Other White': Mexican Americans' Legal Arguments and Litigation Strategy in School Desegregation Lawsuits." *Law and History Review* 21, no. 1 (Spring 2003): 145–194.

Zamora, Emilio. *Claiming Rights and Righting Wrongs in Texas: Mexican Workers and Job Politics during World War II.* College Station: Texas A&M University Press, 2009.

Contributors

Luis Alvarez is an associate professor and the director of graduate studies in the Department of History at the University of California, San Diego. He is the author of *The Power of the Zoot: Youth Culture and Resistance during World War II* (University of California Press, 2008), co-editor of *Another University Is Possible* (University Readers Press, 2010), and co-editor of the forthcoming *A History of Mexican America* (Routledge). Alvarez has published several essays in journals including *Latino Studies*, *Aztlán: A Journal of Chicano Studies*, and *Popular Music and Society*. He is currently working on projects titled "From Civil Rights to Global Justice: Pop Culture and the Politics of the Possible," a study of pop culture and social movements in the Americas since World War II, and "El Tri v. The Stars and Stripes: A History of the Mexico-US Soccer Rivalry," on the sporting history of diaspora, migration, and citizenship.

Carlos Kevin Blanton is an associate professor in the Department of History at Texas A&M University in College Station. His book *The Strange Career of Bilingual Education in Texas, 1836–1981* (Texas A&M University Press, 2004) won the Texas State Historical Association's 2005 Coral Horton Tullis Award for best book on Texas history. Blanton recently published *George I. Sánchez: The Long Fight for Mexican American Integration* (Yale University Press, 2014). He has also published scholarly articles in the *Pacific Historical Review* (2003), the *Journal of Southern History* (2006), the *Teacher's College Record* (2012), and the *Western Historical Quarterly* (2009), the last winning the 2010 Bolton-Cutter Award from the Western History Association for the best article on borderlands history. Blanton's next project explores the long history of US intellectual thought concerning Chicana/o people.

Lilia Fernández is an associate professor in the Department of History at the Ohio State University and is affiliated with its Latino/a Studies program; Department of Women's, Gender, and Sexuality Studies; and Comparative Studies Department. In addition to being an award-winning classroom instructor, Fernández is also the author of *Brown in the Windy City: Mexicans and Puerto Ricans in Postwar Chicago* (University of Chicago Press, 2012), as well as several published articles (in the *Journal of American Ethnic History* [2010] and elsewhere) and book chapters on Mexican American community formation, Mexican and Puerto Rican labor migration, Latino/a education, and Latino/a youth culture. Her next book project is on Latina/o panethnic politics.

Perla M. Guerrero is an assistant professor in the Department of American Studies and the US Latina/o Studies Program at the University of Maryland, College Park. In 2010 Guerrero was awarded a Latino Smithsonian Postdoctoral Fellowship and a Goldman Sachs Junior Fellowship at the National Museum of American History. In 2014–2015 she won a Ford Postdoctoral Fellowship for her first book project, *Nuevo South: Latinas/os, Asians, and the Remaking of Place*, an interdisciplinary investigation showing how immigrants and refugees negotiated race, labor, and community and other issues of place during the late twentieth and early twenty-first centuries. Her work has also appeared in *Race and Ethnicity in Arkansas: New Perspectives* (University of Arkansas, 2014).

Sonia Hernández is an associate professor in the Department of History at Texas A&M University in College Station. In 2014 Hernández's *Working Women into the Borderlands* (Texas A&M University Press, 2014) earned the Sara A. Whaley Book Prize of the National Women's Studies Association and also the Liz Carpenter Book Award for research in the history of women from the Texas State Historical Association. Hernández has published several journal articles and book chapters in English and Spanish in the United States and abroad. Her latest is forthcoming from *Frontiers: A Journal of Women's Studies*. Hernández's next book examines the intersections of feminism and anarchism in Chicana and Mexicana labor and political organizations in the first half of the twentieth century.

Felipe Hinojosa is an associate professor of history at Texas A&M University, where he is also the director of undergraduate studies. In 2010

Hinojosa won the Louisville Institute Postdoctoral Fellowship to work on his book *Latino Mennonites: Civil Rights, Faith, and Evangelical Culture* (Johns Hopkins University Press, 2014), which won the Américo Paredes Book Award of the Center for Mexican American Studies at South Texas College in 2015. He has published several book chapters and journal articles, including pieces in the *Western Historical Quarterly* (2013). His next project is a national, interethnic analysis of the way in which civil rights struggles informed Latina/o religiosity in the 1960s and 1970s and how those movements were, in turn, influenced by faith.

Michael A. Olivas is the William B. Bates Distinguished Chair in Law at the University of Houston Law Center. He is the author or co-author of fifteen books. His *Suing Alma Mater: Higher Education and the Courts* (Johns Hopkins University Press, 2013) won the 2014 Steven S. Goldberg Award for Distinguished Scholarship in Education Law from the Education Law Association. Olivas also recently published *No Undocumented Child Left Behind: Plyler v. Doe and the Education of Undocumented Children* (NYU Press, 2012); coauthored, with Ediberto Román, *Those Damned Immigrants: American's Hysteria over Undocumented Immigration* (NYU Press, 2013); and edited *In Defense of My People: Alonso S. Perales and the Development of Mexican-American Public Intellectuals* (Arte Público, 2013) and *"Colored Men" and "Hombres Aquí": Hernandez v. Texas and the Emergence of Mexican-American Lawyering* (Arte Público, 2006). He is also "The Rock and Roll Law Professor" in his weekly radio show, *The Law of Rock and Roll*, on Albuquerque, New Mexico, National Public Radio station KANW, which reviews developments in music and entertainment law. Olivas's next book is *Perchance to DREAM, A Legal and Political History of the DREAM Act* (NYU Press, forthcoming).

Index